Performing the News

Performing the News

Identity, Authority, and the Myth of Neutrality

ELIA POWERS

Rutgers University Press

New Brunswick, Camden and Newark, New Jersey

London and Oxford

Rutgers University Press is a department of Rutgers, The State University of New Jersey, one of the leading public research universities in the nation. By publishing worldwide, it furthers the University's mission of dedication to excellence in teaching, scholarship, research, and clinical care.

978-1-9788-3668-6 cloth)
978-1-9788-3667-9 (paper)
978-1-9788-3669-3 (epub)

Cataloging-in-publication data is available from the Library of Congress.
LCCN 2023053813

A British Cataloging-in-Publication record for this book is available from the British Library.

References to internet websites (URLs) were accurate at the time of writing. Neither the author nor Rutgers University Press is responsible for URLs that may have expired or changed since the manuscript was prepared.

∞ The paper used in this publication meets the requirements of the American National Standard for Information Sciences—Permanence of Paper for Printed Library Materials, ANSI Z39.48-1992.

rutgersuniversitypress.org

Contents

Performing the News

Introduction

• •

"You have a good radio voice" is a compliment I thought I would never hear.

As a child, I spoke so fast with such a high-pitched voice that people often asked my parents for a translation. "Slow down," my grandma implored me. "Take deep breaths and enunciate," my elementary school teachers said. I did my best, but I always reverted to speeding through sentences. On report cards, teachers diplomatically wrote that my speech clarity "needs time to improve."

As an adolescent, I often spent time talking to an audience of zero, announcing make-believe baseball and basketball games alone in my basement. I had a strong imagination, a sophisticated sports vocabulary, and a voice only my pretend listeners could love. Unlike in reality, I was never asked to slow down and repeat myself as play-by-play announcer for my fictional radio station. I desperately wanted to become a sports broadcaster. I tried emulating the dulcet tones of Dave Niehaus, the voice of my beloved Seattle Mariners, but I talked more like a prepubescent John Moschitta Jr., aka Motormouth from the Micro Machines commercials.

As a teenager, my voice deepened and my speech rate slowed slightly. But I began to stutter, shattering my self-confidence. I hated speaking to an audience and being called on in class. I had to rehearse responses to avoid getting stuck on certain sounds and words. Cruelly, I had a speech block on one unavoidable word: my first name. Talking to people I knew well was manageable; introducing myself to strangers was a nightmare. I dreaded the blank stares, concerned looks, and callous responses to my stutter ("Did you forget your name?"). I recall my misery trying to conduct a routine interview during a high school journalism program at Northwestern University. Even this, as with other basic tasks, made me so anxious that I dialed and hung up several times before the call went through. I feared stuttering through my introduction and sounding unprofessional or, worse, unintelligent. On this call, like others before it, I had such a severe speech block that the person lost patience and hung up, leaving me in tears—and without a source for my article.

As a journalism major at Northwestern, I took a broadcasting course, worked for the campus radio station, and interned at a Chicago television station. Yet I recognized that print journalism was my only realistic route. No one explicitly advised me against pursuing an on-air radio or television career, but it was easy to reach that conclusion. Broadcast journalists sounded nothing like me. They spoke effortlessly and rarely stumbled. I still spoke too fast and enunciated poorly. Speech therapy helped me, but my stutter was pronounced when I felt anxious. Forget reading a script or hosting a show, I still felt uncomfortable doing phone interviews in private. Broadcasting seemed out of the question. I even wondered whether the energy I expended to manage my stutter would prevent a print journalism career.

As a young professional, I became a capable reporter despite self-doubt. I worked at a handful of newspapers and online outlets. My stutter gradually subsided, although my speech still limited what I felt comfortable doing and saying. I e-mailed sources in advance to avoid awkward phone introductions, called them when no one in the newsroom was listening, and pulled them aside after press conferences so that if I stuttered, only one person rather than a roomful of people would notice.

As a not-so-young professional, I did something that had previously seemed impossible: I switched to a career that requires public speaking. By the time I became a college professor, my stutter had all but disappeared. Being in mass communication, I felt pressure to talk clearly and confidently in front of an audience. That was no easy task. I still spoke at a caffeinated pace, so I had to learn to slow down in the classroom. I went from hating how I sound to finding it passable.

I also took a step that brought me close to my original on-air aspirations. A devoted podcast listener, I attended an intensive audio production workshop that motivated me to freelance and start a narrative podcast series. With training and experience, I finally began viewing my vocal delivery as an asset, not a liability. Occasionally, I get feedback like "you have a good radio voice" or "you sound like one of my favorite hosts"—most memorably, a student compared me to longtime National Public Radio (NPR) host Ari Shapiro (not that I agree, but I am flattered).

Reflecting on why I prefer my podcast presentation to my "normal" presentation and why I receive positive comments on the former but not the latter, one obvious reason is that in postproduction, I can edit out flubs, filler words, and other imperfections. More to the point, when I record narration, I emulate the warm-sounding voices I often hear on public radio and podcasts, which I and others have been conditioned to consider "good radio voices." I try to be conversational even as I read a script. I speak slower than normal, pause for effect, enunciate as best I can, and vary my intonation to emphasize important points. In all of these ways, I am performing the news. I am not acting so much as I am presenting a polished version of myself. Specifically, I am performing what is known as "public radio voice."

Public radio has many voices, but that soothing, understated vocal style— satirized skillfully in *Saturday Night Live*'s "Schweddy Balls" sketch—is undoubtedly the one most associated with NPR and its member stations. I am so accustomed to it that I view it as natural, authoritative, and aesthetically pleasing. Yet I know I am part of public radio's core demographic—affluent, well-educated, middle-aged, and White—and that many others find public radio voice unnatural and perhaps even unpleasant.

My goal when developing a podcasting course was to teach students to sound like their best selves rather than to imitate hosts I am used to hearing. In giving feedback, I tried to avoid the phrase "good radio voice" because it implies there is a right and wrong way to speak. Yet I sometimes caught myself praising students who sound like they could be on public radio and subtly nudging others toward that vocal style. When I encouraged students to "be conversational," I generally played examples of journalists who came up through public radio. Many sounded similar. Most, I realized, were White. I feared that my students—who are racially and ethnically diverse—concluded that this is *the* right way to perform.

That was not the message I wanted to convey. Exposing students to diverse podcast hosts with different speaking styles was an easy but insufficient response. I wanted to initiate a conversation about acceptance of accents and dialects throughout the news industry. I wanted to give constructive feedback on voicing and assure students like me who struggled with self-doubt that they belonged behind the microphone. Yet I was not sure what to say to prepare them for the reality of working in news. My research to date had found that employers expected journalists who performed for audiences to have "smooth, well-controlled" voices and "flawless, fluent" speech.[1] Journalists I interviewed for another study felt that stuttering limited their career options.[2]

I decided to widen my research lens beyond experiences of journalists who stutter and notions of what it means to "sound right" in journalism. Television journalists are also expected to "look good" on camera. Reading online, I came across journalists who objected to news industry leaders' narrow conceptions of looking good and sounding right. Journalists from historically marginalized groups (e.g., women, people of color, people with disabilities, people in the LGBTQ+ community) have long resented having to conform to be considered professional. In recent years, more have pushed back publicly, using news articles, op-eds, and social media posts to share experiences of being advised (or instructed) to hide their accent, cover up their natural hair, tone down their mannerisms, and avoid outfits that challenge traditional gender norms. These expectations have come under increased scrutiny as news organizations reckon with their past and confront their inability to recruit and retain journalists from marginalized backgrounds.

Journalists in a variety of sectors, news markets, and roles describe barriers and difficult experiences stemming from differences in how they want to present themselves and what their managers expect. Few studies have examined how norms for appearance and vocal delivery restrict how journalists from historically marginalized groups express their identity. I wanted to know how these norms took shape and evolved, how journalists became aware of them, and how they negotiated their on-air presentation. I was interested in how journalists who defied well-established norms and who in some cases broke barriers went about doing so, how they viewed their experience, and what actions they felt would promote further progress. So I decided to write this book.

Aims and Central Argument

Performing the News: Identity, Authority, and the Myth of Neutrality explores how journalists who perform for audiences on television, radio, and podcasts (or who aspire to do so) learn about expectations for self-presentation and manage their public image. This book contributes to conversations on diversity and inclusion in journalism and intersects with ongoing debates about journalistic authority and neutrality. Specifically, it examines how journalists' self-presentation affects their perceived authoritativeness and how they are rewarded for adhering to well-established, purportedly neutral forms.

How journalists present—from the way they dress and style their hair to their pronunciation, intonation, and rate of speech—contributes to the look and sound of news. These visual and verbal elements are what I refer to as forms. By choice or out of perceived necessity, journalists attempt to perform neutrally. They speak with a flat, "neutral" accent, modify their delivery to hide distinctive vocal attributes, dress conventionally to appeal to the "average" viewer, and maintain a consistent appearance to avoid unwanted attention. In short, they stick to forms that are familiar to news audiences. Their aim is what I refer to as *performance neutrality*—self-presentation that is deemed unobjectionable, reveals little about journalists' social identity, and supposedly does not detract from their message.

Journalists strive for neutrality because they are told that it makes them appear authoritative and trustworthy. Repeated exposure contributes to forms of self-presentation being viewed as neutral or normal. Yet what we hear and see on the news often reflects decisions and institutional norms from a period that predates changes in demographics and societal values. What is considered neutral has historically reflected tastes of White male news managers and assumed tastes of predominantly White, middle- to upper-class audience members. We are conditioned to uncritically view forms like public radio voice, television anchor voice, and the anchor bob hairstyle as acceptable standards.

This book's central argument is that performance neutrality is a myth that reinforces the status quo, limits on-air diversity, and hinders efforts to make newsrooms more inclusive. The pressure to conform to restrictive forms of self-presentation leads journalists from historically marginalized groups to cover. They downplay their differences and conceal aspects of their identity in order to appease managers and avoid alienating audiences. They sense the need to ask permission to be themselves. Feelings of disempowerment lead to disillusionment, prompting some to switch jobs or pursue other professions. As a result, the news industry does not fully reflect our increasingly diverse society.

To truly reflect the communities they cover, news organizations—starting with management—must discourage covering and embrace diverse forms of self-presentation. As I further discuss in chapter 1, when journalists have some agency over how they present themselves publicly and do not feel pressure to assimilate, they are likelier to feel they belong and remain in the industry. They do better work and produce a more distinctive news product that is likely to appeal to underserved audiences. Their presence in high-profile roles can help newsrooms attract diverse candidates, normalize diverse voices on the news, and change public perception about what looks and sounds authoritative.

Primary Focus and Target Audience

While this book is not about me, it is personal given my struggles with self-doubt. Writing it helped me better understand what drove my decision—which I sometimes regret—to abandon my initial goal of working in broadcast journalism. I realized the extent to which I had felt embarrassed about my stutter, feared rejection, and assumed that avoidance was the solution.

Revisiting this was hard but would have been even more so had I received criticism from audience members or news colleagues. Few commented on my stutter and no one said directly that it was off-putting. I also never heard that I sound too shrill, too ethnic, too urban, or not masculine enough, or that I look unprofessional. I cannot put myself in the position of journalists who often receive such comments, but I can tell their stories. In doing so, I hope to raise awareness of how some journalists are induced to cover up their differences and suggest ways to make journalism more inclusive and representative of diverse audiences.

To do that, I focus primarily on public radio and local television—sectors of the news industry that often are at the center of conversations about diversity and self-presentation. Dialogue on the Whiteness of public radio tends to focus on NPR, which is often criticized for failing to speak with many voices and dialects, as its original mission statement promised. NPR's member stations and other public media institutions receive similar complaints about lack of vocal diversity. Local television leaders have been criticized for restricting how journalists express their identity on air and for failing to back them when confronted with audience complaints.

While this book is largely about journalists who work in broadcasting and podcasting, it is *for* a much broader audience, including:

- *Scholars in journalism studies and related fields.* The following chapters explore, among other contemporary topics, the Whiteness of news organizations, the treatment of individuals from groups historically underrepresented in journalism, the role of practitioners, educators, and peripheral actors in socializing new entrants to the profession, and the evolving relationship between journalists and their audiences. I also suggest ways for journalism educators to have productive conversations about self-presentation and industry expectations. Those outside journalism can benefit from understanding how organizational gatekeepers shape standards of occupational practice, how forms become institutionalized, and how those who perform for the public manage their working identity.

- *Practitioners and aspiring journalists.* Anchors, hosts, and correspondents have long had to consider how to manage their on-air image. The growth of podcasting and digital video makes people across the industry (including those who work at newspapers, magazines, and digital outlets) increasingly likely to be seen and heard by the public. Anyone considering a job that puts them behind the microphone or on camera needs to consider how they present themselves and how they are, or will be, received by audiences. While this is not a how-to manual (for that, I point readers to books on vocal technique and image management), it can help practitioners and aspiring journalists navigate their careers and understand legal protections for individuals who feel compelled to cover.

- *Newsroom leaders (e.g., station managers, news directors, and editors) and other influential actors (e.g., voice coaches, image consultants, media trainers, and talent agents).* Anyone involved in hiring and promotion, performance reviews, and/or performance advising can benefit from better understanding how their actions and guidance influence journalists' careers and affect their self-image and what meaningful actions can help reduce inequities.

Data Sources

The best way to understand the impact of restrictive institutional norms is by examining journalists' lived experiences and hearing from those who employ, advise, and work with on-air talent. In-depth interviews ($n = 80$) with journalists in broadcasting and podcasting and those who shape their performance are this book's primary data source. I also analyze a range of written texts that signal to journalists what constitutes professional self-presentation.

In-Depth Interviews

This book draws heavily on in-depth, semi-structured interviews with current and former journalists who perform for audiences on television ($n = 21$), radio ($n = 17$), and podcasts ($n = 15$) and those who advise on or direct such performances: producers ($n = 13$), editors ($n = 8$), managers/directors ($n = 7$), industry analysts ($n = 3$), voice/speech coaches ($n = 12$), media trainers ($n = 4$), image consultants ($n = 2$), talent agents ($n = 3$), and professors ($n = 12$).[3] Participants are diverse in terms of age, race, ethnicity, gender, sexual orientation, and disability. The vast majority grew up and reside in the United States, representing all regions. My definition of a journalist is anyone who reports on, edits, produces, or oversees the production of news, as well as those who provide commentary, including many podcasters.

I found participants using purposeful sampling, a nonrandom technique used in qualitative research to identify information-rich cases related to a specific phenomenon.[4] Researchers commonly use multiple strategies to select participants who are knowledgeable about and may have personal experiences with the phenomenon of interest. I used a combination of criterion sampling and snowball sampling strategies.

The objective of criterion sampling is to identify cases that fit a predetermined criterion of importance.[5] I first sought out journalists, activists, and other thought leaders who had written or spoken publicly about negotiating their on-air presentation. This enabled me to gather insights from some of the most prominent, influential voices in the conversation about diversity, equity, and inclusion in journalism. To find potential participants, I used a range of search engines and online databases, a strategy that produced dozens of news articles, blog posts, editorials, and podcast episodes. I also did a targeted search on Facebook, Twitter (rebranded as X), Instagram, and TikTok using two popular hashtags: #customerservicevoice (on performative, fake work voices) and #pubradiovoice (on the iconic public radio voice). I contacted those who had shared personal experiences through these platforms for interviews. To cast a wider net, I used snowball sampling to find on-air journalists at various stages of their careers who had not yet shared their experiences publicly, those in behind-the-scenes newsroom roles (e.g., producers, editors, and news directors), performance advisers who in many cases worked with journalists interviewed, and professors who teach broadcasting and podcasting courses.

Interviews took place from June 2021 to August 2023. I asked journalists to describe their interpretation and understanding of lived experiences—a hallmark of the interpretive phenomenological approach to qualitative inquiry.[6] This approach calls for open, exploratory interview questions that enable participants to explain phenomena of interest and researchers to "make sense of the participant trying to make sense of what is happening to them."[7] The approach is useful for exploring nuanced questions like the ones I posed to journalists: How did they interpret instances when they felt pressure to cover? What were the sources of that pressure? How did they make meaning of feedback on their vocal delivery and appearance and how did it shape their on-air presentation? What were the consequences of covering or refusing to do so? Questions to managers and performance advisers focused primarily on their feedback to journalists, their conceptions of the news audience, and their views on industry norms.

I examined transcribed audio recordings using interpretive phenomenological analysis (IPA), which produces an account of participants' experiences on their own terms rather than ones prescribed by preexisting theoretical preconceptions. IPA involves multiple readings of interview transcripts, initial note taking, development of emergent themes, searching for connections across themes, and creating a final list of superordinate themes and subthemes.[8]

This book contains many direct quotes and paraphrased statements from journalists and others interviewed. How they express their thoughts and describe their experiences provide insights and nuance that are necessary in order to fully understand the topics discussed. This is particularly so for direct quotes from journalists who describe the impact of covering.

Analysis of Relevant Texts

To examine what attributes and performance skills employers value, I conducted a qualitative thematic analysis of U.S. journalism job advertisements ($n = 510$) on JournalismJobs.com, LinkedIn, Indeed, Mediabistro, and Public Media Jobs. The listings I analyzed were for positions requiring substantial verbal communication with the general public (reporters, anchors/hosts, and multimedia journalists) or within a newsroom (editors/directors and producers). I identified listings on job websites through keyword searches and job category filters. Using an inductive approach to data analysis, I looked for references to verbal communication attributes and skills. I generated frequency counts of recurring language and examined passages that referred to verbal communication to identify patterns in how language was used. I also looked for references to physical appearance, attire, and other aspects of image management.

Additionally, I analyzed advice from authors of English-language journalism and mass communication textbooks on how to look and sound professional. I obtained textbooks ($n = 47$) by visiting the websites of publishers and media trade groups, examining online syllabi, and using keyword searches on search engines and library databases. This qualitative content analysis primarily focused on references to verbal attributes and skills needed to succeed in broadcast journalism. Specifically, I examined how textbooks described industry expectations for appearance and vocal delivery.

To understand how news audiences historically have perceived journalists' self-presentation, I analyzed research from the archives of McHugh and Hoffman, the first and most prominent television news consulting firm. These research records, which span 1957–1995, include sociological and demographic data for local media markets and viewer attitudes toward newscasts and newscasters. I primarily focused on qualitative viewer comments on journalists' appearance and vocal delivery.

These data sources help answer this book's central questions: What signals do those who manage, coach, and train journalists send about how to look and sound authoritative? What assumptions do they make when advising journalists about how to appeal to audiences? How do journalists from historically marginalized groups manage their working identity, weighing their desire to present as they wish with the need to satisfy managers? In what ways do journalists feel compelled to demonstrate performance neutrality? When they cover, what is the cost to individuals and institutions?

Overview of Chapters

I address these questions in the following chapters, which are split into three parts. Part I focuses on critical perspectives, including theoretical frameworks, key concepts, essential actors, and sites of socialization.

Chapter 1 explores White normativity in journalism, the cost of covering, and the case for diversity of form. Chapter 2 focuses on performance as an expression of identity, the role of aesthetics and form in journalism, and the concept of performance neutrality. I examine how research on self-presentation, aesthetic capital, and aesthetic labor helps explain journalism's preoccupation with performance, how journalists signal authority through their performances, and how forms become institutionalized and considered neutral.

Chapter 3 explores how journalists learn about performance norms. The chapter introduces key actors/gatekeepers who influence journalists' self-presentation as well as sites of socialization. I examine what signals these information sources send about how journalists should look and sound authoritative.

Chapter 4 focuses on the influential imagined audience, specifically how demographic data and assumptions about listener and viewer preferences influence on-air presentation. I review decades of research on how audiences evaluate journalists' appearance and vocal delivery and explain why news stations may have less access now to such information. I explore the influence of unsolicited audience feedback and the implications of news managers imagining themselves as the audience.

Part II focuses on norms and practices, detailing how journalists perform the news on television, radio, and podcasts. I explore the evolution of performance norms, the barriers journalists still face, and the progress they have helped accelerate.

Chapter 5 examines how television journalists manage their personal appearance (e.g., attire and hair/grooming) and body language (e.g., mannerisms).

Chapter 6 explores vocal presentation on television (e.g., accent, pitch, and speech fluency). Chapter 7 is about radio performance, specifically the dialogue on public radio voice. Chapter 8 examines how podcasting has created opportunities for journalists to perform in ways that challenge broadcasting conventions.

Part III focuses on laws and suggested actions. Chapter 9 looks at how current law applies to the pressure to cover. I also identify the limits of legislation. Chapter 10 explores how those in or in close orbit to newsrooms can support and advocate for journalists.

Part 1

Critical Perspectives

• •

1

Covering (on) the News

• •

Deion Broxton is best known as the television journalist who justifiably bailed as a herd of bison approached. It was March 2020 and the NBC Montana reporter was recording a stand-up at Yellowstone National Park. Out of the corner of his eye, Broxton spotted danger, prompting him to say the lines that led to TV news and internet fame: "Oh my god. Oh my god. Oh no, I ain't messin' with you. Oh no. Oh no." He grabbed his equipment and took refuge in his car as his camera kept rolling, providing millions of viewers a moment of levity. He understands why his social media post went viral and why he instantly became a meme. A Black reporter from Baltimore living in Big Sky Country has a close encounter with dangerous animals, reacts instinctively, momentarily ditches his broadcast persona, and instead has an authentic and amusing response.

In the following days, Broxton dutifully gave interviews about his brief encounter with bison. He referenced it in his professional biography to show a sense of humor. But he grew tired of talking about it. He did not want those eighteen seconds to define his career. After moving from Bozeman, Montana, to Cedar Rapids, Iowa, for an on-air reporting job, he was sitting in a break room when a new colleague approached. "The first thing he said to me is, 'Hey, it's the bison guy.' I looked at him like he was crazy. It just felt so dehumanizing."[1]

One reason why this interaction bothered Broxton so much is that he had a much more consequential story about his career to share. As a journalist with a self-described "hood Baltimore accent" who spent years struggling to find an on-air job, he was told by a news director that to get hired, he needed to change how he talked—essentially, to sound less Black. Following that advice, he spent thousands of dollars on a speech coach, learned to hide his accent, and changed his broadcast delivery to sound like he is from anywhere, USA. "I worked tirelessly for months," Broxton says. "To change how you talk is hard, and I can't tell you how many times I second guessed myself. I had to constantly think, 'What am I saying? How am I saying it?' I was driving myself crazy. It was so hard to reinvent myself."[2]

Broxton considered his actions a necessary means to an end. "I viewed that my accent and the way I talked wasn't good enough. All I was thinking is, 'What do I need to do to get into this industry?'" He observed that journalism is a mostly middle- and upper-class profession. Gatekeepers at news stations are typically White. Broxton grew up on food stamps in East Baltimore, which he describes as "The Wire," after his favorite television show that filmed in his neighborhood. He elongated vowels, skipped over syllables, and sometimes left the *g* off the end of words. He pronounced his hometown "Baldimore." Where he is from, his way of speaking—"a mix of city accent and southern accent with a Black flair"—was the norm.[3]

But in television news, Broxton was an anomaly. "As a young, urban-sounding African American, there were just very few places for him," says Cathy Runnels, a speech-language pathologist who coached Broxton.[4] Once Broxton changed how he spoke, the results were immediate. Within a week of sending new demo reels to news stations, he had three job interviews. Those interviews led to job offers, and in 2018 he accepted the position in Bozeman. "I don't think I changed myself," Broxton says. "I think I just conformed to fit this mold. Once the cameras go off and I'm off the job, I'm still back to being Deion. But like in any profession there's a way you're expected to behave."[5]

When Broxton began as an on-air reporter, he did not speak publicly about his experience. "I had tunnel vision. I was in a survival mentality. I wanted to be in the house so bad I didn't care what I had to do. I finally got in the house and realized, 'This isn't right.'" The more time he spent in newsrooms, the more he resented having to conform. "I've worked with White people who have all sorts of accents. They slur their words and have jobs on TV. When I slurred my words, I couldn't get a job. That's when I realized that it's discrimination. If you're White and you talk kind of funny, it's OK. But if you're Black and you talk kind of funny, it's a negative. . . . Because of where I grew up, I couldn't get a job. I had to take extra steps, which is what a lot of Black people have to do to succeed."[6]

One lesson Broxton learned: "You may have to conform at first, but once you have a bigger platform, you can say and do what you want." Broxton commemorated the one-year anniversary of the bison video by sharing the story he wanted to tell. Quote tweeting his original bison post, he commented, "A year later. I get tired of talking about this video. But it's a reminder of my journey. I couldn't get a job on TV because of my hood/Baltimore accent. . . . Fast forward, this week I learned I won an award from the Iowa Broadcast News Association."[7] That post, he says, "changed the narrative from me being the bison guy to look what this Black man had to go through just to get here."[8]

Broxton's story illustrates a troubling reality for many journalists from historically marginalized groups: succeeding professionally requires downplaying identity-based differences. Through observation, training, and performance reviews, many journalists perceive—or, like Broxton, are flatly told by others in the field—that their appearance or vocal delivery is unacceptable. Their voices are shrill and lack authority. Their accents are unpleasant and unrelatable. Their speech is halting and distracting. Their natural hair is unsightly and unprofessional. Their attire and mannerisms are too flamboyant. Their performance lacks credibility. They are advised and sometimes directed to change how they look, talk, and act to avoid alienating audiences.

As the news industry reckons with its treatment of journalists from underrepresented groups, it must address the compulsion some feel to mute their differences and hide markers of their background when applying to jobs and presenting to news audiences. Broadcast journalists, podcasters, and program guests face decisions and directives about how to perform the news.

Performing the News

I do not describe journalists as performers to suggest that they step outside themselves and into the role of someone entirely different, as actors do. Nor do I contend that their main objective is to entertain, like musicians and comedians. Journalists *are* like many performers in their use of voice, appearance, and body language to present an appealing version of themselves. They seek to communicate clearly, come across as credible, and be captivating. They need directors to accept their performance and audiences to validate it.

Journalists may perceive that there are right and wrong ways to perform the news. Among the ways that news institutions establish authority—and journalists assert their professionalism—is by legitimizing or delegitimizing particular practices or forms.[9] In defining parameters for appropriate self-presentation, the journalistic community has largely excluded those from underrepresented groups.[10] When journalists hear their voice described as unauthoritative, their manner of speech as improper, or how they dress or wear their hair as unprofessional, the implication is that their self-presentation lacks legitimacy.

Feedback on journalists' self-presentation can be constructive (e.g., how to have a strong and healthy voice, how to have good posture, how to wear colors that translate well on camera). Yet journalists commonly hear comments about physical and presentational attributes that are prone to being more subjective, based on personal preferences (e.g., what sounds pleasant and looks appealing). Whether someone has a suitable voice for radio or is attractive enough for television (as opposed to having a "face for radio") is partially a matter of aesthetic taste. Views on this may reflect a manager's bias—or assumptions of audience bias—with regard to race, ethnicity, class, gender, sexual orientation, or disability.

Notions of ideal self-presentation change over time, reflecting shifting social and cultural norms. Compared to previous eras, journalists today sound more conversational and dress less formally. Acceptance of diverse voices, speaking styles, and appearance attributes is greater in some newsrooms, markets, and sectors than others. Yet throughout the industry, journalists still feel pressure to conform, in large part because the news product reflects the tastes of predominantly White newsroom managers and their assumptions about audience tastes.

White Normativity in Journalism

Sociologists commonly consider those who are White a distinct social group with experiences shaped by their "White habitus," which conditions their perspectives, cognitions, and sense of beauty.[11] In White-dominant fields, White tastes and standards of decency serve as the norm for social acceptability, known as White normativity. Whiteness defines the "normal or accepted range of conduct and characteristics" and all other racial categories are contrasted with Whiteness as deviations from the norm.[12] When non-White groups gain admittance into White communities, the ideology of Whiteness and its privilege quietly become second nature or habitual. "Simply put, Whiteness constitutes normality and acceptance without stipulating that to be White is to be normal and right."[13]

News organizations have long been "White in tone and perspective."[14] Despite public pronouncements and costly initiatives, progress toward diversity in journalism has been limited.[15] While the broadcast news workforce has slowly become more diverse, industry surveys show that still the vast majority of people identify as White and a plurality identify as male. General managers and news directors are consistently the least diverse. Results reveal an industry lagging behind an ever-increasing minority population in the United States.[16] Journalists I interviewed perceived that because newsrooms remain largely White spaces where the White perspective is dominant, institutional norms are slow to change.

Sociologists Carlos Alamo-Pastrana and William Hoynes have argued that "news has been racialized in the United States, that is, defined as a White field, staffed largely by White professionals, which ultimately reaffirms its own legitimacy."[17] In public radio, the White-dominant mindset has influenced speech standards.[18] Regionally and ethnically marked features of journalists' speech have been suppressed.[19] Across the news industry, Standard American English is considered preferable to "nonstandard" dialects.[20] African American English is often thought to be unprofessional.[21]

Television journalists historically have been expected to fit into established White newsroom environments.[22] As a result, anchors and reporters "spoke in the same clipped diction as their White counterparts" and "bore no traces of African-American culture in their mannerisms or appearance."[23] Newsroom leaders still police how Black journalists talk, dress, and wear their hair in an effort to cultivate an image of "palatable Blackness."[24] Which raises the question of palatable to whom?

Journalists often assume that their primary audience is White, middle- to upper-class, and well educated.[25] This demographic is one that many news organizations rely on for financial support and feel they cannot afford to lose. Even though news consumers are increasingly diverse, affluent White audiences still have disproportionate influence, particularly in public radio and to a lesser extent in television news.[26]

The Prevalence of Covering

White normativity creates significant hurdles to achieving diverse, inclusive newsrooms because journalists feel compelled to mute their differences and assimilate. Sociologist Erving Goffman defined this behavior as covering. Instead of attempting to conceal aspects of their identity, or pass, those with a "known stigmatized identity" may try to "keep the stigma from looming large."[27] Goffman described stigma as disqualification from full social acceptance because of an attribute that is considered unfavorable or discrediting. Society creates normative expectations about attributes that are felt to be natural. Those possessing attributes that do not match assumptions about how individuals should look, sound, or behave are "reduced in our minds from a whole person to a tainted, discounted one."[28]

Discredited attributes are often easily discernable, such as skin color, hair, body size, and markers of disability. Broxton was discredited because gatekeepers perceived that he sounded too Black, an example of a stigma attached to identification with a particular race or ethnicity.[29] Being stigmatized radically changes a person's self-concept, which helps explain why Broxton perceived that the way he spoke was not good enough.

People from marginalized groups experience public stigma through negative stereotypes, prejudice, and discrimination. Some fear negative evaluation regardless of whether it is justified; this is known as felt stigma. They may also experience self-stigma, or shame associated with a personal attribute or characteristic.[30] Stigmatized individuals sense the need to always be "on" and aware of the impression they are making.[31] As a result, they are likely to cover.

Building on Goffman's work, legal scholar Kenji Yoshino has defined covering as toning down a disfavored or stigmatized identity to fit into the mainstream. This pressure to conform, Yoshino argues, is a hidden assault on our civil rights.[32] It is hidden because entire groups are not discriminated against, only those who fail to assimilate to mainstream norms. "Outsiders are included," he writes, "but only if we behave like insiders." This new form of discrimation targets "minority cultures rather than minority persons," so it is generally not proscribed by law.[33]

Law professor Russell Robinson has argued that covering is wholly or largely self-imposed. Managers and others in positions of power create a norm. Employees may feel pressure to follow that norm, but they ultimately decide whether to adhere to it. Many instances of covering are not precipitated by any articulated demand. The demand, rather, is "in the air. . . . It is perceived by the individual based on [their] prior experiences, intepretations of ambiguous statements, and readings of body language, silence and gestures, among other things."[34]

Covering is commonplace, according to surveys. In 2013, more than 60 percent of employees across industries said they covered at work and roughly half said that leaders in their workplace expected workers to do so.[35] Most said covering was vital to their professional advancement but detrimental to their sense of self.[36] Covering was most common among members of marginalized groups, most notably those who identified as LGBTQ+ (83 percent), African American (79 percent), female (66 percent), and Hispanic or Latino (63 percent).[37] A similar survey conducted a decade later found progress to be minimal. In 2023, still roughly 60 percent of employees said they covered at work. Comparatively fewer (40 percent) indicated that their team leaders expected them to do so. Covering was less common than before for some groups, most notably African Americans (65%), but across the board, nondominant groups reported higher rates than those who identified as cisgender, heterosexual, male, non-disabled, and White.[38]

Yoshino, who was involved in both surveys, has found that people often refrain from being viewed as activists at work. In some situations, they avoid associating with coworkers who share their stigmatized attributes. This book is not about advocacy-based or association-based covering that may occur off air. Instead, it focuses on what happens when journalists who are in studio or in the field perform for audiences. Individuals avoid behaviors widely associated with their stigmatized identity to avoid being stereotyped. Yoshino has referred to this as covering up affiliation or cultural identification, which 40 percent of employees surveyed in 2013 said they did. People sometimes alter their self-presentation to blend into mainstream culture. Yoshino has described this as appearance-based covering, which nearly 30 percent of employees reported doing.[39]

The Cost of Covering

The cost of covering is substantial. "When journalists are told, 'You need to change your appearance or the way you sound,' that has a deep, lasting impact, not just from a professional standpoint, but also in terms of their identity," says former television journalist Vanessa Ruiz.[40] Simply put, it reinforces their status as second-class citizens. Making major changes to vocal presentation and appearance can be costly and physically damaging. Covering puts journalists at a competitive disadvantage because they spend time and effort managing their identity in addition to doing their job.[41] Many do this early in their career, interviews revealed, when they feel most professionally vulnerable and view challenging norms as too large a risk. Those who refuse to cover commonly miss out on professional opportunities and leave the field. Aspiring journalists who feel pressure to cover may choose other careers.

Covering tends to be overlooked in discourse on diversity, equity, and inclusion. More often the focus is on representation. Communication scholar Theodore L. Glasser has argued that "we trivialize diversity by treating it as something that can be neatly packaged or easily measured," such as by quantifying the percentage of women or racial minorities. This, Glasser wrote, is the "folly of reducing diversity to physiographic criteria for admission or employment, which . . . hardly qualifies as evidence of diversity in any seriously cultural sense."[42]

The problem of covering cannot be solved through increasing newsroom diversity alone. Newsroom leaders must consider how individual actors and their organizational culture contribute to an environment in which journalists feel unable to bring their whole selves to work. They must reevaluate processes for hiring, training, and promotion and assumptions about audiences that drive decisions about whose stories are told and *how* they are told. They must rethink institutional norms that are unnecessary, outdated, harmful, and often discriminatory and embrace diverse forms of self-presentation.

The Case for Diversity of Form

Journalists benefit from being able to present in ways that feel genuine. Their employers benefit as well, although the reasons why might be less evident. Below I lay out the moral, financial, and editorial cases for diversity of form.

The Moral Case: Minimizing Harm and Normalizing Diverse Forms

News organizations should strive to minimize harm to journalists and normalize diverse forms of self-presentation. Doing so is both morally right and serves the institution's interests. Many news organizations profess to value diversity, equity, and inclusion but fail to live up to their ideals when journalists are encouraged or directed to cover. Removing this pressure reduces harm and demonstrates an organization's commitment not just to hiring diverse talent but to airing diverse voices and styles of appearance.

News organizations have a responsibility to put people on air (or on podcasts) who broadly look and sound like the communities they cover. Exposure to different types of voices and appearance attributes can help reduce bias and stigma. That is what motivates print journalist John Hendrickson to make media appearances, even though he finds them nerve-wracking because of his stutter. "Anytime a person who looks or sounds different goes on TV or radio or a podcast, they are normalizing it for everybody else," he says.[43]

Broadening notions of what looks and sounds professional and removing outdated restrictions allow news organizations to fulfill their mission to serve diverse audiences. "Our world is so globalized right now that it seems narrow to have a standard radio sound," says radio journalist Gretel Kahn.[44] The same is true on television. "People want to see themselves represented," says Carolyn Kane, a broadcast journalist turned talent coach/agent. "I don't feel like the White, New England, 'accentless' way of speaking is a good representation of who we are as a nation, so it shouldn't be a complete representation of who we are as broadcasters."[45]

The Financial Case: Attracting Diverse Audiences

The ability to attract diverse audiences by ensuring that they feel represented is central to the financial case for diversity of form. Political theorist Hanna Pitkin has found that politicians are rewarded for reflecting their constituents. One way to do so is by sharing similar physical characteristics.[46] Media scholar Amy Jo Coffey applied this concept to local television, arguing that physical representation is important in a news story (e.g., who is interviewed) and for the journalist who appears as the community's representative. Broadcasters, she argues, should physically resemble the communities they serve.[47] Viewers who see themselves represented on the news may become loyal to a local station if they feel it stands for them.[48]

When audiences do not hear or see people on the news who represent them, they may feel marginalized and tune out. Maria Hinojosa saw this happen first-hand. The longtime anchor and executive producer of the radio program *Latino USA* observed that one of the reasons listeners turned away from public media is because they "didn't hear their real voices."[49] Former *This American Life* producer Stephanie Foo wrote in a 2016 manifesto on diversity in public media that program directors have finally realized that a market of people of color exists and that if they do not cater to it, they will not grow their audience.[50]

News organizations not only have missed opportunities to broaden their reach, but some have also passed up chances to differentiate themselves in the marketplace. News products are "experience goods," and journalists are an important part of the package that news outlets sell to audiences.[51] As public faces and voices of news programs, journalists become recognizable personalities.[52] Their appearance and vocal delivery are part of their personal brand, which sets them apart from other on-air talent and helps their news program distinguish itself from competitors.[53]

Personalities do not stand out and programs tend to blend together when there is sameness of form. "I always dislike when radio sounds the same in every market," says former public radio journalist and trainer Catherine Stifter. "If you drive around the country and you are listening in Phoenix or Poughkeepsie, it should sound different, like the local place."[54] Audiences tend to gravitate toward news personalities they identify with and feel they know well. These parasocial relationships help increase audience loyalty. Journalists can leverage their unique attributes to cultivate such relationships. "Our audience, they look like us, they are us," says television journalist Sia Nyorkor. "They identify with us because of our differences."[55] Broxton says that part of his appeal is that he is "not the norm." Viewers have told him, "It's so refreshing to see something different on television. We're thankful for you because we never felt like someone spoke for us."[56]

The Editorial Case: Better, More Genuine Journalism

Journalists who present in diverse ways can offer different perspectives on the stories they tell. Yet they often are constrained by conventional forms. Radio journalist Joe Wertz knows that well. He learned early in his career to "write to your voice" and tried doing so by using colloquial language in his scripts. But on air, he used an unnaturally formal tone to conceal his Oklahoma accent, which listeners critiqued. He even tried avoiding words and phrases that brought out his "Okie-ness." "I realized how much work I was doing to not sound like myself. None of that was in service of the story—it was in service of some jerk on Twitter who said mean things." Wertz says once he stopped trying to hide his accent, his storytelling improved.[57]

News stories are more vivid, personal, and genuine when journalists do not try to conform. Longtime radio producer and voice coach Viki Merrick recalls that while she was co-producing the *Moth Radio Hour*, her colleague Jay Allison told a host, "Don't forget to put your Alabama on." The host had been trained to tone down her accent, but as Merrick observed, "When she's herself and there's some Alabama in her voice, it's a completely different energy."[58] Public radio journalist Diana Opong has a similar reaction to hearing NPR's Ayesha Rascoe. "I love that she doesn't sound buttoned up and perfect. She sounds like herself, which lends credibility to what she's saying."[59] In other words, it sounds less phony. "A diversity of different kinds of voices, styles, and speaking patterns is what adds to the authenticity of a show," says podcast showrunner, host, and reporter Dan Bobkoff.[60]

Sources tend to identify with journalists who do not hide aspects of their identity. Journalist Noor Tagouri often heard that wearing a hijab made her approachable. "Showing up as myself and sounding like myself helps me connect with people," she says. Journalists who stutter say that because they "don't fit the stereotype of a journalist," as one reporter put it, sources are often at ease and inclined to divulge information. "A lot of people over the years who I've interviewed have said I felt like I could be myself because you were yourself. . . . They felt more comfortable talking to me because I was not some super-polished professional."[61]

Summary

When journalists can be themselves, they spend less time managing their identity, freeing them to do better work and form stronger connections. The news product is more interesting and authentic. News organizations are better able to recruit and retain diverse talent, demonstrate a commitment to diversity and inclusion, normalize performance attributes and styles that have long been stigmatized, differentiate themselves from their competitors, and attract audiences who previously felt unrepresented.

Journalism benefits from less covering and more diversity of form. However, journalists have ample incentive to remain silent on this topic. Especially early in their career, they may feel powerless, fear being penalized for criticizing colleagues, and want to avoid being labeled an agitator, which may limit their advancement. They may wish to avoid revisiting difficult experiences that put them in the media spotlight and in some cases drove them from the profession. Still, many have spoken out against covering, have challenged well-established norms, and have performed in ways that feel genuine. Chapter 2 further explores how journalists perform the news and how forms become sanctified and viewed as neutral.

2

Performance, Form, and the Myth of Neutrality

• •

Starbucks baristas and Disney World employees were doing it. So were restaurant servers, receptionists, and retail workers. Scores of TikTok users were peeling back the curtain to demonstrate the difference between their "real voice" and their work #customerservicevoice. Jeannette Reyes, a morning television anchor known on TikTok as "MsNewsLady," starred in some of the genre's most viral videos. Reyes used her news anchor voice in settings where it was comedically out of place: at home, with her anchor husband, and with in-laws and friends, who were not amused. She used it off air in the newsroom and asked colleagues to join her (they declined). "Even anchors get sick of the anchor voice," she quipped.[1] On air, Reyes deepens her voice and hides her accent. She demonstrated that accent—"a mix of Rhode Island . . . plus a little bit of Rosie Perez"—toward the end of one video.[2]

Viktoria Capek also wanted in on the action. "I kind of work in customer service," she began her TikTok video. "I work in news." Capek used her off-air voice (which is relatively high pitched) and speaking style (fast-paced and casual) before switching to her decidedly deeper on-air voice. She spoke deliberately and with impeccable diction. Gone were her "ums" and any trace of upspeak. "Hey, guys" was replaced with the formal greeting, "Well, good morning to you."[3] Capek went from sounding like a twentysomething to a prototypical newscaster. She recorded the video as a PSA of sorts on behalf of broadcast journalists. "We might sound like this and look like this all the time," she says, "but we're not robots—we're real people, too."[4]

News anchor voice is a familiar and much-parodied form (think Kent Brockman on *The Simpsons* or the entire *Anchorman* cast). What the TikTok videos illustrate is how greatly these journalists' on-air and off-air presentations differ and how seamlessly they switch between styles. Broadcast journalists are skillful performers. They do not all go to great lengths to transform their vocal delivery like Capek and Reyes do when on camera. They generally do not consider themselves to be in customer service—they serve "the public." But like many public-facing professionals who participated in the TikTok challenge, journalists are strategic about their self-presentation. Some more or less perform as they please. Many others feel pressure to appease managers; they may perform to conform.

This chapter covers performance—why it matters so much in news, how journalists use it to manage their image, and what that reveals about their industry's values. Guided by Erving Goffman's self-presentation theory, I explore how appearance and vocal delivery are expressions of identity and how we form a working identity. I use the concepts of aesthetic capital and aesthetic labor to show how certain performance skills and attributes have been considered more appealing and authoritative than others. Finally, I build on previous scholarship on the form of news and argue that in the context of self-presentation, there is no neutral form.

Performance as an Expression of Self

Many journalists object to the intense focus on their self-presentation.[5] Some downplay the performance component of their job and emphasize parts that seem more substantive.

But those who advise broadcast journalists and podcasters have a clear warning: ignore performance at your own peril. "It is on the basis of your performing ability that you will be judged by your audience and your employer," a broadcast journalism textbook proclaims. Reporting and writing matter, but on-air work "will ultimately decide your success."[6] As an NPR trainer once warned, "If you don't want to perform—at least a little bit—you're probably in the wrong business."[7]

Journalists often pursue on-air positions because they have an affinity for performing.[8] Some work hard at it and others "seem to have been born with the performance gene and sound like old hands almost as soon as they start reporting."[9] What exactly is performance? Goffman's dramaturgical model, which used theater as a metaphor to explore social interactions, provides useful insights.

Goffman's Self-Presentation Theory

Goffman defined performance as an individual's activity in front of a set of observers, or audience. During such interactions, the individual plays a pre-established role and hopes that observers consider the performance credible.[10]

Journalists commonly think in terms of performing a part and earning audience approval. When Renata Sago began a public radio job in a predominantly White community, she told herself, "I need to please this audience—this is the character I must play."[11] Dmae Lo Roberts considered the narration she did for her radio stories to be a performance. "You have to decide who your character is and how to present it and be comfortable portraying that character."[12]

Performances allow individuals to manage their public image. They accentuate certain attributes and conceal others in the hope of creating a favorable impression. When journalists read a script aloud or engage in unscripted talk, they make choices about vocal delivery (e.g., pitch, inflection, rate of speech) that affect how they are perceived. Appearance (e.g., attire, hair/grooming) and other nonverbal cues also convey information to audiences. Journalists use their "expressive equipment" to project an image of themselves. Goffman referred to this as a front—the part of an individual's performance that defines a situation for the audience.[13] To present a compelling front, performers need to convince the audience that the way they look, speak, and act is appropriate for their role. When performers take on an established role, such as a news anchor or reporter, they often find that there are already well-established fronts—or familiar forms— from which they must choose.

Goffman focused primarily on face-to-face interactions that occur in everyday life. I use his concepts to examine self-presentation in news studios and in the field, settings where journalists publicly act out their roles.[14] The performance of self is never a solo act, Goffman explained, because it depends on the setting, the audience, and the cooperation of others. Yet journalists' public performances commonly involve one-way communication. When doing a live shot on location, reading from a teleprompter while behind a news desk, or recording a voice-over in studio, journalists must imagine their audience as they perform.

As Goffman observed, "Because talk is learned, developed, and ordinarily practiced in connection with the visual and audible response of immediately-present recipients, a radio announcer must inevitably talk as if responsive others were before his eyes and ears (TV announcers are even more deeply committed to this condition)."[15] Goffman noted the difficulty of "self-constructed talk projected under the demands, gaze, and responsiveness of listeners who aren't there."[16] The goal is to produce a "spontaneous, fluent flow of words—if not a forceful, pleasing personality—under conditions that lay speakers would be unable to manage."[17]

All of this occurs in frontstage settings, where individuals perform a specific role for their imagined audience. Backstage, individuals can step out of character because they are out of public view. The humor in Reyes and Capek's TikTok videos comes from their staying in character and maintaining their front (the rehearsed, artificial-sounding anchor voice) even when backstage in ostensibly private settings. We are amused—and people in the video are annoyed—because Reyes refuses to give the performance a rest.

Authenticity and Agency in Performance

The binary that backstage journalists can be authentic but when frontstage they must put on an act assumes that they are either "on" (they are performing, which is inherently inauthentic) or "off" (they are not performing and can be who they *really* are). This implies that authenticity is an "intrinsic quality of the free individual" rather than how it is increasingly regarded—a "matter of appearance that is constantly in need of negotiation between the individual who has claims to authenticity and the surrounding world."[18] Media studies scholar Mark Deuze has argued that authenticity is manufactured. It is less a commitment to being "true" to oneself and more an effort to distinguish oneself and accentuate one's uniqueness as a trademark.[19]

Some interviewees referred to authenticity as trueness. A voice coach said, "Authentic is a fancy word for 'be yourself.'" Others aimed to help journalists "find their authentic voice" and "be true to themselves." Several journalists said that at times in their career they could not be their authentic selves on air. My intent is not to criticize the advice of voice coaches (I have told students to "be yourself") or to minimize the frustrations of journalists but to associate myself with Deuze's view that authenticity is a social construction and that there is not just one self to be.[20] In other words, there is no one true or authentic way of speaking, looking, and acting.

Many expressions of self are deliberate performances.[21] We commonly alter our appearance based on the image we wish to convey. We design our voices, "varying pronunciation and prosody to suit differing interlocutors and situations." While this is often done unconsciously, it is sometimes a conscious and calculated decision, such as when journalists work with a voice/dialect coach or image consultant.[22]

In broadcasting, authentic talk is intended to approximate naturally occurring conversations[23]—informal, intimate discourse that usually takes place in private and is brought into the public sphere.[24] Broadcast talk is, however, staged for performance.[25] Research suggests that even when newscasters claim to speak the same in private as they do in studio, they unconsciously adjust to the conventions of the discourse genre, replicating a familiar standard of on-air speech. They speak slower, enunciate more clearly, and change their vocal inflection more than they do in everyday conversation.[26] What constitutes natural talk varies based on context. "We have different voices for different situations because not every voice works in every situation," says Rob Rosenthal, a story editor, reporter, and producer for radio and podcasts.[27] "We change how we sound in different environments, but it's still us," says radio journalist, educator/trainer, and voice coach George Bodarky.[28] Even Capek, who sounds dramatically different on camera and off, says she feels like "my news voice is my voice—it's just an elevated version."[29]

How we speak is not a "pure reflection of who we are," says Chenjerai Kumanyika, a professor and podcast host/executive producer. "It's very tempting and seductive to think that I have an internal spirit that's uniquely me and the voice is my expression of that. But I think the voice is a construction and a performance. Rather than expressing an authentic voice, I think it's about choosing a performance that's appropriate to the moment."[30] The question arises: who should make this choice and on what basis?

Employees often must sacrifice some autonomy to fit with their organization's needs and culture. But managers and consultants should not tell journalists how to look or sound like themselves. Journalists should be allowed some agency in selecting a performance that is appropriate to the moment. "It still feels like to some degree we need to ask permission to be ourselves," television journalist Michelle Li says. "Instead, we should be giving ourselves permission to be ourselves. Help me be the best version of myself, but please stop telling me to change."[31] Asking journalists to change their appearance or vocal delivery to closely conform to that of a dominant group is also fraught. Coerced assimilation, Kenji Yoshino argues, is a threat to personal autonomy, which he defines as giving individuals the freedom to elaborate their authentic selves rather than adhering to a rigid notion of what constitutes an authentic identity.[32]

Self-Presentation and Identity

Identity is best understood as a set of characteristics that defines one's sense of self or a group's sense of self in relation to a complex social environment.[33] Our identity is socially constructed—formed not just by asking "Who am I?" but also "How do others view me?" and "How do I fit into the world?" Several types of identities are relevant to this book. One is social identity, or self-categorization in relation to group membership. Society classifies people by broad criteria (e.g., race, gender, class), and individuals often affiliate with these identity groups.[34] Personal identity is how individuals define and view themselves in relation to others—in essence, the interests, values, characteristics, and traits that make them unique. Goffman described personal identity as relatively fixed and differentiated it from felt identity, which a person adopts because they see it as the most suitable identity in a given situation. Identity is often fluid not only because one's performance of it may change based on setting, but also because one's self-concept, or evaluation of self, may change over time.

Identity is communicated and negotiated through self-presentation.[35] Physical appearance is central to defining personal identity. Increasingly, the self is defined in aesthetic terms, how one looks rather than what one does.[36] People express their individuality—and in some cases their group identity—through their personal style (e.g., clothing, accessories, hairstyle, body art). The feedback people receive on their appearance—not just stylistic choices but also physical characteristics (e.g., height, weight, facial features)—can shape their sense of self.

Identity is also tied to speech. "The way we speak reflects our identity to a certain extent, but also it creates that identity," says Rob Drummond, a linguist who studies spoken language and identity. "It helps create the way we're perceived within society. We then manipulate the way we speak depending on the identity we're trying to perform."[37] Criticizing a person's speech can be viewed as an attack on their identity. "To say something negative about how someone talks feels like I'm critiquing who they are as a person," Rosenthal says. "That feels unfair."[38]

How a person talks may not be a pure reflection of who they are, but it reflects how they view themselves and want to be viewed in a particular setting. It also reflects where they have lived, who has influenced them, and what feedback they have received.[39] Accents, in particular, are an important part of a person's social identity,[40] often signaling regional affiliation.[41] As psychologist Katherine D. Kinzler explains, "A good deal of our speech—and hence, large swaths of our social identity—is baked in, showcasing our early upbringing, which is very difficult to escape."[42] That became evident to television journalist Deion Broxton, who found it difficult to change his vocal delivery after having spent most of his life in one part of Baltimore. As he worked with a voice and communications specialist, he was still in close contact with friends and family who reinforced speaking habits he was trying to break.

Working Identity

In the months before and after he moved to Montana for his first on-air job, Broxton carefully managed his working identity. In newsrooms and other organizational settings, individuals signal their identity to coworkers.[43] People from marginalized groups often feel extra pressure to do this "shadow work" to appear professional because they perceive themselves as subject to negative stereotypes.[44] "Both the nature of the work and the pressure to do it, the 'working identity' phenomenon, is a form of employment discrimination," law professors Devon W. Carbado and Mitu Gulati write.[45]

Companies extract a diversity profit by hiring workers from minority groups who have "palatable working identities"—for instance, those who are Black but not "too Black" in their employer's view.[46] Brittany Noble felt that to be palatable to her managers, she had to tone down her Blackness by straightening her hair and speaking like a prototypical newscaster. Her friends thought that her on-air persona seemed fake. "By the time I was a television anchor I didn't even know who I was," Noble says. "I was changing myself just to be this presenter on the news, and it wasn't working."[47] When media studies scholar Libby Lewis was in television news, she managed her working identity by "talking more White than the whitest White person." The alternative: "Work in fear of being sent to a voice coach or worse, fired for breaking one of the unwritten rules of adopting the White mid-Western speech pattern."[48]

Noble and Lewis are among the many Black Americans who have felt pressure to code switch—a common covering technique in which people change how they express themselves around those from different racial and ethnic backgrounds,[49] often to conform to culturally dominant White styles of speech.[50] Research shows that Black college graduates under the age of 50 are most likely to feel the need to code switch.[51]

Name as an Identity Signal

To manage their working identity, employees may engage in racial or ethnic distancing. Someone who is bilingual may decide not to speak Spanish at work. A person with an ethnic-sounding name may feel pressure to anglicize it.[52] Television journalist Tahera Rahman at first did not pronounce her name on air the way she did with family and friends. "When you start in this industry you're thinking, 'let's not make this hard,'" she says.[53] Once Rahman felt more secure in her role, she decided to use a more authentic pronunciation. Growing up, Jorge Valencia spent a lot of time trying to fit in. "Changing my name was the easiest way to do that," he says. In high school, he went by George because no one could pronounce his name. During college he switched to the anglicized pronunciation of Jorge. He still says it that way on air and in other work settings because "it's easier for people to understand and it saves me time having to repeat my name," but he defers to sources if they want him to use the Spanish-language pronunciation of their names.[54]

Sia Nyorkor says journalists now face less pressure than before to change their names. When she was in college in the late 1990s, she remembers a student shortening her last name so it sounded less Jewish. Professors and journalists advised Nyorkor to change her name before she applied for television news jobs. At the time, ethnic-sounding names were increasingly common on television, but "not so much African names," Nyorkor says.[55] She ignored the advice, kept her name, and eventually got hired to work on air. During that same era, when Gloria Riviera got engaged, a television news executive asked her to keep her last name because it sounded ethnic. "More diverse names were valuable to the network," Riviera says.[56]

An anchor's name can have value to a news station because it signals diversity. Michelle Li, who is Korean, grew up in the Midwest with adoptive parents. She went by the family surname, Sherwood. Mentors told her that she would fare better on the job market with a more Asian-sounding last name. As one said, "If news directors are going to hire an Asian person, they really need to get more bang for their buck." The implied message: looking Asian is not sufficient. "The idea was that I'd reach Asian viewers if I had an Asian name or that my name as Michelle Sherwood was too distracting for people because then they would have to think, well, that doesn't match."[57]

Li resisted at first. "My name is a key identity factor for me," she says. "I'm not ashamed of [Sherwood]. It's not hard to pronounce. It's my parents' name. It felt fake to change it—like faking to be an Asian person. It's like, you can only be Asian if we put you in this box." She kept her name through her first two television jobs but relented after not advancing fast enough. On air she was still

Michelle Sherwood, but she began sending out tapes as Michelle Li. Her Korean last name is Park, but to more clearly signal her Koreanness to White male news directors, she decided on Li. Not Lee, her birth mother's maiden name, because she thought those news directors might not recognize that as Korean. Li says the name change was "strategic" and "felt really cheap." She resented having to do it. "It felt like I was selling out adoptees by not being able to represent as who I am. But I thought, 'if this is what I have to do, I'll do it.'" Once she did, the response rate increased for tapes sent out with her new name prominently displayed. "They saw my name and probably thought, 'oh, this is an Asian person. We need an Asian person. This is a diverse hire.'"[58]

Li feels that in her role, "you're too Asian or not Asian enough"—the latter in reference to her name, the former to her cultural identity on air. In one high-profile instance, after Li mentioned dumpling soup as a favorite holiday food tradition, a viewer criticized her for being "very Asian" in a voicemail telling her to "keep her Korean to herself." Li played the viewer's message on social media, prompting an outcry and a flood of users expressing pride in being #VeryAsian. "I'm always bobbing and weaving," Li says, "trying to appease the audience, to make myself less Asian or more Asian."[59]

That identity work is common among journalists of color. As Tavis Smiley is quoted as saying about his time at NPR, "I have to be authentically Black, but not too Black."[60] Journalists often confront expectations about what they should sound like based on their race or ethnicity. Radio journalist Diana Opong says it "feels terrible" when people talk to her on the phone and then are surprised she is Black when they meet her in person.[61] Tanya Ott, who helped select programming for a public radio station, said managers were hesitant to pick up a show because they thought the host sounded White and they "wanted diversity on their air." When Ott explained that the host is Black and gay, someone responded, "Well, he doesn't sound Black." Ott says the person "immediately realized how offensive the comment was and got a horrified look on their face. So did everyone else around the table."[62]

As these examples illustrate, journalists often are expected to represent a social identity group to which they belong. Yet within an identity group, there is no one authentic way of speaking, dressing, or behaving. "To say otherwise would be to participate in a reductive and inaccurate essentialism of which I want no part," Kumanyika wrote in an essay about identity and performance.[63] Just as it may be discriminatory to deny someone the right to be on air because their voice sounds too Black, "including a voice [on air] that is deemed as sounding Black can also be another site of discrimination."[64]

Aesthetic Presentation and the Form of News

Many journalists expend significant energy on identity work and image management because their industry places a high value on aesthetic presentation.

News serves more than a utilitarian function; it is not just the sum of its informational content.[65] It has aesthetic appeal; there are intrinsic delights in consuming it.[66] On television, aesthetic presentation includes not only graphics and set design but also journalists' appearance and vocal delivery. On radio and podcasts, journalists' voices set the aesthetic tone along with music, natural sound, and effects.

The news industry covets journalists with highly valued aesthetic traits. Those who possess traits of beauty that are perceived as assets capable of yielding privilege, opportunity, and wealth are said to have aesthetic capital,[67] a form of embodied cultural capital—corporeal clues of class that are "written onto the body."[68] Sociologist Pierre Bourdieu described cultural capital as a collection of symbolic elements such as skills, tastes, and styles of speech and dress that indicates membership in a social class.[69]

Aesthetic capital is similar to cultural capital, sociologist Tammy L. Anderson and her coauthors argue. "We live in a society with well-defined preferences and attitudes regarding individual beauty and aesthetics. Though such tastes and viewpoints change over time and vary by social context and group, people are made keenly aware of them on a daily basis."[70] Evaluations of aesthetic beauty are partly a reflection of taste—what carries cultural value within a certain context or field.[71] Those in positions of power typically determine what is regarded as "tasteful" or high status.[72]

In journalism, newsroom leaders often are the arbiters of aesthetic taste. They consider aesthetic appeal when hiring, then instruct new employees on appearance and manner of speech, a practice called aesthetic labor. Early research on aesthetic labor focused primarily on frontline service workers but has more recently expanded to include employees in other "style" labor markets.[73] Companies use aesthetics to build brand culture and express a corporate identity.[74] Hiring managers screen for applicants with an appealing personality package, including pleasing manner of speech and stylish appearance.[75] They prefer those who "look good and sound right," those whose embodied capacities and attributes at the point of entry to employment conform to an organization's brand image.[76]

Employers develop and commodify workers' capacities and attributes through recruitment, selection, and training, transforming them into competencies and skills aimed to produce a style that is visually or aurally appealing to audiences.[77] Workers not deemed an aesthetic fit are often excluded during recruitment and selection, relegated to nonvisible roles in the workplace, or fired.[78] Organizational gatekeepers who determine aesthetic fit help set standards of occupational practice by advocating an ideal type. When those who do not fit this ideal are discouraged from entering the profession, this may limit diversity.[79]

The idea of aesthetic fit is one way discriminatory attitudes impact the labor market.[80] The ideal worker is often thought to be middle or upper class, conventionally gendered, and White.[81] Thus, workplace demands for aesthetic labor can serve to legitimize discrimination based on gender, race, and class.[82] News managers' aesthetic standards inevitably reflect their tastes and assumptions about audience tastes. Because managers typically are White and may view the audience they must cater to as middle or upper class and White, the range of forms that are considered aesthetically appealing often is narrow.

Form and Journalistic Authority

In journalism studies literature, form typically refers to how print news is designed and packaged. In *The Form of News: A History*, Kevin G. Barnhurst and John Nerone examine the enduring visible structures of the newspaper (e.g., layout, color, typography, graphics, and photography).[83] To them, form is everything a newspaper does to present the look of news. The newspaper provides a three-dimensional experience and the form becomes reassuring through repeated exposure. Content changes daily, but the newspaper's physical arrangement, structure, and format remain roughly the same. Headline size, story placement, and other design elements connote importance. Thus, form becomes "sanctified"; it "encodes a system of authority."[84]

In *Journalistic Authority: Legitimating News in the Digital Era*, Matt Carlson defines form as the persisting visible and narrative structures of news, including design elements, narrative conventions, and image use across different media. Standardization of form helps tame the continuous demands of news production, Carlson explains. News forms help signal legitimacy and provide insights into the workings of journalistic authority, which is always open to contestation and change.[85]

Writing about journalism as performance discourse, Marcel Broersma defines form as the structure, design, and genre of a news article. Journalists are in a continual battle for symbolic power, Broersma argues. One way they assert their authority over and autonomy from actors in journalism and other fields is by contesting conventions of form and style. To retain and strengthen their social position, journalists employ stylistic innovations and invent new forms without greatly challenging professional rules.[86]

Broadcasting and Podcasting Forms

Broadcasting and podcasting also have distinct forms. Instead of focusing on the packaging of news content, this book explores how journalists' aesthetic traits and presentation styles contribute to the three-dimensional experience of consuming news. Journalists do not just produce news; they are an essential part of the news product. Whether or not we find a performance appealing, we notice it. Every host's voice has a unique texture and tone. Their style of speech becomes part of their trademark. They are the institutional voice. When they are away, their show sounds and feels different. An anchor's appearance, mannerisms, and on-air presence make a show aesthetically distinct and appealing to audiences. Journalists focus on self-presentation in order to be perceived as authoritative as well as aesthetically pleasing. News anchors with deep, resonant voices and "accentless" speech are often praised for sounding authoritative. Those who follow appearance conventions—straight, medium-length hair for women; short hair and a clean-shaven face for men; gender-normative attire for both—are often perceived as looking authoritative.

Just as forms in print news become reassuring through repeated exposure to them, so do forms in broadcasting and podcasting. Content changes daily, but a newscaster's physical appearance and vocal delivery often remain the same. Talent changes, but the aesthetic experience of watching or listening to journalists perform the news remains consistent. Forms of news presentation become sanctified; they encode a system of authority.

Forms vary depending on medium and genre.[87] Morning television has a less formal feel than evening television. Journalists typically sound more casual in narrative audio than on hard news programs. As voice coach Sora Newman tells journalists who try to perform like *This American Life* host Ira Glass, "You're doing news—Ira is not. He's just talking to people in their living room, telling them stories. . . . In news, you can't talk that way."[88] When students ask journalism professor Sally Herships for voicing advice, she asks them, "'Are you going to a tiny local radio station? Is it a national show?' In design, there's a saying: the form has to fit the content."[89] Journalists' voices are expected to suit the station that employs them.[90] When Antoinette Lattouf worked at an Australian national public broadcasting station, she was taught to speak naturally. Later, at a commercial television station, she was encouraged to perform with a vocal inflection that she found phony and overly dramatic. "Whenever I was in public broadcasting, I was a bit too commercial, and whenever I was in commercial, I was a bit too public broadcasting," she says.[91]

Within a given sector (e.g., local television, public radio), news often looks and sounds similar across news organizations. This homogeneity is known as institutional isomorphism. In many fields, organizations are rewarded for being similar to others. This can make it easier to be acknowledged as reputable. Institutional isomorphism is important for public legitimacy because it reflects widely accepted norms and behaviors and promotes the success and survival of organizations.[92] However, it can be problematic when it restricts diversity or limits new forms from emerging, as it has in broadcast journalism. Forms of self-presentation associated with marginalized groups (e.g., ethnic accents, natural hairstyles for Black women) are sometimes deemed unprofessional, while other forms (e.g., "accentless" speech, the newscaster anchor bob) have become normalized and are considered legitimate.

These familiar forms are widely referred to as neutral. Yet form is never neutral; it reflects what journalists value and consider appealing.[93] Aesthetic practices and principles are socially constructed.[94] Yet journalism's highly developed aesthetic tradition has gained the mark of objectivity. Because it is ubiquitous, news consumers may no longer regard it as aesthetics and instead accept it uncritically.[95]

Conceptualizing Performance Neutrality

Critiques of neutrality commonly focus on journalists' approach to news coverage—specifically, impartiality and detachment. To forestall accusations of bias or partisanship, some journalists avoid revealing personal opinions, taking sides in debates, inserting themselves in stories, or influencing events.[96] They may try to use neutral language and give equal voice to competing viewpoints.[97] Because nonverbal cues can influence viewers, television journalists often strive for nonverbal neutrality.[98] When covering traumatic events and conducting emotional interviews, they are expected to appear calm and unaffected and instead allow their sources to inject opinions and emotions into a story.[99]

Related to nonverbal neutrality is performance neutrality, defined in the introductory chapter as self-presentation that is deemed unobjectionable, reveals little about journalists' social identity, and supposedly does not detract from their message. Interviews with current and former journalists revealed that performance neutrality has dimensions primarily associated with speech and appearance.

Sounding *placeless*—like you are from everywhere but nowhere—is commonly considered neutral. Being regionally unidentifiable has long been desirable in broadcasting. In the mid 1900s, authors of an influential training manual advised announcers to adopt a "neutral" accent, writing that "it should be impossible for the listener to tell from which section of the country you come from."[100] Expectations have changed little over time. In the early 2010s, then-NPR vice president of programming Eric Nuzum used the phrase "ambiguously genuine" to describe his ideal announcer. "They sound like a real person, but they don't sound like a specific age, or as if they were from a specific region."[101] Radio journalist Gretel Kahn equated a "good voice for radio" with someone who speaks neutrally, "like I don't know where you're from."[102] Chapter 6 further explores the notion of a "neutral" broadcast accent.

Vocal *flatness* is also considered desirable. Interviewees used the term to describe the ubiquitous, vaguely midwestern or mid-Atlantic news anchor accent, which is often viewed as the "neutral norm for the middle class nationwide."[103] Those who were raised to speak with this flat accent told me they considered themselves fortunate. Others who were not felt they had to adapt. As the lone Black journalist at his first on-air job, Don Champion knew he had to follow a speech coach's advice to sound midwestern. "I wasn't thinking, 'why do I have to conform?' I was trying to do whatever it took to get my next job and get out of a small market."[104]

Related to detachment and nonverbal neutrality, flatness also refers to sober, restrained speech. Former radio journalist Kim Fox "played it straight" when covering hard news. To sound authoritative, she spoke flatly, "removing emotion from anything I said."[105] Gabrielle Jones, who described her delivery as intentionally "personality-less," consistently received positive feedback, which she said speaks to "how that very bland, rootless way of speaking is praised."[106] Former trainer Catherine Stifter disagreed that a monotone voice sounds unbiased: "That's just boring," she told them. "Energy is neutral."[107]

Journalists of color reported being pressured to "flatten" their voice and "tone down" their delivery. When she worked in public radio, Stephanie Foo felt that those who advised her on voicing wanted her to "dial back" her presentation to make it sound flat and unaffected. "I struggled with it and against it. I would try to inject tiny instances of myself and they would always cut it out, which enraged me."[108] Other women of color, told they sounded too young and casual, were advised to slow down and speak more formally, which they found unnatural. Chapter 7 details how journalists have attempted to fit in by, as one host put it, "flattening the interesting aspects" of their voice and delivery.[109]

Some journalists reluctantly attempted to hide their sexual orientation from audiences. Advisers viewed *ambiguity*—being unclassifiable—as an asset. Former television journalist Harrison Hove recalls his agent recommending that he "toe this line so that as many women like you as possible and as many men like you as possible. You want to be this middle ground. Are you gay? Are you straight? Who knows."[110] Hove, who is gay, tried early in his career to find that middle ground and perform neutrally.

Another dimension is *conventionality*, often referring to appearance. For decades, journalists have learned to present in ways that are broadly palatable, unobjectionable, and stylistically down the middle. Many try to look conventionally attractive, like whatever is deemed mainstream in their market, to avoid alienating audiences. Television news executives have long believed that the key to retaining viewers is to "build them up early and don't offend them."[111] "Them," in this context, referred to the predominantly White "Middle Majority," members of the working class and more educated white-collar professionals who made up the bulk of the television audience in the mid- to late twentieth century. These loyal viewers generally expected journalists to look clean cut, with mid-length hair and traditional, "tasteful" attire. Appearance norms have changed in recent decades, with style generally becoming less conservative. News stations increasingly target diverse audiences. Yet as chapter 4 explores, some journalists perceive that newsroom leaders still fear alienating White, middle-class viewers or the wealthy, well-educated listeners who have traditionally supported public radio.[112]

Chapter 5 covers another dimension of performance neutrality: *consistency*. Journalists who behave inconsistently or unpredictably risk attracting unwanted attention and, in rare cases, becoming the news. Concerns about potential distractions shape not just what journalists write and say but how they present themselves publicly. Television journalists are advised to maintain continuity in their appearance. Many are contractually obliged to get their employer's approval if they wish to do otherwise. How journalists look when hired often becomes the "neutral" baseline, setting the standing for what is considered normal appearance. Consistency is particularly stressed for women and journalists of color, whose bodies and stylistic choices are most heavily scrutinized.[113] Many journalists I interviewed initially decided against switching hairstyles or straying from their usual wardrobes because they sensed, or heard directly from managers, that viewers would find them unpredictable and untrustworthy.

The Myth of Performance Neutrality

Performance neutrality is a myth that benefits those in positions of power. While the industry-standard anchor voice is referred to as "neutral," it actually reflects a distinct aesthetic choice that was socially constructed almost a century ago when radio news became widely consumed and White men created newsroom norms. "Standard" appearance on television has long reflected White beauty norms. One example: Black journalists commonly use chemical straighteners and wear weaves and wigs that emulate White European hair textures and hairstyles—part of their effort to achieve "palatable Blackness."[114]

Appearance norms designed to prevent journalists from alienating loyal audiences can block many forms of identity expression. Journalists often maintain a consistent look because they are told it helps viewers focus on their message. Yet interviewees often viewed this as an unnecessary form of institutional control that limits the way Black women, in particular, express themselves through their hairstyles. Journalists are accustomed to finding a supposedly safe middle ground—both in their reporting and their self-presentation. Yet journalist Lewis Raven Wallace aptly describes centrism of any kind as "more a marketing tactic to reach broad audiences than actual neutrality," arguing that "we are past the point where [audiences] expect us to speak to a fictitious and ever-shifting center in order to be neutral."[115]

In many fields, middle-class White men are considered the "standard category of human beings." Whiteness serves a normative function by defining the "neutral" range of human attitudes and behaviors.[116] Wesley Lowery observes that in journalism, "the views and inclinations of Whiteness are accepted as the objective neutral."[117] As public radio journalist Tonya Mosley writes,

> Every person of color in your newsroom has a story about how a manager questioned either their news judgment, their diction, or whether they could be neutral or objective.... This flawed way of thinking assumes that White journalists have a neutral point of view. News as we know it was built on this idea—that cultural norms, ideas, and points of view, which have historically come from White journalists, are neutral.[118]

Given this dynamic, Wallace and others argue that neutrality is a myth that serves the powerful.[119]

Summary

Interviews reveal similarities between neutrality in reporting practice and performance neutrality. Just as journalists signal impartiality and detachment by keeping their personal opinions private and not inserting themselves in stories, many interviewees initially tried to reveal little about themselves when performing. They felt pressure to speak in a flat, neutral accent, tone down their delivery, keep aspects of their identity private, look conventional, and maintain a consistent appearance. This was especially so for early career journalists who wanted to advance in the industry. Research shows that the longer journalists work, the less they embrace neutrality as a core professional value.[120] Interviewees were likelier to challenge aspects of performance neutrality when they felt more established professionally or had left the field.

Performance neutrality becomes a particularly unuseful goal when its characteristics remain static while audience composition changes and norms evolve. Chapters 5–7 examine how a variety of news forms became institutionalized and how journalists have pushed back against expectations that they perform neutrally. The next two chapters explore how journalists learn about these expectations and the pressure some have felt to appeal to newsroom leaders and news audiences.

3

Learning How to Perform

• •

Deion Broxton decided he wanted to be a television news reporter in college after covering protests over Freddie Gray's death. Broxton was drawn to the broadcast journalists who joined him in the streets. He watched in awe as they reported live and felt moved to become one of them. Broxton was bothered by the lack of Black journalists covering the unrest in his hometown of Baltimore. He had wanted to become a sportscaster, but after this experience he shifted his focus to news, where he thought he could make a difference and set himself apart. "The rarer you are," he assumed, "the more in demand you can be."[1]

Broxton never figured that how he talked would interfere with his career goals. He thought little about performance when he began in news. But over time, his observations, interactions, and experiences clarified industry expectations for getting and keeping an on-air job. He got advice from managers about improving his vocal delivery, and in his spare time he found people to coach him. His on-air presentation always seemed to be a work in progress.

How do journalists like Broxton learn to perform the news? There is no authoritative guide to looking and sounding professional; no industry-wide appearance code or *AP Stylebook* entry on voice and speech. One can major in journalism and learn little about performance. Sora Newman learned to refine her radio voice the way many journalists learn how to perform: "trial by fire."[2] Once on the job, it is common to receive vague feedback and unhelpful criticism rather than constructive coaching. Changing jobs means adjusting to new expectations. Journalists may learn as much from jobs or promotions they do not get as they do from successes. In journalism, the socialization process is messy and often frustrating to those trying to understand professional norms and practices.

This chapter is about occupational socialization, the process for learning about appropriate or legitimate modes of practice.[3] I explore how and where journalists are trained, what information sources they access, who they turn to for advice, and whose directives they must consider. I identify influential actors who shape the look and sound of news and examine the signals they send about self-presentation. I also identify key sites of socialization—places where journalists absorb information about industry expectations.

Aspiring and early career journalists often reach a similar conclusion: the path of least resistance, at least at first, is to follow well-established norms when performing. Many signals point in that direction. Mentors with professional experience often feel obligated to share pragmatic advice about how the industry is, not how they wish it was. Journalism is competitive and bosses can be blunt. Institutions are hard to change. Those who challenge norms are commonly met with resistance. Yet as some norms change with the times, so too has advice about looking and sounding professional.

The best explanation for why journalists encounter varied signals as they learn how to perform is that journalism lacks formalized standards. Unlike professions such as law and medicine, journalism has no credentialing requirement—there is no entrance exam or professional license. Many journalists never study journalism. News organizations often lack time to train new hires. Codes of ethics exist but often are not followed or enforced.[4] What constitutes professional journalism is ambiguous and contested. Journalists regularly circulate knowledge among themselves through channels other than textbooks and training courses.[5] Much of what they learn about performance comes from observations, conversations, and experiences that occur outside classrooms and newsrooms.

Yet journalists tend to identify as members of a profession because it lends status to their work and helps maintain communal boundaries.[6] In the absence of a governing authority and formalized codes of conduct, newsroom leaders look to industry norms and set their own standards to assert their legitimacy and articulate a shared understanding of acceptable practices.[7] Scholars describe this as "de facto professionalization"—the development of educational and behavioral standards that are not imposed and controlled by authorities.[8]

Journalists primarily learn about performance norms and standards through vocational anticipatory socialization, a process by which individuals intentionally or unintentionally receive messages from their environment about the profession that affect their career expectations.[9] Below I explore how, as historically has been the case, journalists discover and internalize institutional norms, often without being directly told what those norms are.[10] I also consider the role of peripheral actors such as voice coaches, image consultants, and talent agents who advise journalists about self-presentation. First, though, I look at the important role of observational learning in the socialization process.

The Observation-Imitation Cycle

Social behavior is often learned through observation. According to psychologist Albert Bandura's social learning theory, individuals observe those around them and encode their behavior. They are likely to model behaviors that come with rewards.[11] Many aspiring journalists first learn what looks and sounds professional and who they need to imitate by observing prominent newscasters. Early in his career, Broxton closely observed how news anchors looked, talked, and comported themselves. Television became his "in-home campus," as a news director once put it, for studying how broadcasters perform.[12]

One of Broxton's first observations was that few Black journalists have dreadlocks or long hair of any style. Both he and Don Champion, a former television correspondent, gleaned from watching news that as Black men, they needed to keep their hair short. "I sensed that looking 'clean-cut' was the expectation in the business," Champion says.[13] Black female journalists often draw similar conclusions. Whitney Miller assumed that she had to stop wearing braids when applying for jobs, in part because she did not see anyone on television news wearing them.[14]

Journalists from historically marginalized groups often observe that they are outsiders. Early in her career, television journalist Sia Nyorkor noticed a uniformity in Black female journalists' appearance. "Everyone looked the same—light skin, straight hair, size six. I didn't fit into any of those boxes."[15] Diana Opong observed that no one in broadcast news sounded like her family. "I never heard West African accents. I heard traditional American and British accents, which were considered acceptable." One reason why she decided to work in radio was that she saw few television journalists who looked like her. "I think I had a sense that there wasn't room for someone like me."[16]

Noor Tagouri was captivated by female journalists like Lisa Ling, Christiane Amanpour, and Soledad O'Brien, "women of color who didn't look like the mainstream and didn't sound like them, either." But they were the outliers; she remembers seeing little racial or ethnic diversity on television. "You want to see yourself represented when you're watching television, but I never experienced that. For the longest time, I never thought I was going to cover my hair [with a hijab] because I had never seen anybody on TV do it."[17]

To Viktoria Capek, the archetypal newscaster was skinny, wore a tight dress, and had short, bobbed, blonde hair. "I was never told this is what I should wear. It just became normalized because it's what I saw around me."[18] Jana Shortal says that from watching television growing up, "I knew it was important to be a White male, but that was going to be difficult for me." The women she observed on television played gender-normative roles. "I knew what uniform I needed to put on. The example had been set for 50 years."[19]

Journalists' observations about their news market can give a false sense of what it is like elsewhere. Watching local television news in Miami, Vanessa Ruiz viewed multiculturalism on air as the norm. "You have people of all backgrounds, nationalities, and experiences coexisting, and that's reflected in the local media," Ruiz says. "It creates this false perception that we live in a diverse and welcoming country. When I left Miami, I realized that is not true."[20]

Problematically, such observations can lead journalists to stop pursuing on-air careers. "People aren't applying because they think, 'Why would I ever get hired with my accent, with my Black skin, with my Asian background, with my very Muslim name? I just wouldn't get a look,'" says Antoinette Lattouf, an Australian broadcast journalist, diversity advocate, and author of the book *How to Lose Friends and Influence White People*.[21] Journalists who stutter made similar observations. "I believed that I could be a great TV anchor," a print journalist says. "But in the back of my mind, from seeing who was on TV, I knew there was no way a person was going to hire me."[22] Before ultimately becoming a radio anchor/host, another participant assumed that "my stutter meant that I could never pursue this line of work."[23]

During Khalon Richard's time at NPR, early career journalists—particularly those with accents—counted themselves out from on-air positions. "With the NPR voice, people kind of know if they have it or if they don't." Richard says those in the latter category assumed that "this isn't going to be my path because I don't sound like what I hear on the radio."[24] Huo Jingnan, Richard's colleague at NPR, had similar self-doubts. In college, she thought that print journalism was her only realistic path. "I didn't think I would have a future in TV, so I didn't even try."[25] She figured that her foreign accent was a strike against her. She learned English growing up but it was British English. "You don't sound like an American," her father told her. "People are going to think you're an outsider." No one sounded just like her at NPR, but some had accents, which, as a producer trying to become a reporter, she found encouraging. Yet when she finally got on air, she tried to imitate NPR voice, which she considered the standard.

Imitating the Standard

Such imitation is commonplace. When Dorothy Tucker started an on-air television job in Chicago, she tried to emulate her White male colleagues. "They clearly were the stars. I thought if I sounded like them and presented like them, I would be as successful."[26] When Dana Adams began as a broadcast journalist, she learned how to dress, wear her hair, and sound confident by watching network news anchors. As a consultant and agent, she advises clients to "observe other broadcast journalists, take a little bit from each person, and create your own on-air persona."[27] Talent coach/agent Carolyn Kane similarly advises clients hired in a market that is new to them to "look around them and see how people on air are doing it."[28]

Brittany Noble took her cues from a local anchor turned television legend. "My hair was the perfect Oprah situation. I knew I needed to have straight, bouncy, flowy hair. That's what I thought a news anchor was supposed to look like."[29] Shortal remembers that at her college, women who aspired to become on-air journalists modeled themselves on Jane Pauley and Katie Couric. "They all looked the right way. I didn't and I knew it," she says. "Rather than be humiliated, I just quit."[30] Shortal stopped studying broadcast journalism but eventually was persuaded to return. Early in her career as a television reporter, she felt that she could not stray far from the Pauley/Couric look.

When journalists imitate those they observe and are professionally successful, they may become the model others follow. The observation-imitation cycle helps legitimize the status quo. Repeated exposure causes performance attributes to be viewed as neutral or naturally occurring. "It's never questioned that women in broadcasting are slim and blonde and talk a certain way," Lattouf says. "People imitate that cookie-cutter person and it becomes a never-ending cycle. A certain type of person applies for a role and sounds like they do because they think that's the way it was meant to be."[31]

Early career journalists imitate voices and speaking patterns perceived as authoritative, a phenomenon known as phonetic imitation.[32] Some think that they must sound important, so they give over-the-top performances. "I see journalists trying to put on this hard-hitting reporter voice, but it sounds so fake," says voice coach Sally Prosser.[33] Coaches generally advise against imitation, even when it does not involve exaggeration. "At some point, you outgrow that and decide who you want to be," consultant/coach Marilyn Pittman tells her clients.[34] "If you like a voice, don't mimic it," voice coach George Bodarky says. "Mimicking is trying to be something that you're not."[35]

Yet some aspiring journalists consider imitation to be necessary. Growing up in Puerto Rico, Javier E. Gómez wanted to work in commercial broadcasting— ideally, an on-air job at an English-language station. To do so, he figured he needed to greatly reduce his Spanish accent. Gómez recorded himself reading news scripts and tried to imitate anchors in New York, where he attended college. He later worked with a speech coach on accent reduction. Gómez expended so much energy trying to sound like someone else that he felt he was starting to lose some of his identity.[36]

Michelle Faust Raghavan, who grew up in a bilingual household and was used to code switching, felt the need to sound White to succeed in public radio. "I wanted to sound like a real, serious NPR newscaster, so I mimicked the way people spoke on the radio."[37] During commutes, Dan Bobkoff practiced talking along with news radio hosts to sound "normal and decent." Bobkoff, who stutters, thought that the better he could imitate others, the more comfortable he would be with his delivery. "I lowered my voice and I emphasized every other word. I tried to make myself sound like I'm 60 years old. I was drawn to people who didn't have a generic radio voice, who weren't Edward R. Murrow wannabes. But what I was actually doing was trying to emulate some sort of idea of what an authoritative anchorman sounds like."[38]

Generations of journalists tried to emulate Murrow, Walter Cronkite, and other anchors of that era whose voices suggested gravitas. "For a long time, that was the definition of a good voice," says voice coach Ann S. Utterback.[39] There were no female role models to emulate in the early 1970s when NPR's Susan Stamberg became the first woman to anchor a national nightly news broadcast, so she tried deepening her voice in order to talk more like a male anchor.[40] She struggled to put on the booming "voice from on top of the mountain" that she assumed station managers wanted to hear.[41]

Breaking the Cycle

Stamberg's supervisor told her to speak naturally, which she did, ending the observation-imitation cycle. When that happens and new forms are introduced, the status quo can change. Ira Glass grew up hearing that authority comes from enunciation and precision. But he found that speaking style to be phony.[42] Glass was drawn to Stamberg, who sounded to him like "some Upper West Side New York lady leaning into the microphone, mensch-ily talking into the radio."[43] When he heard Stamberg and other NPR hosts "talking like real people," he thought, "That's the direction I have to go in."[44] Glass followed his instincts. His vocal delivery—"understated, conversational, pause-friendly," suggesting "intimacy and rumpled authenticity"—stood out.[45] With *This American Life*, Glass "launched a thousand radio geeks who heard the message loud and clear: be yourself and tell good stories."[46]

Podcast executive Kathy Tu recalls a time when people in narrative radio and podcasting "were all trying to sound natural like Ira was."[47] Former *This American Life* producer Stephanie Foo observes that "all these imitators popped up because that's what people associated with success."[48] Former NPR senior producer Juleyka Lantigua says that while Glass is rightly considered a standard, "not all journalists can sound like that and remain true to themselves. There's a process of both filtering and diluting that happens when you try to sound like something else, versus trying to cultivate and elevate the natural [speaking] patterns that occur as you tell your story."[49]

The voices journalists imitate have changed over time. But as many have noted about public radio, those voices have consistently been White. "[Ira Glass] completely challenged this idea of what NPR should sound like but in a very White way," says Celeste Headlee, a podcast host and longtime public media journalist. "Most of the people we know from *This American Life* are White. Black and Latino people don't talk like that. It's great every time someone breaks through NPR's bastion of sound, but it's still monochromatic."[50]

Chapter 7 takes up the question of whether public radio sounds predominantly White. The extent to which journalists who present in diverse ways have broken through in broadcasting and podcasting is explored throughout part II of this book. The following section explores signals from a range of sources that early career journalists are likely to encounter.

Vocational Anticipatory Socialization

Throughout high school, Broxton thought little about his vocal delivery. In college, his friends gently teased him about his accent and dialect and mimicked his deep voice. But he was not offended; he took pride in being unique. The first hint of roadblocks ahead came from a professor's suggestion that midwestern speech is preferred in broadcast journalism because "it is not even an accent" and "it is the model for Standard American English."[51] That professor also advised students to look "nice and groomed" and avoid dreadlocks on television. That lesson stuck with Broxton. (He keeps his head shaved.)

Through vocational anticipatory socialization (e.g., studying journalism, doing journalism internships, applying to journalism jobs), journalists learn important lessons about performing the news. These signals are influential because the start of a journalist's career is a vulnerable stage that is intimately connected to personal branding and identity building.[52]

Lessons from the Classroom

Performance and aesthetics are part of the journalism school curriculum. In production courses, students learn the basics: where to position a microphone for optimal sound, what backdrops work best for stand-ups, how to compose a good shot, and how to stay composed during breaking news. Lessons like these are uncontroversial and nearly universal. There is no such consensus about how professors should cover appearance and vocal delivery. Instruction on voicing is common in the performing arts but has historically been overlooked in journalism.[53] Professors often feel unqualified to teach students about vocal technique because they never received such training. That leaves students in a bind. "They're expected to have a great voice, which is their number one tool of the trade," says voice coach Prosser. "But they're not getting feedback."[54]

Even if professors feel qualified to teach voicing and give advice on appearance, determining what to say—or whether to say anything—is tricky. Jill Olmsted acknowledges that these conversations can be challenging to navigate. However, the former broadcast journalist feels it is her responsibility to prepare students for comments they might hear when they go on the job market and get into newsrooms. Hair, makeup, clothing, even physical features are not off limits. "There was a girl with a space between her teeth. I told her that a news director might tell her to fill that in, and she got insulted. I wasn't telling her she had to do that. I was telling her this is what the industry is like. . . . It's more accepting now, but it's still a very judgmental place." What Olmsted tells students about vocal presentation: "I'm not saying you can't succeed with your voice as it is, but you should be aware that you have a twang or that you talk fast, because a news director is probably going to have that conversation with you. Or you won't even get the chance because you won't be hired."[55]

Students sometimes perceive that professors' feedback is intended to deter them from pursuing—not prepare them for—a broadcasting career. That was the case in a high-profile 2020 controversy involving an incoming dean at Arizona State University. The school rescinded its offer to Sonya Forte Duhé after students at her former institution alleged that she made inappropriate comments about their voice and appearance. Duhé, a former broadcast journalist, was accused of telling students of color that they did not look presentable and speak properly. A black female student says that Duhé called her natural hair "messy" and unsuitable for television. A gay student considering broadcast journalism alleged that Duhé described his voice as "too theatrical." Duhé denied these allegations but explained that she expects students to follow industry standards for attire and grooming.[56]

Some professors have suggested that students should cover in order to be employable. When Lena Pringle studied journalism, she was told that she would not be hired in television news with her natural hair because it looked "too urban."[57] Tagouri, the former broadcast journalism student, says a professor who taught and worked with her at a news station told others, "I don't know who she thinks she is wearing that [hijab] on her head and thinking that she's ever going to get a job [on television]." Another professor asked Tagouri why she wanted to work in broadcast news without taking off her hijab while reporting when it took only one "crazy person" to kill her.[58]

Former students said that professors' comments influenced them even when they were not directed specifically at them. Nyorkor recalls reviewing videos of White newscasters in journalism school and being told, "This is how you need to look—she's articulate, she's clean looking."[59] A broadcast journalism professor advised Diana Opong and her classmates to "sound normal—like the majority of people who are listening." She was the only student of color in her class. "I had been excited to be in front of the camera, but I decided to do production because I was like, 'I'm not meant to be in front of the camera.'"[60] A student who stutters switched out of the journalism major due in part to a professor's comment about how journalists should sound. "She said, 'I want clear speech—tell me your main points and be really fast about it.' She was trying to prepare us for reality. I don't think her intention was to be rude, and she didn't know I was a stutterer. But sitting there in class, hearing a portrait of how journalists should present, I'm thinking, 'That's not who I am at all. How can I do this?'"[61]

Television journalist Tahera Rahman recalls a professor making no effort to challenge stereotypes of how broadcast journalists should look. "The message was just 'try to look like whomever you see on TV.'" Another professor was supportive of her goal to be a TV reporter. "But her advice was 'try *Al Jazeera*' or 'try Detroit,' where there is a large Arab American population. She named other big, diverse cities with ethnic populations that she thought would be more likely to accept me on TV. I don't think it was coming from a bad place but it was just the reality of the industry that we didn't have anyone like me yet."[62] Likewise, Michelle Li was advised to target television news markets like Seattle that were known to accept Asian American journalists.[63]

Others recall professors who reassured them that most employers would be accepting. A broadcast journalism professor advised Gómez not to worry about his Spanish accent as long as people could understand him. Gómez appreciated the support but in retrospect feels the professor was unrealistic about how employers would respond. He and many of his classmates with accents had trouble finding on-air work.[64] Nyorkor's graduate school professors advised students to "be themselves" and did not suggest that they needed to cover—a far different message than what she had heard years earlier as an undergraduate. She attributes the differences to changes in industry norms and a graduate program with more diverse faculty.

Those who learned little in college about self-presentation typically had mixed feelings. They appreciated the focus on their work's substance. Yet some later felt blindsided by the amount of attention paid to their appearance and vocal delivery. "It would have been good to have some sort of emphasis on delivery and presentation," Li says, "because the people who have it, they go farther."

Textbooks

Textbooks used in broadcasting and podcasting courses often emphasize performance. Commonly written by former journalists, these resources help set the agenda for classroom discussion and socialize students into the profession, potentially influencing career decisions. By articulating norms and practices and presenting ideas as indisputable, authors legitimize a belief system that students may interpret as natural.[65] This section explores authors' advice on self-presentation.

My content analysis of journalism and mass communication textbooks revealed that many avoid the topic of appearance or reference it vaguely, recommending that students "dress sharply" or "look presentable." Those that provide specifics generally identify appropriate appearance as being neatly groomed and conservatively dressed. One textbook advises journalists to "avoid extremes of taste." Hair should be neither too long nor too short; clothing should be stylish but not "flamboyant." Broadcast journalists should not be overweight, have "unusual features," or have obvious scars or other "physical defects," the authors write. They advise journalists to correct any "defect" that can keep them from being considered for a position.[66]

Textbooks tend to be specific about what sounds authoritative. Many recommend "neutral" midwestern or mid-Atlantic accents and use of General American English.[67] One advises journalists to avoid "sloppy diction," such as dropping a letter at the end of words, citing as an example, "While 'lookin' might be acceptable in conversational speech, it is not usually acceptable on air."[68] Regional accents may even disqualify journalists from broadcast work in their hometown, and "in a city on the other side of the country, you may literally be laughed at."[69] More recent textbooks tend to have a nuanced message: regional accents may be accepted locally but limit a journalist's geographic mobility. Authors generally warn that strong foreign accents can interfere with clear communication and stall a journalist's career.[70]

Broadcast journalism textbooks describe speech disorders as a roadblock to career success and in some cases as a disqualifier from landing an on-air job. "Minor speech impediments such as weak 'Rs' or 'THs' that become 'Vs' could be barriers to an otherwise promising career," authors of one book write.[71] Others state that broadcasters should not have "obvious speech problems, such as a lisp or a stutter."[72] Several textbooks advise journalists who have such "problems" to seek out speech therapy and to "manage expectations" and "be realistic" about their on-air career prospects. Authors who do not directly reference speech disorders still communicate that impediment-free speech is desirable by stating that journalists should "speak fluently under pressure," "sound clear and crisp," and go at a "steady tempo."[73]

Many textbooks mention the importance of pleasing tone or pitch. One notes that "generally speaking, low-pitched voices are more pleasant than high-pitched voices," and advises broadcasters to speak at the lowest comfortable pitch level and to "eliminate harsh or shrill sounds."[74] Another explains that while broadcasters were once expected to have a deep, bass voice, more range is now accepted. "Certainly, a deeper sounding voice is advantageous, especially for female announcers," the authors write, "but as long as your voice is not difficult to listen to, you should have no trouble working as a broadcast performer."[75] Others point out that audiences accept nontraditional broadcast voices if the message is compelling.

On balance, textbook authors advise journalists to stay within the mainstream and avoid extremes in self-presentation. Doing so, they argue, helps journalists avoid turning off employers and distracting audiences. Textbooks often implicitly—and in several cases explicitly—encourage covering.

Internships and Other Vocational Training

Journalism students also receive important signals outside the classroom. Newsroom internships are a site of socialization. Interns learn about professional norms and practices from industry veterans who are considered to have tacit expert knowledge. Veterans share their expertise through interactions and interns also learn through observation and imitation of behaviors.[76]

Journalists recalled observations and memorable conversations about how to appear professional. "Nobody was saying, 'Wear this type of jacket or wear this type of hairstyle,'" says Whitney Miller, who interned at a television station. "But I would look around the room and see how people were dressed and that's how I figured out how to dress." One lesson she gleaned about appearance: "Straight hair is professional hair, period."[77] During a television internship, when a producer asked Rahman whether she would take off her hijab if she were offered her dream job as a television reporter, she said no. The producer's response: "Well, it's going to be hard for you—get ready for a lot of nos." Rahman says she appreciated the honesty. "I already knew it would be difficult, but that really prepared for me for rejections."[78]

Journalists also recalled learning about vocal delivery. When Opong worked at a public radio station on her college campus, she observed a host toning down her accent and women of color trying to emulate the station's dominant sound.[79] A journalism professor noted that at radio internships, many of his students learned to "adopt the sensibilities that will make them suitable for the newsroom" and "modulate their voices to be appropriate for broadcasting purposes."[80] As an intern, Gretel Kahn learned about her radio station's audience from listener feedback. "They would complain about a guest host with an accent. This was someone who spoke English as their first language. As someone who didn't, I found that nerve wracking if I wanted to be on air."[81]

Those who do not study journalism or have traditional news internships rely primarily on early work experiences. Rob Rosenthal did not attend journalism school, "where they taught you back in the day to sit up straight and speak in a stentorian voice." He trained in community radio, "where the station is supposed to sound like the community it serves." Rosenthal says that while he was at the station, "no one sat me down and said, 'Well, you know, you're supposed to sound like this.' Your individuality was welcomed."[82]

Job Advertisements

For students starting in the industry and young professionals trying to advance, job advertisements provide some of the clearest signals about self-presentation. Job seekers often have limited knowledge about hiring organizations. Recruitment materials help shape their first impressions of potential work environments.[83] Employers use listings to convey job requirements and define the "personality package" employees should possess. Candidates assess themselves against this package and against the organization and the job description to determine fit.[84]

To explore how appearance and vocal delivery are part of this desired personality package, I conducted a thematic analysis of journalism job advertisements. Not surprisingly, news organizations sought applicants with excellent communication skills. Yet the specific skills desired and how excellence is defined and measured were largely unstated. Many television and radio job postings referenced only vague attributes such as a "quality broadcast voice," "dynamic on-air performance," or "superior on-air presence." Without clarification, some postings sought "professional" news delivery and "relatable" voices.[85] Postings with vague descriptions and insufficient specificity about the speech characteristics desired of applicants can deter some from pursuing a job. In a separate study I conducted, journalists who stutter cited job advertisements seeking highly skilled speakers as a reason they did not apply.[86]

Some job advertisements were more specific in describing desirable vocal characteristics and skills. Clarity was the most commonly referenced characteristic. Employers sought applicants who "speak clearly and concisely" or have "clear enunciation," who "connect with audiences" and "attract and retain viewers" by delivering news clearly, concisely, and authoritatively. "Smooth" was another frequently cited vocal characteristic, such as having a "smooth, pleasant delivery" or "smooth presentation skills."

Employers also sought applicants who could go off script and remain poised under pressure. Job advertisements set a high bar for improvisational skills, desiring employees who can "flawlessly" or "effortlessly" ad lib. Implicit in these references is the need for verbal acuity in stressful situations. Job listings did not explicitly identify speech disabilities as incompatible with journalistic work. Yet in describing ideal broadcast speech, employers used euphemisms for impediment-free speech, including "fluent," "well-controlled," and "without stumbles." Listings suggested that audiences will connect only with journalists who deliver the news without faltering. This profile of the ideal type may limit the diversity of applicants by excluding people who have speech disabilities who could perform duties with adaptations and employer support.

Job advertisements contained few references to appearance. Several sought telegenic applicants who can "connect on camera" and have "superior on-air presence" without specifying desirable appearance attributes. One listing stated that applicants "must meet professional appearance standards as prescribed by company policy" without identifying what specific standards the policy includes. Another sought applicants with "consistent on-air appearance" that meets "professional standards regarding wardrobe, hair, cosmetics, and grooming." Whether "professional standards" referred to a specific company policy was unclear. The lack of clarity about appearance expectations in job postings prevents meaningful analysis of the impact on potential applicants.

Job Interviews

Journalists also received informative feedback when they applied for jobs. Tagouri typically got no response when she asked news stations why they turned down her application. The few newsroom leaders who responded said that audiences were not ready to see a journalist with a hijab. During one interview, a news director stated proudly that he had not hired a prior candidate with a hijab and would consider that candidate only if she reapplied without it.[87] Rahman had similar experiences. A television news director told her after a final-round interview that while the station was impressed with her qualifications, they had decided to "go in a different direction." Rahman viewed that as coded language. "To me, it meant they did not want to go the breaking-the-stereotype direction."

Years later, the news director confirmed that Rahman had been one of the best candidates but said that the ultimate decision was made by "men in suits above me." The news director was glad that Rahman persisted and eventually made it on air.[88]

After receiving his mass communication degree, Broxton worked at FedEx before taking jobs as an assignment editor and a web producer for Baltimore TV stations. He applied for dozens of on-air jobs, primarily in smaller markets, and desperately tried to get the attention of news directors through e-mail, calls, and a DVD demo reel. Broxton's two-and-a-half-year job search produced just one inquiry from a Florida news station. Revealing the likely reason why few hiring managers called him back, the station's news director told Broxton, "I like you, but your accent, it's kind of strong. If I bring you down here, you have to prove to me that you're going to work on that."[89]

Broxton bought a CD with exercises from a dialect coach. He listened to it while driving, repeating the coach's phrases. He felt he was progressing, but he learned weeks later that the news station had filled the position without interviewing him in person. Broxton has mixed feelings about his experience. He wishes his speech was accepted, but as a realist, he appreciates the news director's candor. "If he didn't give me that feedback, I might still be a web producer in Baltimore," Broxton says. "I'm not angry at him, I'm thankful. He was the first person with power to tell me to change my voice and see a speech therapist, and it made a difference."[90]

Influential Voices Outside the Newsroom

Within days of his conversation with the news director, Broxton sought help from Cathy Runnels, a speech-language pathologist he had met at a National Association of Black Journalists conference. Runnels dispelled Broxton's notion that he spoke incorrectly, telling him that "the way you talk isn't wrong." Runnels's goal for Broxton was for him to be understandable in any market. "He had a lot of informal styles that worked really great in his environment," she says, "but in a more formal setting, he just wasn't able to switch."[91]

Runnels commonly helps journalists speak in a way that will increase their professional opportunities. She and many other performance advisers exist in close orbit to—though often work outside of—newsrooms and shape journalism practice.[92] Lacking newsroom authority, these peripheral actors are valued because they have institutional knowledge (an understanding of what news managers want) and technical expertise that few journalists possess. Their advice can factor prominently into whether journalists from historically marginalized groups feel compelled to cover. This section examines how performance advisers reinforce and challenge institutional norms and practices. Given that vocal communication is common to all news performance, the role of voice coaches warrants particular emphasis.

Voice Coaches

Voice coaching blossomed toward the end of the twentieth century to meet a rising demand for polished newscasters. As network news programming expanded and cable news outlets flourished, coaches worked with former print journalists who were "novice newscasters" and broadcast journalists with little or no voice training.[93] Because few journalism educators and newsroom leaders are experts on vocal delivery, training of on-air talent has long been outsourced to speech and language therapists, journalists turned consultants, and other professionals with performance backgrounds.

Voice coaches decipher vague critiques and help journalists identify their goals. Coaches often confront hot-button issues like vocal fry and accent reduction. They must ultimately be responsive to the objectives of their client, who may be a student or recent graduate on the job market, an early career journalist struggling to advance their career, a journalist transitioning to broadcasting or podcasting, or a news manager concerned about their talents' appeal.

Technical training and translating concerns. Voice coaches train journalists to have clear and expressive voices. They teach them about vocal hygiene and posture. They help journalists breathe properly and warm up their vocal cords. They work with them on projection, articulation, pronunciation, and finding optimal range. Coaches help journalists identify what they—or others—dislike about their presentation and suggest modifications. Prosser wants to change the mentality that "you get a voice coach because your voice isn't right or good," but in many cases, clients come to her after receiving harsh criticism. "I had one client tell me, 'I got this horrible e-mail saying that I mispronounce all my words and I sound like a shrieking banshee. What can I do?'"[94] Journalists often struggle to pinpoint problems they hear in their voices. "So, they're just like, 'Something doesn't feel right with me or doesn't sound right,' and they lose confidence," says coach Mary Chan.[95]

News managers have difficulty identifying solutions to perceived problems. "They know what they want to hear, but they don't know how to articulate getting someone there," says Bodarky, a voice coach who has years of experience as a radio news manager.[96] Utterback described similar experiences. "News directors say, 'This voice is awful or needs work,'" often in response to audience criticism. "Ann, I have fiery letters on this woman," managers told her. "[Listeners] say she sounds young and doesn't know what she's talking about. You've got to fix her."[97]

Making sense of unspecific feedback is a significant part of coaches' work. Managers commonly tell journalists, "I need you to sound more engaged" or "sound warmer and make it connect with the audience," which offers little guidance on how to make vocal changes. For that reason, the advice to "pretend you're talking to a friend" is also unhelpful, Prosser says.[98] Comments such as "sound like yourself" and "be natural" can be confusing, voice coach Dara W. Allen says. "Someone may have a preconceived idea of what a news person should sound like and is trying to do that voice and then also put this conversational sound on top of that."[99]

Managers may also identify a problem but misdiagnose it. "I often hear from news directors that female journalists' voices are too high pitched and nasal," Allen says. "The person is left trying to figure that out on their own and they can develop bad habits vocally, so that is not helpful advice." Often the issue is not pitch (how high or low the voice sounds) but rather resonance (placement of the voice—e.g., whether sound resonates from the chest or throat). Runnels says the issue could also be inapt intonation; for example, describing a funeral in a tone that is more suitable for a joyous event.[100]

Representing the listener. Voice coaches often tell journalists that how they speak should not distract from what they say. To determine what is distracting, coaches may position themselves as audience representatives. Imagining themselves as the average listener, they gauge whether they are paying more attention to form than content. "Everything I do is about the audience," Pittman says. "I represent the audience to make sure they hear what journalists say." When Pittman heard a woman's voice that she found "too squeaky, high, and folksy" on a radio show, she advised the station to shorten the segment. "I listen for a living and she's getting on my nerves," Pittman responded. "I've started to tune out the content because the form is not pleasing to my ear."[101] As Bodarky tells journalists, "If someone is paying more attention to how you're saying something than what you're saying, it's an issue." He recalls a workshop attendee telling him, "This is how I talk and I shouldn't change that." His response: "That's the way you talk, but I don't want to listen to it because it's piercing my ear and I'm going to turn you off. I'm not saying change who you are, but let's adjust your voice so I can listen to you a little bit better."[102]

Utterback is candid about what turns audiences off: "If the person has a heavy accent, a really fast or slow voice, a really high voice, a thin voice, a monotone voice, any of those things, it's going to distract from a person's ability to listen to the message." In Utterback's experience, people with distracting voices are hired less often and stay on air for less time. Audiences get fed up, tune out, and news directors hear complaints. "So, to me, it was that simple," she says. "My job was to get [clients] to the point where they're not going to be distracting."[103]

Women who use vocal fry, characterized by a deep, breathy, creaky sound, often hear that the way they speak is distracting and unappealing. Voice coaches tend to focus on another concern, telling clients that vocal fry indicates poor technique and can lead to health problems. Prosser records videos about vocal fry. "I get a lot of people saying, 'Oh, the internalized misogyny.' But at the core, vocal fry is bad because it is air moving haphazardly through the vocal cords. When I hear vocal fry, I hear restriction. It's not about misogyny or sexism. It's just not a healthy way to speak."[104] Allen says that people who speak with vocal fry are likely to suffer from vocal fatigue and develop bad vocal habits. "It can really mess up your voice," Utterback says. "It's not just my personal prejudice that I don't like the sound—there's an anatomical reason [to avoid vocal fry]."[105]

Pittman says vocal fry is not only potentially damaging but makes speakers "sound weak" when their voice drops off at the end of sentences. As she tells her clients, "It means you're losing your power. Reporters need to have authority and power in their voice. . . . You need to breathe to project your voice." Her female clients sometimes push back. "They say, 'That's my authentic voice.' I say, 'Is it? Because I didn't hear you speak that way during normal conversation.'" The bottom line, as Pittman tells clients: "People listen to the radio while doing other things. So if you can't be easily heard, if you lose me and I tune you out, then I miss the important content you have to deliver."[106]

As a practical matter, voice coaches tend to advise journalists based on their perception of the world as it is rather than as they wish it existed. They may condemn but feel unable to ignore biases when advising clients about how to sound appealing to audiences and improve their employment prospects. "It's fine to say, 'I'm from the South and gosh darn, I should be able to use my accent anywhere and be respected,' but it's not the reality," says Utterback, who shed her southern accent when she was young. "There comes a point when realism overrides idealism. You can't be holding onto ideals you believe if they aren't true in the real world."[107]

Yet determining what is distracting often involves subjective judgments. Voice coaches' tastes—and their assumptions about audience tastes—may factor into their evaluations. Several journalists observed a problematic lack of diversity among coaches. "I've never had a voice coach who isn't White," Opong says.[108] Others complain that voice coaches try to "correct" journalists who do not conform to White midwestern speech patterns.[109] "There's talk in the industry about vocal diversity," says Gabrielle Jones, a public media executive, "but the problem is the system of voice coaching, which is created to eliminate individuality, to take ethnic and cultural elements out of your voice."[110]

Voice coaches disagree with that characterization. Many describe their intention as helping journalists sound like the best version of themselves. "It's a performed voice," Bodarky tells clients, "but it's still you. Instead of changing who you are, it's just ironing out the wrinkles."[111] When journalists asked Catherine Stifter how to get their stories on NPR, she responded, "It's not sounding like NPR, it's working with the voice you have."[112] Jessica Hansen, NPR's former in-house voice coach, had a similar message: "I'm not going to teach you to imitate someone else. My job is to make you the fullest expression of you that you can be."[113]

Balancing interests. A voice coach's job can be more difficult when journalists and their managers disagree about what needs to be addressed. Coaches are used to balancing interests and advising clients about whether manager concerns—or audience complaints—have merit. For practical reasons, they ultimately may recommend that journalists defer to managers and adhere to well-established norms. For instance, some coaches advise journalists to sound vaguely midwestern—not because they believe it is a superior way of speaking but because it is what news directors and audiences have long expected. "There is a standard of radio speech," Pittman says. "It's clean, crisp diction. If you're on the radio then you have to be understood and you have to be liked and you have to develop an audience. When you're doing news on an NPR station, I think you have to have some of that Nebraska-sounding thing."[114]

Utterback also advises journalists to consider employer expectations for appearance. A client who worked at a Miami news station said managers wanted her to show cleavage and wear shiny fabrics. Utterback says she told the client, "If you want to keep your job, give them what they want." As she advised a different client who had come from New York City and was now working in a small Pennsylvania town, "Part of the problem is you look like you're in New York. You need to look like you're in a small market. You need to dress like the women do here when they go to church."[115]

In some situations, coaches challenge norms they view as outdated and unfair. Several advised female journalists against deepening their voices to sound more authoritative. "I hear that often and it drives me bonkers," Hansen says. "I tell them, 'You did the research and reporting. You have the authority to tell the story; you don't have to do anything more.'" When Hansen hears that someone's accent or dialect is difficult to understand, she asks, "Difficult for whom to understand? Is it most people or a couple of people who write cranky e-mails? Unless most people can't hear parts of the story, I don't think it's a problem. I don't want people to give up who they are and where they come from."[116]

Who coaches work for and under what circumstances often affect whether they reinforce or challenge institutional norms and practices. The perceived need for realism about demands the existing landscape imposes on journalists leads some coaches to give advice that does more to encourage than discourage covering. Yet as norms change, they increasingly advise journalists to find employers who will not ask them to conform.

News Consultants

News consultants have long been part of the system that socializes journalists.[117] Consulting firms became powerful forces in broadcast journalism in the 1960s, and by the early 1990s, roughly three-fourths of local television stations used consultants.[118] Some journalists resented consultants' presence, objecting to their fixation on ratings and their focus on cosmetics over substance. Yet these "TV news doctors" became a fixture in newsrooms, where some had offices and attended meetings with television management.[119] Consultants primarily used audience research to advise news stations about how to appeal to audiences, focusing on the production values of a newscast and the performance of news presenters.[120]

During the 1960s and continuing for decades, consulting firms flew anchors to their headquarters during non-ratings periods to be coached intensively.[121] Described as part elocution coaches and part cosmeticians, consultants held seminars on how to dress and speak, apply makeup, and style hair. Large consulting firms teamed with boutique agencies that specialized in grooming and coaching potential star anchors but generally did not conduct audience research.[122]

News stations still hire consultants, but their role in advising journalists on self-presentation has been reduced for reasons explained in chapter 4. Large media companies may have one or more consultants working across their stations. Some larger stations have in-house cosmeticians and stylists or contract with specialists. Consulting sessions tend to be most common in medium and large markets and for lead anchors in markets of all sizes.

Some journalists perceive that if they are directed to work with an image consultant, management has found fault with their appearance. "You just have to read between the lines," says Tucker, the television journalist. "If they keep bringing in consultants who do nothing but focus on hair and clothing and makeup, that tells you something."[123] Yet image consultants, like voice coaches, view their role as more than just fixing perceived problems.

Managers and agents have referred many clients to Barbara Allen-Rosser, a consultant in the cosmetic and image business with more than thirty years of experience advising television journalists on aspects of appearance (e.g., hair, makeup, attire) as well as verbal presentation. Allen-Rosser views her role as helping clients "connect" on air and feel confident about their appearance. She takes pictures of them from all angles to "see how their body works," reviews wardrobe and hairstyle possibilities, and asks for their feedback on what looks best. Like voice coaches, Allen-Rosser focuses on ensuring that journalists do not distract audiences. "If people can't get past their looks, they aren't going to hear a word they say."[124]

Allen-Rosser often meets with clients' news directors to discuss their concerns and to learn more about ratings and viewer preferences. She generally recommends that clients defer to those in charge. "News directors should know the [television] market better than anyone. They're the ones who will help make the ultimate call." Allen-Rosser wants clients to think of ways to compromise. For instance, if a female anchor cuts her hair short but her news director objects, she advises: "On the weekend, when you're out, you can wear your hair how you want, but on television, wear a wig and you can look like you always have."[125]

Several journalists raised concerns about lack of diversity within the consulting industry. "It seems like they all go to the same convention and have similar taste," Li says. "Most are not people of color."[126] Nyorkor was bothered by the lack of Black consultants. White consultants often told her to "have slicker, smoother hair. . . . They went around telling the GM and news director what everybody should wear, and [management] listened. When the consultants came back every quarter, they wanted to see those changes made."[127] As this comment illustrates, consultants not only reinforce but in some cases shape institutional norms and practices.

Talent Agents

Agents are best known for helping clients find jobs and negotiate salaries, but they also advise on self-presentation.[128] Many are former broadcast journalists who tout insider credentials, including connections with newsroom leaders and consultants, and first-hand knowledge of how news stations evaluate talent. After a short stint as a broadcast journalist, Liz Hart learned about talent evaluation as a headhunter working with station management to identify candidates for on-air positions. She watched tapes of anchors and reporters from around the country, assembled reels for news stations, and saw what appealed to hiring managers. After working for a talent agency, Hart started her own firm.

When advising clients on their appearance and vocal delivery, Hart and other agents echo the advice of coaches and consultants: do not distract the audience. Hart gives clients tips on attire before they have on-camera job auditions. She typically advises men to wear a dark suit and a white shirt, and women to wear colors that complement their skin and to go easy on accessories. "I want an audience to watch my client, not their earrings or necklaces," Hart says.[129] Kane has a similar perspective: "I just don't want to notice your clothes or makeup first."[130] Adams says there is a looser dress code now than when she was in television, "but the same idea applies: you shouldn't be distracting. It's a subjective assessment, but it's a subjective business," so she advises clients to keep their attire "simple and elegant."[131]

Agents describe themselves as realists. "I'm a no-BS kind of person," Adams tells clients, "because it only benefits you."[132] Hart, like many coaches and consultants, views her job as preparing clients for the profession as it is, not as she wishes it was. That means accounting for preferences and biases rather than ignoring them when advising clients about their vocal delivery. "If their voice is too high, if it sounds too young, that is a problem," Hart says. "Audiences don't want to hear from a child." She corrects clients when they drop letters from words or do not use standard English. "You can't say 'dat.' It's not a word. I'll tell clients, 'We have to work on your dialect. If you're going to speak the English language, do it properly.' It's not a race thing by any stretch. It's an English thing." Hart's view on accents: "The bottom line is, you have to sound like me" (in her view, "accentless"). She tells clients with southern twangs or northeastern accents, "If you want to go to work in LA, you have to get a voice coach because your accent isn't going to work there."[133]

Agents often advise journalists to defer to managers. "I always say that if your news director is telling you to wear nonsense purple jackets every day, then you do it," Kane says. "You have to do what your boss wants."[134] In other situations, however, she wants journalists to have more agency over how they present. For instance, Kane encourages Black clients to wear their natural hair so it can become normalized. Adams may do so depending on the market and on feedback from news directors. "If a journalist says, 'I'm wearing my hair this way, like it or not,' they have a right to do that, but they might have to find a place where [managers] don't mind you wearing your hair that way."[135] Agents commonly reinforce existing norms and practices while encouraging clients to find stations where they feel accepted.

Newsroom Leaders

News directors and other top-level managers often have the most influence over journalists' self-presentation. These newsroom leaders typically waste no time in giving feedback to talent. Broxton heard from his manager soon after starting his first on-air job. He was doing his best to fit in. "No one ever said anything about my accent in Montana because I hid it," Broxton says. "I was in an all-White state, so I'm reading my script and I'm just trying hard not to sound like my normal Baltimore self." It was difficult enough for Broxton to be "accent-free" on air, but then his news director also asked him to loosen up and be less robotic—to sound conversational and "be himself." Broxton had just spent months training himself *not* to talk the way he does in casual conversation with people from Baltimore. "It was like, 'You're speaking Standard American English. Now we need you to be more conversational.'" Broxton worked on that in Montana with a retired news anchor and a speech-language pathologist. By the time he got to Iowa for his next job, Broxton says he felt more comfortable on air. Sounding conversational remains a work in progress.[136]

Early in his career, Broxton heard lots of advice about how to perform. Sound natural without alienating viewers. Lose the regional dialect. Adopt a "neutral" accent that works in any market. Maintain a clean-cut appearance. Newsroom leaders giving such advice may be well intentioned, but the result is that journalists may feel compelled to cover.

Summary

This chapter has shown that journalists encounter varied signals as they learn how to perform. Through observations, interactions, and experiences, many conclude that to succeed, they must follow well-established norms and conform to the so-called mainstream. Performance advisers reinforce some norms and practices but push back on those they feel are outdated or unfair. They commonly advise journalists to defer to managers and avoid distracting audiences. Chapter 4 further explores how managers' tastes and audience feedback shape the look and sound of news. Chapters in part II provide greater detail about managers' advice and directives to journalists.

4

The Influential
Imagined Audience

• •

Michelle Li learned a lot about her former television station's priorities from a stock photo on the wall of a conference room. The woman pictured was Karen, a forty-five-year-old suburban mother of two. Station leaders created her identity to fit the demographic profile of their target audience. The photo was a visible reminder of the viewer journalists should imagine when performing. Wherever Li worked, she always knew the target viewer profile. "It's always a Karen, Dave, or Bill. It's never Kyung-Sook. I've never seen that person reflect someone who looks like me." In local television news, Li says, "you're trained very early to know that your audience is probably White, probably in the suburbs, and probably middle class."[1]

Early in Eric Nuzum's public radio career, he had a clear picture of his audience. The program director at the station where Nuzum worked asked colleagues to clip from a magazine and display in their cubicle a photograph of a person they imagined as their average listener. Revealingly, everyone chose roughly the same person: a middle-aged, Volvo-driving liberal with an advanced degree and a successful career; someone who is civically engaged and a lifelong learner. "It was a very elitist profile," Nuzum says. A racially homogeneous one, as well. "Was that person White? Yes, because [in the late 1990s], more than 80 percent of public radio listeners were White." As Nuzum explains, "When writing a promo or a news story, you would look at that photo and ask, 'How would that person want this explained to them?'"[2]

Journalists can often point to a photograph or conjure up an image of their imagined audience, the person or people with whom they assume they are communicating.[3] In public and commercial broadcasting, this audience has long been as Li and Nuzum described: White and middle to upper class. In digital media, the profile tends to look different. When Juleyka Lantigua started LWC Studios, the listener she and her colleagues imagined was Keni, a twenty-six-year-old Afro Latina who is the oldest of three children of immigrants and the first in her family to graduate college. When LWC considers launching a new podcast, the guiding questions are: Will Keni like and share this? Lantigua knew from audience research that "there are a lot of Kenis who aren't being served well by traditional radio."[4]

Many broadcast news organizations want to attract young, diverse, historically underserved audience members like Keni and remain appealing to older, less diverse audience members like Karen who have long helped sustain their stations. Some journalists I interviewed sensed that when performing, the latter took precedence. They felt that managers wanted them to present in ways that would satisfy the aging segment of the audience to avoid losing their financial support, although others who led newsrooms or worked closely with managers said that in their experience that was not a consideration.

This chapter examines the influential imagined audience—specifically, how conceptions of audiences and the economic pressure to please them have shaped the way journalists perform. Data show that broadcast audiences tend to skew older now because young people are migrating to digital media. The body of research on audience preferences provides no clear conclusions. The trend is toward a greater acceptance of journalists who present in diverse ways. Yet ample evidence from the recent and distant past indicates that audiences are critical of journalists from historically marginalized groups who deviate from the "neutral" norm. Study participants are "psychoanalyzed as experiencing feelings of alienation" when evaluating journalists who look and sound different than them.[5]

There is less current research than before on how audiences evaluate on-air talent and no publicly available data on how—or even if—such evaluations affect donations, subscriptions, or ratings. News outlets infrequently conduct such research internally. Listeners and viewers call stations and go online to comment on journalists' self-presentation, but the views of a vocal minority may not reflect broader audience sentiment. Given this uncertainty about what audiences want, managers may rely on instinct and intuition, imagining audiences as people who share their tastes. As a result, audiences are given what newsroom leaders *think* they want.

Managers often do not indicate how they conceive of their outlet's audience and how assumptions about listener and viewer tastes shape their advice to journalists. This chapter does not assess the relative influence of audience data, personal preference, and implicit bias in managers' decision-making. Instead, it focuses on what the information they have access to reveals. I explore what early research showed about audience demographics and preferences, how influential news consultants advised stations to cater to loyal audiences, what recent research reveals about shifting audience expectations, and how individuals and institutions have responded to unsolicited audience feedback. I also share what journalists have gleaned about managers' tastes from conversations about appropriate self-presentation. First, I provide an overview of why and how news outlets try to please their imagined audience.

Pleasing the Imagined Audience

Communication professor Sherman Paxton Lawton observed in the early 1930s that broadcast stations cannot make money without pleasing their audience.[6] This observation remains relevant. Across much of the broadcast industry, audience numbers have flatlined or fallen, threatening steady revenue streams and long-term sustainability. To maintain relevance in an age of immense competition for attention, news outlets must seek to please audiences and keep them engaged. Appealing news presenters may help this effort. Newsroom leaders have adopted a marketing orientation that seeks to make news responsive to consumer preferences.[7]

Yet giving audiences what they want can be difficult. Lawton once remarked that "the huge and indefinable, unmeasurable entity called the audience is not easy to analyze."[8] Journalists typically perform without receiving immediate feedback from listeners or viewers. The less an actual audience is visible or known, the more individuals become dependent on their imagination.[9] Broadcast audiences are a vague abstraction, an imaginary entity constructed from the vantage point and in the interest of institutions.[10] Because journalists can never know precisely who consumes their work and why they do so, discussions of what audiences want are inherently speculative.[11] Even so, journalists form mental constructions of audiences that have material consequences, such as who gets hired and promoted and how programming is shaped.[12]

Broadcast news audiences are often imagined as hurried by busy routines, easily sidetracked, and quick to tune out if they become displeased or disinterested.[13] Because radio listeners are multitasking, "all types of things can pull them away," voice coach Sora Newman warns.[14] Listeners can be picky about how—and with whom—they spend their time. "You're a guest in someone's house," Rob Rosenthal tells radio journalists, "and that someone can uninvite you quickly by the press of a button."[15] According to a radio programmer's adage, it takes years to build an audience and only a few seconds to drive them away.[16]

The same is true with television. Viewers have long been able to choose among programs and to watch a lot or a little with more or less attention.[17] Home television viewing is characterized by distraction. With ample options, viewers are constantly tempted to change the channel.[18] Digital and mobile media promote diverse forms of distracted viewing, including second screening.[19]

This perception of audiences as highly distractible, selective, and inundated with options puts pressure on journalists to avoid drawing unwanted attention to themselves. Distractions are undesirable, but the ultimate fear is alienating audiences. Studies show that journalists form an understanding of who audiences are, what they prefer, and what might alienate them primarily through audience research, direct feedback from listeners and viewers, and their own tastes and instincts.[20] The following sections explore these influences.

Audience Research

Audience research has notable limitations. Listener and viewer tastes are notoriously difficult to gauge. Audiences are cumulatively conditioned by what they are accustomed to seeing and hearing on the news.[21] The more they are exposed to newscasters, the more they tend to perceive them as trustworthy and authoritative.[22] Therefore, results may reflect the extent of audience familiarity with the options presented instead of what they most prefer. Heavy reliance on such research creates a self-perpetuating feedback loop that disadvantages journalists who do not conform to fit the mold.

However, research on audience demographics and preferences has long informed journalistic practice and has been used to rationalize managerial decision-making.[23] To examine findings over more than half a century, I draw upon two primary sources: peer-reviewed research and proprietary data collected for media clients by private firms (accessed through library archives or described by sources with access to such data).

Early Research on Television Audiences

Television news executives have long justified the importance of ratings by asserting that estimates of audience size are more or less direct reflections of audience tastes. As cultural historian Ien Ang wrote, "In a particularly self-serving leap of argument, ratings are celebrated as guardians of the public interest, as instruments which require that the television industry 'give the audience what it wants.'"[24] Although ratings reveal whether programming resonates with audiences, they do not reveal *why*.

Before the 1960s, when consultants became influential in broadcast news, stations did not know the extent to which an anchor's appeal helped attract viewers. Then research funded by the consulting firm McHugh and Hoffman (M&H) reached an unexpected conclusion: perceptions of newscasts often were determined by responses to news anchors more than by responses to the content of the news. Audiences could not recount details from news stories but could provide detailed descriptions of anchors' voices, outfits, and hair.[25] Research from

Magid, another large consulting firm, found that many viewers chose news for the on-air personalities.[26] Appealing newscasters were likelier to be trusted and draw larger audiences.[27] With this understanding, television general managers and news directors became increasingly interested in the ability of anchors to attract ratings with their presentation skills and became increasingly reliant on the data news consultants provided to make personnel decisions.[28]

Consulting firms created detailed reports for news stations about viewer habits, attitudes, and preferences. Researchers surveyed audience recall of on-air personalities. M&H reports included statistics on viewers' familiarity with individual journalists, how likable they found them, and how they assessed their on-air presentation. Research showed who was the best-known and most popular journalist at a news station and in a news market. Consultants invited viewers to newscast screenings to give real-time reactions to journalists' performances.[29] They conducted focus groups, asking participants about an anchor's hair, wardrobe, and demeanor and about their favorite anchor pairings.[30] Based on these results, consultants made clear to news managers who they should consider their core audience and what these viewers found appealing.

Catering to the Middle Majority. Consultants advised journalists to create programming that was broadly appealing and inoffensive to working-class Americans—the so-called Middle Majority. W. Lloyd Warner, a sociologist and anthropologist who coined the term, identified the Middle Majority as people in the upper part of the lower class (mostly high school graduates in blue-collar jobs) and the lower part of the middle class (slightly more educated white-collar or high-end blue-collar workers). In the mid- to late twentieth century, these two social classes represented roughly two-thirds of Americans and were the most likely to be loyal television viewers. Warner's social class analysis greatly influenced M&H's advice to broadcast stations. Its audience reports included a detailed breakdown of Middle Majority viewership trends and identification of the class of each directly quoted respondent. According to former television news director and consultant Craig Allen, "Under Warner's tutelage, McHugh and Hoffman began the process of taking news out of the hands of newsroom bourgeois and passing it to the masses."[31]

Research showed that viewers generally changed channels when a program aroused their anger or inflamed their prejudices. Therefore, the goal was to create unobjectionable programming that would not turn them off.[32] This finding also shaped personnel decisions. If audiences found a newscaster objectionable, managers were held responsible. As a news director once said, "If the ratings don't work, they aren't going to fire the production manager for screwing up the news, they are going to fire me."[33] Many newsroom leaders considered it safer to stick with the status quo—in most television markets, a White male news anchor—than to take a chance on someone unconventional. As author Ron Powers wrote in the late 1970s,

Station managers are not notable for their bigotry as a group; only their slavishness to presumed mass-audience tastes stands in the way of inroads against the color and ethnic barrier. The surveys and ratings books make it clear that the most important buying segment of TV news watchers are middle-class Whites. Best not to court their disapproval with an unpleasant symbol at the anchor desks, especially when an archetype of White American is just a flick of the dial away.[34]

Television newsrooms diversified after consultants found that Middle Majority audiences were more accepting of minorities on air than the news establishment assumed. Instead of hiring minority anchors, some station managers tested the waters by hiring a reporter from their market's largest minority group to fill a "minority specialist" position.[35] Managers also resisted hiring women as anchors until evidence suggested audience approval. Research in the 1960s and 1970s found that viewers perceived female newscasters as enthusiastic and nonthreatening; they helped to humanize broadcasts.[36] Viewers described a local female anchor as "sweet" and "personable and friendly, the type of person my wife would choose for a friend."[37] Such comments prompted stations nationwide to hire women as coanchors.[38]

Female anchors had to play a particular role. Managers in Detroit replaced a departing female anchor with a woman whom audiences found "warm, friendly, almost like a neighbor" rather than candidates audiences described as cold and harsh.[39] Former news anchor Christine Craft alleges in her memoir that the owners of the Kansas City station where she worked felt she was not bringing "warmth, teamwork, partnership, and comfort" to the news program, so they proceeded to measure audience sentiment in a manner designed to elicit negative responses. She claims that news executives justified removing her as coanchor because research showed that viewers found her "too old, too unattractive, and . . . not sufficiently deferential to men."[40] Craft says the news director told her that "when the people of Kansas City see your face, they turn the dial."[41]

Some viewers, conditioned to see men behind the anchor deck, struggled to accept women in top on-air roles. In Columbus, female viewers told researchers that a female anchor had "eye appeal" but seemed unfit to anchor the news. "She presents the news all right," one viewer said. "I have nothing against her but I prefer men for newscasting."[42] A female viewer in Chicago said, "I don't like girl forecasters—any of them. They don't belong in the business. It's out of their realm. It's a man's job. They don't fit in."[43]

Authority and credibility. While women were often viewed as personable and comforting, research from the 1970s found that audiences generally perceived male anchors as more credible than female anchors and older White male newscasters as most authoritative.[44] In Baltimore, a young Oprah Winfrey was paired with seasoned male anchor Jerry Turner at WJZ-TV. Viewers found both coanchors physically attractive, stylish, and pleasant to listen to but otherwise viewed them differently. Turner was described as poised and authoritative; Winfrey as being "unsure of herself" and "in too deep," with a shallow understanding of the news. White men were not the only group to criticize Winfrey; some Black male and female viewers also voiced their disapproval. When Winfrey was replaced by Al Sanders, who was also Black, audiences approved, commenting positively on his authoritativeness.[45]

Female anchors who were considered to be authoritative walked a delicate line. Summarizing audience comments, an M&H research report stated that a female Houston anchor "conveys a nice sense of authority without seeming superior to the viewer or pushy, always a danger for a newscaster and especially for a woman in this role." The report described her as "warm, personable, and feminine without being gushy or girlish in her manner."[46]

Physical appearance. People who are considered physically attractive are typically perceived to be more intelligent and trustworthy than others.[47] M&H research in the 1960s and 1970s found journalists' appearance important to viewers, although less so than being interesting and believable.[48] According to Allen, the Middle Majority expected news anchors to dress "middle of the road." Audiences wanted them to "look good but not steal the show."[49] Viewers praised local news anchors for being "clean and wholesome"; "a very sharp dresser, but never flashy"; and "neat, well-groomed, and conventionally dressed."[50]

Gender. In the 1950s and 1960s, television viewers described their ideal newscaster as a clean-shaven, neatly dressed middle-aged man of medium height and build, reflecting what audiences were accustomed to seeing on air with anchors such as Chet Huntley, David Brinkley, and Walter Cronkite.[51] Participants in one study rated male broadcasters significantly higher on the physical dimension of interpersonal attraction than women.[52] In M&H research, viewers praised male anchors for looking "All-American," "neat, clean cut, and tall," and "poised and silverly haired." Reports sometimes included no qualitative feedback about a male anchor's appearance. That rarely was the case for female anchors, whose looks were a focal point. One local anchor was described as a well-groomed, "attractive blonde with a good figure." Descriptors such as "serious" and "intelligent" were secondary.[53] Another female anchor's perceived qualifications were her striking looks and stylish clothing. The M&H report indicated that "her strongest assets are physical."[54]

Men were not spared from such critiques. Baltimore viewers described a male news anchor as having a "chubby little face" and looking like an "overgrown baby."[55] Buffalo audiences complained about an anchor's "swelled head."[56] Yet women bore the brunt of criticism. A Houston journalist who was praised for her reporting was criticized as a "sloppy" dresser, having "poorly styled" hair, and not wearing enough makeup.[57] A female anchor in the New Haven–Hartford market was described as unkempt and as having messy and dirty hair.[58]

Race. Audience members rarely referenced the race of White journalists but commonly did so when evaluating minority journalists. One comment identified a journalist as "Carol Hall: Channel 13's Black newswoman."[59] An M&H report noted that a Chicago weathercaster was "highly stereotyped, racially and sexually. . . . Blacks tended to react to her mainly as a Black and Whites tend to react to her mainly as a female. Blacks, thus, may endorse her because, they say, she is Black or may reject her because she is not convincingly Afro-Black."[60]

Black journalists who conformed to White beauty standards typically were viewed as more acceptable than those who challenged conventions. A White female viewer who described a Houston field reporter as "striking" added, "I am not sure I like her Afro hairdo," a sentiment that Black male viewers also expressed. Like other Black journalists, the reporter was criticized for being "cold, stiff, and humorless."[61] The reporter's presentation, researchers noted, led some to conclude that she is "not really an appealing or admirable newscast figure or spokesperson for the community."[62] Research consistently showed that Black journalists were perceived as being more introverted and anxious and less cheerful than White journalists.[63] A Black female journalist, who later became a network news correspondent, was described as professional and articulate but "having no personality." A White female viewer found her "too uppity."

Vocal delivery. Television viewer preferences have long shaped how journalists talk on air. In the 1970s, when stoic anchors with deep, booming voices were the norm, viewers told news consultants they wanted journalists to sound conversational instead of being "granite newscasters who spoke from Mt. Olympus."[64] Local news stations then sought out coanchors with good on-air chemistry and a conversational speaking style that was attractive to the Middle Majority. Viewers also wanted newscasters to be familiar-sounding, like ordinary people they would encounter. Journalists who did not fit that profile were considered potentially alienating. An M&H research report pointed to a New York news anchor's "cultured accent, which no doubt serves to make her seem more distant from the bulk of Middle Majority viewers."[65]

Gender. Female broadcasters tend to speak at lower mean pitch levels than women in the general population. Researchers posit that women in on-air roles are influenced by studies showing that audiences consider voices that are lower in pitch to be more confident and trustworthy.[66] Research on whether television viewers prefer male or female voices has produced mixed results. Some studies reveal a preference for male newscaster voices, yet others have found no significant difference.[67] A 1973 study found that while many people had no opinion about which gender's voice was most credible, those who preferred male voices were conditioned to hearing them on television.[68]

In M&H research from that era, respondents generally preferred deep male voices to high-pitched female voices.[69] Viewers felt that many female newscasters lacked gravitas. The delivery of female newscasters, the report noted, "may lack the authoritativeness many viewers want."[70] Even female audience members described male anchors as more forceful sounding and thus more authoritative. One report described the ideal female newscaster's voice as "forceful but feminine" without operationalizing those terms.[71]

Race. Black journalists often received negative feedback on their vocal delivery. In an M&H report, a Black anchor in Houston was criticized for "not losing her native accent—Texas, Southern, or Black." Viewers complained about her lack of fluency and "poor enunciation," which, the report said, "reflects poorly on the Houston area and its inhabitants, White and Black."[72] A Black television journalist in Washington, DC, was criticized for having an "irritating" voice that sounds "artificial, even masculine."[73]

Fluency and clarity. In M&H reports, viewers praised journalists for speaking smoothly, criticized them for stumbling, and commented on speech that they perceived to be abnormal. As a viewer said of a local news anchor, "She talks well, doesn't stutter around like the ones on the other stations."[74] An anchor in another market was described as "lispy."[75] Audiences complained that Barbara Walters had poor diction and was hard to understand.[76] As one viewer said, "I'm surprised she got this far with a speech impediment."[77]

Television viewers have long expected anchors to have a "smooth" vocal delivery and to seldom make errors in grammar or diction.[78] A study from the 1970s found that newscasters with fluent, clear, and slow speech were rated higher in the competence and composure factors of credibility.[79] Decades later, research found that news consumers have little tolerance for delivery mistakes, especially from male newscasters. Misspeaking or stumbling even a few times called into question journalists' command of the language or script, leading to perceptions that they were less experienced and hence less credible.[80] Radio audiences also identified the ideal characteristics of radio performers' delivery as flawless enunciation, smooth vocalization, and a medium rate of speech.[81]

Decline in audience research. For decades, audience research from large consulting firms shaped television news managers' personnel decisions and influenced journalists' self-presentation. By the early 2000s, however, demand for such research had begun to wane. The television news industry consolidated and large station groups produced more in-house research. As audiences fragmented and viewership declined in some markets, station management realized that "talent didn't move ratings anymore," according to Allen, the former news consultant. "There's no reward [in doing research] if it's not going to boost ratings."[82] Consultants began producing fewer reports for news stations. As a result, less reliable data now exists on audience preferences.

Contemporary TV Audience Research

Research consistently shows that television news audiences skew older. Pew Research Center surveys from the late 2010s found that Americans above the age of 50 primarily turned to television for local news, while younger respondents gravitated toward online sources. Black Americans, women, and those with a high school diploma or less education were more likely than their counterparts to express a preference for local television.[83]

Publicly available data on how modern audiences perceive television journalists mostly come from academic research, though the volume has decreased in recent decades. Findings indicate that audiences still judge male and female newscasters differently in some respects. One study found that after controlling for physical attractiveness, male newscasters rated higher in competence, composure, and extroversion than women.[84] In another, viewers also considered male newscasters to be more credible (with older male newscasters deemed most credible) but perceived news items read by female newscasters to be more credible. Contrary to prior research, message credibility was not determined by the speaker's credibility. This distinction was identifiable because, unlike prior studies, subjects in this study had to evaluate the message as well as the newscaster. The researchers concluded that "this suggests that there is an indirect, unconscious part in the process of judging credibility, which has not yet been considered by current literature" and that the issue warranted further study.[85]

Research also indicates shifts in appearance preferences. Television viewers, aware that female newscasters often are chosen for their looks, told researchers that they wanted more diverse representation than the narrow version of beauty offered.[86] Another study found that viewers care more about journalists' competence than their looks. Fewer than one-third of respondents thought that female newscasters needed to be physically attractive—and even fewer felt that male newscasters did. Appearance was not irrelevant (being "smartly dressed" was valued), but respondents wanted more balance in newscaster selection.[87] Other research shows that when female journalists looked glamorized as opposed to looking "more natural," viewers took them less seriously and often assumed they were less intelligent.[88] A different study, however, found that men perceived "sexualized" female newscasters to be more professional but less suited for war and political reporting than nonsexualized female anchors.[89]

Early Research on Radio Audiences

Researchers who studied radio audiences predated television consultants in recommending that journalists appeal to the middle class. In the late 1940s, journalism professor Mitchell V. Charnley wrote that radio must "achieve a common denominator . . . that will hold appeal for everybody," adding that "on the negative side, it must avoid offense." He advised presenters to imagine a middle-class family listening in the living room while doing household activities.[90] Others with access to audience data came to a similar conclusion about radio's primary listenership. In later decades, the conception of audiences for commercial news as predominantly middle class largely remained the same.

Many journalists assumed that noncommercial stations, which are often licensed to or affiliated with colleges and universities, served a different type of listener. Yet for decades, these stations had limited data on audience demographics and preferences. "We were guessing what people wanted to hear," says Steve Olson, a former public radio executive whose company helps stations interpret and act on audience research. "It was throwing darts at a dartboard."[91] Audience research became influential in the 1980s when public radio stations, working with the newly created Radio Research Consortium, gained access to detailed data on listener habits. Public radio was never as ratings driven as commercial radio, but managers used audience data when making programming decisions.

As part of a "research revolution" in public radio, a cottage industry of consultants emerged to help stations professionalize the sound of their programming.[92] Consultants focused more on programming than on personalities. They rarely probed listeners' perceptions of anchors and hosts because there was little evidence that hosts drove ratings. "Public radio has never been personality driven," Olson says. "The hosts aren't anonymous, but with a few exceptions at the national level, people generally listen for the content, not the host." Consultants did, however, provide stations with insights into audience demographics and psychographics.[93]

Research showed that public radio's most loyal listeners were well educated, wealthy, middle aged, and interested in social causes.[94] NPR's first employee, Jack Mitchell, described a "symbiotic" relationship between public radio and these core listeners who "feel so connected to their medium that they are willing to support it financially."[95] As Michael P. McCauley wrote in his history of NPR:

> The American public radio industry began to soar when its leaders realized that people who were highly educated, socially conscious, and politically active were most likely to listen to their brand of broadcasting. Audience research helped public radio fuse its programs more snugly to the values, beliefs and attitudes of the people who tuned in and pledged their financial support.[96]

That those people were primarily White was unintentional, says Abby Goldstein, president and executive director of the Public Media Content Collective (formerly the Public Radio Program Directors Association). "It's not like public radio said in the 1970s, 'Oh, we want to make sure only White people get access to our content.' It was all based on education level. Public radio has been looking back and asking, 'What did we unintentionally do? Who has had access to higher education in this country?'"[97]

Nuzum, who managed on-air programming at an NPR affiliate and later at NPR, recalled internal conversations about the lack of audience diversity. "The excuse used to be that the percentage of African Americans and Latino Americans in our audience roughly equaled the percentage of the general population. So the public radio audience was reflecting that demographic."[98] That is not the case in many markets where audiences now are less diverse than the local population.

Data made public by NPR showed that in 2012, people of color represented less than 15 percent of the radio audience.[99] Nearly a decade later, it was roughly 20 percent.[100] "There's no question that [the public radio] system succeeded by targeting affluent, highly educated White folks at the exclusion of people of color," says Maxie Jackson III, a public radio executive with content and audience development experience. "Some of the early researchers who created this targeted approach said that when people of color become more highly educated, they will aggregate into our audiences." That has not happened to a large degree, Jackson says. "We are still struggling to become relevant and authentic to people of color."[101]

Attracting younger listeners has also been difficult. Data from 2015 showed audience growth on digital platforms and among radio listeners who are sixty-five and older but a loss of radio listeners under forty-five, a trend that was expected to continue.[102] Before Nuzum left NPR, he warned board members that the organization could not count on people in their late twenties and early thirties aging into the audience, as had long been the case.[103]

The Impact of Public Radio's Audience Demographics

How does the presumed public radio audience affect guidance given to journalists? "I have never sat down with a reporter and said, 'You don't sound educated enough,'" Goldstein says. "I don't think any news director says, 'We've got to get this reporter to sound more White' or 'You have to be understandable to our old White audience.' That's not the way people in this industry work."[104] Olson never heard such comments when working in public radio and consulting with local stations. Audience demographics mattered greatly in fund-raising, Olson says, but not on the news side. "It wasn't really a matter of whether a certain kind of person was listening and I'm going to tailor my programming to them."[105]

Yet some contend that public radio's imagined audience profoundly shapes programming decisions. The default audience profile for public radio remains White baby boomers, Nuzum wrote in a 2022 column for the trade publication *Current*. "They are no longer the majority of listeners, but they still have a stranglehold on public radio's programming. . . . As with younger generations, people of color don't listen as much because the programming doesn't speak to them, even to the point of feeling somewhat hostile."[106]

Khalon Richard feels that her former NPR colleagues often had White, middle- to upper-class, middle-America listeners in mind when they gave journalists feedback like "you don't want to distract the audience with how you sound" or "make sure the audience gets these references."[107] Celeste Headlee, a public radio journalist turned podcast host who founded Headway DEI Training, says that when NPR does something that sounds different, mostly White and male local station managers "become absolutely terrified that it's going to scare away people who have been their biggest donors for the past half-century." Even when stations vow to target communities that better represent their region's diversity, "there's always a sentence in there about 'and maintain our current audience.' The idea that you're going to alienate these upper-class White listeners is frightening to people."[108]

During an early performance review, a colleague advised Renata Sago to soften her voice on air, to be less abrasive, and to "get rid of that urban accent." The implication was clear that the way she spoke would alienate the overwhelmingly White audience. "I learned what this demographic of our audience likes to hear and how to make sure they kept listening and that sponsors kept coming to us."[109]

Sociologist Laura Garbes has found that public radio stations only aired sources who were considered "good talkers," a practice that disproportionately excludes those with ethnic accents from low-income communities of color. Journalists from diverse backgrounds whom Garbes interviewed could easily understand sources with accents but their editors worried that listeners would find the sources unintelligible.[110] "You have to be able to understand them" while driving, these editors often said. As Garbes concluded, "The 'you' presumably belonged to the imagined, White, upper-class public radio listener."[111]

Several journalists I interviewed had similar experiences. Headlee recalls several instances when an editor told her to cut a sound bite because a speaker's accent was too strong. She disagreed but figured it was a losing battle, so she reinterviewed the person in their native language and used a translator's voice in the story. Former broadcast news producer Kris Vera-Phillips says that editors commonly flagged accents she grew up hearing and found easy to understand. "They'd say, 'If I can't understand it, then maybe the rest of our audience can't,' and I'm like, 'Which audience are you talking about?'"[112] The imagined audience is a "powerful ideological tool in the newsroom," says professor and podcast host/executive producer Chenjerai Kumanyika. "'Our listeners won't understand this or receive this'—that can be applied to all kinds of decision-making."[113]

Managers also evaluate whether journalists are good talkers. Working in public radio, Nuzum commonly heard that phrase, which he considered code for sounding highly educated. Those who were not considered good talkers generally responded to that feedback by speaking more formally than was natural to them and using cultural references that resonated with public radio's core audience.[114]

Linguistic Bias

Journalists may have reason for concern that a significant portion of the audience will view aspects of their speech unfavorably. Listeners are prone to linguistic bias, prejudice, or profiling—the auditory equivalent of racial profiling.[115] Implicit bias based on accent, dialect, and speech patterns is widespread, research shows. People with nonnative accents are widely perceived as less pleasant to listen to and less intelligent than those with native accents.[116] Instead of perceiving accented speech as more difficult to understand, listeners often perceive it to be less truthful and the speaker as less credible.[117]

This makes many speakers feel stigmatized. "It's still acceptable in many social circles to mock other people's way of speaking," says Carrie Gillon, language planner for the Squamish Nation and a cohost of *The Vocal Fries*, a podcast about linguistic bias and discrimination. "People don't stop to think, 'What am I actually mocking?' It could actually be a person's class or race."[118] Accent bias, for instance, is often a proxy for other biases. "How we speak is so connected to gender, sexuality, social class, and ethnicity," says Rob Drummond, a linguist who helps run the Accentism Project, which compiles stories about accent bias or other language-based prejudice and stereotyping. "If you think about the other forms of discrimination—the color of someone's skin, their ethnic background, their gender, or sexuality—it's very direct. I don't like this person because they are this or that. But when you're saying you don't like their speech, it's really about something else. Because it's one step removed, it doesn't seem as direct."[119] Or as pernicious. "There's this idea that if you tried a little bit harder, you could change the way you speak and sound more 'correct'—you could fit in," says Megan Figueroa, a research scientist and Gillon's podcast cohost.[120]

Linguistic bias and discrimination reinforce social hierarchies as those in positions of power push others toward their way of speaking. "What form are we directing you to? Generally, it's the one that middle[-class] to wealthy White cisgender men use," Gillon says. "The people at the top of society impose that on people who are lower in the social hierarchy. We're saying everyone should aspire to sound like the person on top." Those who are lower in that hierarchy learn early in their education that they do not speak the correct form of their language. "We just absorb that until we're taught otherwise," Gillon says.[121]

Many people view unfavorably accents that are associated with lower socioeconomic classes. News audiences in one study preferred broadcast journalists who had no trace of a regional accent.[122] However, another study found that audiences in a southern media market liked and found more credible journalists with an accent similar to theirs, suggesting that news outlets should be less prone to require radio journalists to "meet a generic national standard."[123]

Race is salient in many audience preference studies. In the southern media market, White listeners found White-sounding voices more credible, while Black listeners had no racial preference.[124] In other research, participants preferred that candidates for a local radio job use more "formal" White dialect (words ending in "ing") rather than the dropped *g*'s associated with non-White speakers and those in lower social classes.[125] Another study found that listeners across races and ethnicities often correctly identified voices as being from White radio newscasters but were far less able to identify the race of Hispanic and Black newscasters, commonly labeling them as White based on their voice. This

reflects audience conditioning to think of radio journalists as White and journalists' socialization to adopt General American English, which, according to
the researcher, is misguidedly assumed to sound White.[126]

Research on Podcast Audiences

Because of the size and scope of the podcasting industry, there is significant variability in audience demographics. On balance, research suggests that podcast
audiences are younger and more diverse than radio audiences. A 2021 survey
found that the majority of podcast listeners were White but an increasing number were Hispanic and Black, reflecting the diversity of the U.S. population.[127]
That same year, research showed that people of color made up 42 percent of NPR's
podcast listeners, compared to 21 percent of its radio audience. Most NPR podcast listeners were under the age of 45, according to data shared with the *Washington Post*.[128]

Rund Abdelfatah, cohost of NPR's *Throughline*, assumes that her narrative
history series, launched as a podcast and later put on radio, speaks to a range of
listeners. She does not feel the need to choose between serving NPR's traditional
audience (White and upper-middle class) and the "aspirational audience" (young
and more diverse). "There's this assumption that [these two audiences] want
something different, but our show challenges that."[129] When Lantigua worked
at *Code Switch*, an NPR podcast about race and culture, she assumed that her
audience was diverse. The production team debated about whether cultural references familiar to younger, non-White listeners needed to be explained to older
White listeners (Lantigua generally opposed use of the so-called explanatory
comma). "We made sure not to alienate our audience, but we didn't try to cod-
dle White listeners," she says.[130]

Many podcasters I interviewed imagine their audience as people who infrequently hear themselves represented on the radio and are early adopters of
technology. That describes Keni, the avatar for LWC Studios' target audience. Young Hispanic and Latino listeners historically have been underserved by
radio and podcasting despite their growing numbers and collective spending
power, Lantigua says. Increasing wealth and social mobility make such audiences
increasingly attractive to advertisers. Communicators from minority backgrounds are thought to have cultural and social knowledge that enable organizations to reach and represent these audiences effectively.[131] Lantigua looks for
hosts like Mitzi Miller, a young, urban, college-educated Afro Latina who can
reach and represent LWC's core audience. "She has the voice and the life experience of Keni as I imagined her," Lantigua says.[132]

Podcasting companies often conduct research to determine their audience
avatar and make programming decisions but generally do not make such data
publicly available. Academic studies show that listeners form parasocial relationships with podcast hosts, but little is known about how these listeners evaluate hosts' vocal delivery.[133] Podcast audiences from diverse backgrounds seem

likely to accept hosts who perform in diverse ways, but this topic requires more research.

Unsolicited Audience Feedback

Research can be costly and time consuming, so news organizations also consider other data points to gauge audience sentiment. Perhaps the most polarizing is unsolicited feedback on journalists' appearance and vocal delivery. Journalists historically have dismissed those who write letters and call newsrooms as irrational and unrepresentative of the general public.[134] Perhaps justifiably, many feel similarly about the small, outspoken segment of their audience who messages them on e-mail and social media or writes online comments.

Yet research shows that these communications help journalists across news sectors identify their audience and what they are thinking.[135] Several newsroom leaders described this type of audience feedback as useful but unscientific. "It should be taken seriously, but I also understand that e-mails and phone calls are anecdotal," says Jackson, the longtime public radio executive. "I've always measured the quality of my performers more by ratings—whether the person's show resonates with an audience."[136]

Although comments are unrepresentative, they give performers a sense of audience perceptions in a way that ratings do not. Positive feedback tends to stick out because it can feel so rare. Viewers thanked Sia Nyorkor for helping to normalize natural hair on television. Viktoria Capek's social media followers praised her for wearing outfits that challenge television news conventions. A recent college graduate said that Capek's willingness to be herself motivated him to pursue an on-air career.

Criticism seems to drown out praise, although researchers have not studied which is more commonplace. Research shows that negative comments are disproportionately directed at women. A 2018 study found that 88 percent of female television journalists and 57 percent of male journalists were criticized online for elements of appearance such as clothing, hair, or weight.[137]

Journalists routinely hear audience complaints about their vocal delivery, although no study has quantified this. Public radio listeners criticized Joe Wertz's Oklahoma accent, even when he was a reporter in that state. "People say mean stuff and it really gets in your head, especially when you're first starting out." When listeners told him that he mispronounced words, it confirmed his fear. "You can no longer just tell yourself, 'Oh, everyone doesn't like their voice—everybody thinks they sound stupid,'" Wertz says. "It becomes, 'No, I really do sound stupid. I sound like a hick.'"[138] The first time Ari Shapiro guest hosted NPR's *Morning Edition*, a listener wrote him a message that he still keeps on his desk: "Dear Ari, please butch up."[139]

Women's voices are picked apart in ways that men's are not. "I am a White dude on the radio, and no one has EVER tweeted at me critiquing my voice,"

NPR's Scott Detrow once tweeted. "Yet literally all of my female colleagues get constant criticism for how they speak or sound."[140] For a time, it seemed the most common criticism was about upspeak, rising inflection at the end of a sentence. Then listeners moved on to other complaints, many of which audio journalist Sally Herships has heard. "Once you stop speaking like a little girl, you might actually be worth listening to," one listener told her. Another said her "creaky voice makes my skin crawl. Fingernails on a blackboard."[141]

So many listeners complained that female public radio journalists speak with vocal fry that *This American Life* dedicated an act to the topic in 2015. Producer Chana Joffe-Walt was struck by the volume of angry e-mails on the topic, some of which she quoted from in the episode. Listeners called women with vocal fry "unbearable," "excruciating," "annoyingly adolescent," and "distractingly disgusting." Several said it detracted from the credibility of the journalism.[142] Listeners told former *This American Life* producer Stephanie Foo that she sounded like a thirteen-year-old, that her voice sounds like driving on gravel, and that listening to her made them want to kill themselves.[143] At the public radio station where Kris Vera-Phillips worked, listeners often complained about women who had high-pitched, nasally voices. "Unfortunately, leadership considered that as something that needed to be coached, rather than accept[ing] it and normaliz[ing] it."[144]

Journalists noted a clear double standard. "Men use vocal fry all the time, but they're not criticized for it," Headlee says. "Women are." Complaints about women's voices often come from men. "If they aren't complaining about vocal fry, they're complaining about pitch," Brooke Gladstone, host of WNYC's *On the Media*, said during a panel. "You've got this perfect zone that the mostly guys out there who are prone to complain won't like. Anything that's high is painful, or else you've got your fry because women are dropping their pitch."[145]

Journalists of color are also accustomed to audience complaints. The cohosts of *Code Switch* revealed during an episode that listeners have criticized them for speaking too fast and too loud and for using too much slang.[146] Gene Demby is Black and his former cohost Shereen Marisol Meraji grew up in a Puerto Rican and Iranian home where "no one spoke in hushed tones."[147] Listeners "write with a certain sense of possession and ownership of public radio," former NPR host Sam Sanders said in a podcast interview. "What they're really saying is, 'This is my public radio. And I want it to sound the way I am used to it sounding, which is stuff catered just to me, an older, usually coastal, usually liberal, affluent degreed elite.... I only want public radio to cater to my whims.'"[148] When Catherine Stifter did training at an NPR member station, White listeners commonly complained about Black journalists' vocal delivery. "There was definitely a sense that if you didn't sound like NPR, then you were possibly uneducated, which was a criticism leveled especially at people of color."[149]

When audience members criticize how journalists look and talk, institutional responses vary. Some newsrooms prohibit journalists from responding directly to their detractors. Others permit or even encourage such interactions, often on social media. A meteorologist who received audience complaints about her weight responded on Twitter, "I like pasta, bread and cheese too much to obsess over my weight. I like my body and that's all that really matters." A meteorologist with multiple sclerosis responded to a viewer's complaint that her legs are "distracting" by writing, "I'm grateful I have them to walk with. You're right. I don't look like the typical person on TV, and I'm proud to be a size 10. Imagine that! You can always turn the channel if you're offended by my huge legs."[150]

Some managers respond directly to commenters. When viewers vowed to change the channel because Tahera Rahman wore a hijab on air, her manager responded, "You're more than welcome to," adding that the station does not discriminate based on religion, race, gender, age, or anything else.[151] The podcast *99% Invisible* received so many complaints about women's voices that managers created an auto reply, which begins: "Hello! You've written in to voice your dislike of one of our female reporter's voices. You're not alone. We have a filter set up that automatically sends these types of emails into a folder labeled 'zero priority.' We'll review this folder and consider the complaints within, well, never."[152]

Yet in voice coach Ann S. Utterback's experience, managers take audience complaints into consideration in hiring and promotion decisions.[153] Journalists recall how feedback is brought to their attention. At Harrison Hove's first full-time television job, a viewer wrote to newsroom leaders to complain about his "offensive" mannerisms. The viewer, claiming not to be a homophobe, said that seeing Hove made them want to switch stations. A manager printed out the e-mail, redacted the names of the sender and recipient, and put a photocopied version of the complaint inside a station envelope on Hove's desk. Hove assumed that his manager agreed with the comments but was too cowardly to talk to him about it face to face. The experience was "traumatic," Hove says, because he was new to the community and still not comfortable with his sexual orientation. "It was a terrible way to be introduced to the industry."[154]

Public radio managers have often taken listener complaints seriously, according to Goldstein, president and executive director of the Public Media Content Collective.

When you run an organization where you have individuals supporting you with gifts, there's this high degree of sensitivity that if you piss off your audience, they'll stop supporting you. So as soon as you get one complaint, people overreact. There was a tendency to say, 'Oh, well if one listener complained that probably represents the views of dozens of listeners—we should listen to that. . . . What we've learned over the years is that no matter what you do, there's going to be a small, passionate group of people that will give you negative feedback, and you can't overreact to that negative feedback.[155]

Managers may feel pressure to act on audience criticism out of self-preservation. "A lot of executives are terrified for their jobs," says television journalist Javier E. Gómez. "They don't want to risk their livelihood to make someone else's career or to do something that hasn't been tried before."[156] That's why Mariam Sobh, who wears a hijab, thinks she was not able to break into television news. "[Managers] were afraid of their audiences," she says.[157] Whitney Miller observes that "it all comes down to who the manager is and if they're willing to take risks. It's crazy to think that me wearing my hair in its natural state is a risk, but some see it that way."[158]

Instinct, Intuition, and the Influence of Personal Taste

Research and unsolicited feedback offer some insight into news audience demographics and preferences. But to journalists, the imagined audience is not just an avatar based on market research or the outspoken people who help fund their news operation. Many imagine their audience as people like themselves or their family, friends, and peers.[159] Newsroom leaders, in particular, tend to consider themselves the prototypical audience member.[160] Because listener and viewer tastes can be difficult to ascertain, managers trust their instincts and intuition to make decisions as the audience proxy.[161] "I can't make a judgment on what criterion the audience wants to use in hiring somebody," a radio news director once said. "So, I use my own."[162]

In many fields, those who run organizations attend the same universities, have similar professional backgrounds, and approach decisions similarly. This helps explain the homogeneity of organizational forms and practices.[163] Journalists often are attracted by and seek out those who are similar to them, a tendency known as homophily.[164] When managers surround themselves with like-minded people with similar values, "you end up in these homogeneous little bubbles," Goldstein says.[165] As public radio journalist Elena Rivera observes, "Most stations are run by old White men who say this is what we think radio should sound like. . . . They often repeat the advice they were given and are used to the voices they grew up hearing."[166] Adds Foo, "If your ear hasn't been trained to hear certain types of voices, you're going to struggle to understand them or think they sound too strange."

Managers often assume that listeners share their tastes. "What you end up with is defaulting to one type of listener as your primary audience," says podcast executive Kathy Tu, "and that listener is going to be a reflection of the person who is making the product."[167] When Headlee worked in public radio, she included a song from a hip-hop artist in the opening of a show on diversity. "The executive producer comes in and says, 'nobody wants to hear that at 8 o'clock in the morning.' 'Actually, I do and my friends do also,'" she responded.[168] Some interviewees felt that managers conveniently cited the imagined audience instead of being direct about what voices or programming elements they found unappealing.

Even when managers were more direct, journalists were frustrated by their vague explanations. "We live and die by subjectivity in this business," says former television journalist Don Champion. "So often we hear, 'There's something about him or her I don't like,' but there's no explanation why. That's a real problem in this industry."[169]

Managers making broad generalizations about listener tastes to justify programming choices or advice to journalists was a chronic problem, according to longtime television news executive Hugo Balta. "They would frame their feedback as if it was drawn from studies, but they never sourced where that information came from." Balta says that in his experience, managers often invested heavily in data collection but dismissed findings that did not align with preferred narratives. "They would look at ratings and comments and fall back on their gut feeling and subjectivity." He found evaluation of on-air talent to be "very biased," reflecting what appealed to White managers. "When journalists [in Spanish-language media] were told to change or neutralize their accent, I felt that was based on prejudice rather than on sound data."[170]

Other former newsroom leaders cited different reasons why managers disregarded or de-emphasized audience data and relied instead on instinct and intuition. Carolyn Kane says that at her former television station, managers with a good feel for their local market and an interest in fairly evaluating on-air talent overrode audience feedback they considered too harsh. She recalls a Latina anchor being widely criticized by viewers. "We could have looked at that research and gotten rid of her, but she was a local and a large part of the community, and she wasn't bad on air, so we kept her."[171]

Giving feedback or making personnel decisions based on gut feeling and subjective evaluations can be problematic, Headlee says, "because we know from research that it makes a person susceptible to bias."[172] Implicit bias creates disparities in hiring practices and is widely understood to be a cause of unintended workplace discrimination.[173] Headlee feels that public radio managers were sincerely committed to equality and inclusion but "couldn't see their biases and understand that what sounds to them like an NPR sound is an inherently White sound."[174]

Summary

Newsroom leaders must consider their audience given their duty to ensure consistent revenue streams. But as this chapter has shown, it is difficult to accurately identify who the audience is and what they want. There is scant data on how modern audiences evaluate on-air talent and how those evaluations affect news stations' listenership and viewership. Managers make assumptions about audience composition, preferences, and willingness to accept differences. Some news stations now attract more diverse audiences. Yet the imagined audience still often remains White and middle to upper class, and this perception influences journalists' self-presentation. Interviews reveal that some journalists feel pressure to appeal to their managers' tastes and try to avoid alienating aging audiences who have been integral to their news stations' survival. In the absence of reliable current data on audience preferences, newsroom leaders may overreact to online comments, giving a vocal minority of listeners and viewers an outsized role in shaping performance expectations.

Part I has examined how journalists learn to perform and who influences their self-presentation, including imagined audiences and newsroom leaders. Part II explores the origins of performance norms in television, radio, and podcasting, how journalists negotiate their self-presentation in different contexts, and how they are challenging conventional news forms that have long resisted change.

Part 2

Norms and Practices

• •

5

Consistent and
Conventional Appearance

● ●

(Performing on Television—Part I)

In college and as she advanced in her television news career, Sia Nyorkor heard the same advice on appearance: your look must be consistent. No major changes to your wardrobe. No flashy new accessories. If you usually wear contacts on camera, do not switch to glasses. Perhaps most importantly, do not change your hairstyle without your manager's approval. "We're told as journalists that the way we appear on camera always has to be the same."[1]

Whitney Miller heard the same message from mentors who viewed her résumé reel and later from television news colleagues. Restrictions on her hairstyle most bothered Miller. "Black women are known for switching up their hair," she says. "I can wear a ponytail today and colored hair next week and that's normal in the Black community. But in corporate America, that's not normal." Miller kept her hair consistent but struggled to understand why managers resisted change. "My sense was that switching up your hair might make the White person who's going to hire you feel uneasy. You can't be a good reporter because we don't know what you're going to look like next week. It was fed to me that if your look is not consistent, then the viewer cannot trust who you are and what you are saying."[2]

Journalists are not just advised to be consistent; it is often contractually required. Television station contracts commonly include a clause requiring talent to seek management's permission before noticeably altering their appearance. This clause helps stations maintain continuity and control the image they project to viewers. To avoid conflict with managers and unwanted audience attention, journalists commonly start their career with a conventional look. Many women in television news opt for the iconic anchor bob. Viewers are likely familiar with this form: perfectly coiffed straight hair with no natural curls, stopping between the chin and collarbone. It is a high-maintenance hairdo that often requires chemical straighteners and styling tools. The payoff is hair that is sleek, with texture "magically landing somewhere between a helmet and a halo."[3]

The anchor bob is so ubiquitous on television news that it is often called newscaster hair. A 2018 study that examined publicity photos of nearly 200 female on-air journalists found that 96 percent had smooth hair, mostly of shoulder length. Only one Black anchor wore her hair with a natural curl. Very short hair was also rare.[4] These and other styles (e.g., braids, dreadlocks, and Afros) historically have been considered unprofessional. Nyorkor and Miller knew this when they began in journalism. Told that their natural hair might distract or even offend some viewers, they consistently wore conventional newscaster hairstyles.

This chapter explores what I call the consistent and conventional principle in television news. Simply put, sticking with a proven, mainstream look is the surest way to advance in an industry that values stability. Choose a style that is familiar, widely accepted, and unlikely to alienate audiences. Do not wear anything that calls attention to the messenger instead of the message. Consistency and conventionality are two dimensions of performance neutrality. Journalists are commonly told that consistency makes you trustworthy and looking conventional gives you authority and broad appeal. Both help to avoid distracting viewers.

I begin by examining how this conventional wisdom shapes journalists' on-air appearance. I return to the concepts of aesthetic labor (to consider how managers attempt to control workers' public image) and aesthetic capital (to assess what physical attributes and elements of personal appearance are valued in television news). I also explore how journalists have challenged conventions and helped normalize diverse forms of self-presentation.

Consistent Appearance

Television news can be chaotic. The news cycle moves increasingly fast. Journalists chase stories from broad coverage areas to share across platforms. Reports are filed at the last minute. Scripts and show rundowns change for continual breaking news. Live shots are added or cut. All of this is communicated through earpieces in real time before and during broadcasts. Newsroom leaders who manage this chaos prize predictability in any form.

That helps explain why the look and format of television news tend to remain constant. Local newscasts typically feature coanchors sitting behind a curved desk and in front of a recognizable cityscape backdrop. During the half-hour or hourlong program, they make small talk and alternate reading from a tele-prompter between prerecorded news packages and live reports. Standardiza-tion helps tame the demands of news production.[5] For managers, having on-air journalists maintain a consistent look means one less concern in an otherwise stressful job.

Aesthetic Labor and the Appearance Clause

To ensure consistency, managers recruit and hire candidates who are physically appealing and embody their organization's identity. They then seek to control workers' appearance so these employees remain an aesthetic fit.[6] The employment contract helps establish this control, giving employers the right to monitor, evaluate, and sanction workers.[7] In television news, appearance clauses spell out expectations.

Some journalists consider appearance clauses to be antiquated and unfair, part of an effort to control their bodies and limit their self-expression. Talent agent Liz Hart disagrees. As she explains to clients, "[Stations] are hiring a package. If all the sudden [a journalist] shows up and doesn't look like the same person who interviewed, that's the talent's fault."[8] Hart advises clients to get a news director's consent before significantly changing their appearance. Talent coach/agent Carolyn Kane agrees that it is reasonable for stations to seek conti-nuity and have some control over journalists' appearance.[9]

The responsibility to seek consent for change tends to fall more heavily on women, whose hair is more closely monitored and who are at greater risk of being assailed for making a "drastic change" in style or color.[10] What constitutes a dras-tic change in appearance? Kane cited a face tattoo as an example. Miller, the television journalist, says, "If someone wants to wear purple hair and dress like a clown, that can't happen because people won't trust you." But Miller does not view Black women alternating between hairstyles as a change that justifies insti-tutional control. "We wear different styles that protect our hair and keep it growing. We wear some just because they're aesthetically pleasing to us—it's a connection we have with Black viewers who do their hair the same way."[11] Dana Adams, the consultant/agent, says she doubts most stations would take action against talent for wearing natural hair, even if it were deemed a substantial change in their appearance.[12] (Current laws may prohibit such action, as explained in chapter 9.)

Yet even if managers do not cite a contract's appearance clause, there are other ways to signal expectations that journalists maintain a consistent look. When television journalist Dorothy Tucker decided that she no longer wanted to straighten her hair, her manager objected. "He was careful not to say, 'I don't like your hair that way' because he knew that would probably get him into trouble. But he just kept saying that he wanted me to look like my [station website] photo because that's what the public sees." Tucker's hair in that photo was straight. "I told my boss, 'If I keep trying to look like this picture, I'm going to burn my hair out and be bald.'" The manager never explained why Tucker's appearance needed to remain consistent, but Tucker took his comments to mean that he disliked her natural hair."[13]

Rather than dissuade talent from changing their appearance, some managers push for a makeover. If it is deemed to be in her client's interest, Hart tends to accept managers' requests and negotiate with the station to pay for the makeover. Vanessa Ruiz was surprised when a station that hired her immediately wanted her to change her appearance. "After multiple interviews and looking at my reel, they knew what I looked like. And yet when I got there, the very first week, they took me to a hair salon and made me cut my hair. I thought, 'This is how you hired me.' But when you sign a TV news contract, for the most part they own what you look like. I didn't have much room to argue, but it rubbed me the wrong way."[14]

Removing Distractions

One common explanation for why journalists must maintain the same look is that consistency is comforting and change is distracting. Over time, viewers come to associate television journalists with a specific hairstyle or wardrobe. They form a connection with local anchors and reporters and feel reassured by their stable presence. As some contend, even a seemingly minor change in appearance can distract and potentially alienate audiences, jeopardizing the relationship journalists have cultivated.

Many journalists are taught to avoid becoming the center of attention when reporting and performing. Unpredictable appearance can shift focus from the message to the messenger and may compromise the appearance of neutrality. Explaining her consistent on-air appearance, Rachel Maddow said in a news interview, "I don't want to insert myself into the story. I just want to give a useful analysis of it to help people come to their own conclusions. It's why I have a conveyor belt of gray blazers—I try to look exactly the same every day. Don't focus on what I'm wearing. Focus on what's coming out of my face."[15]

Black female journalists are particularly likely to be told to maintain continuity in their look and image so their bodies do not become distractions.[16] Miller bought into that when she was younger. "In my mind, consistency was synonymous with trust. It was so deeply ingrained in me that I told interns to keep the same look to avoid distractions." As her career progressed, however, Miller resented the implication that journalists who change their appearance are distracting and untrustworthy and stopped giving that advice. "Pushing journalists to be consistent is just another way of saying 'don't be Black.' The only people who have a problem with 'inconsistency' are White managers, and the comment is usually directed at a Black woman who's switching up her hair. . . . Regardless of what women do or whether they change their appearance, viewers will comment. Switching up your look is not distracting because [viewers] are already distracted."[17] Yet consistency remains the norm in many markets.

Conventional Appearance

For decades, local television journalists have consistently looked "stereotypically heteronormative" and "not overly sexy," according to the 2018 study of television publicity photos.[18] For example, along with the anchor bob, most women wear minimal jewelry and a modest monochrome top that covers their cleavage and their shoulders. The look for men is also standardized: short (or no) hair, a clean-shaven face, and blazers and ties. With few exceptions, on-air talent abide by these "very predictable" appearance standards.[19]

Form is sanctified through repeated exposure. Television audiences become conditioned to view this unofficial newscaster uniform as authoritative. It is considered to be neutral, to reflect a mainstream, middle-of-the-road style or aesthetic. Attire that is fashionable but not too suggestive. Hair that reveals nothing about a person's background or tastes. Physical characteristics also are viewed as neutral. Skin without visible body art. Physical features and body types that are conventional by television standards.

Aesthetic Capital in Television News

Appearing conventional is not the same as looking ordinary or average. Compared to the general population, television journalists are typically more classically attractive and more sharply dressed. By conventional I mean typical among telegenic newscasters. As the publicity-photo study showed, television newsrooms are filled with journalists with similar aesthetic traits and physical characteristics, and who style themselves in similar ways.

These are all elements of aesthetic capital, traits of beauty that are perceived as assets capable of yielding privilege, opportunity, and wealth. Personal beauty assets include facial features, hair, body/physique, and elements of personal style such as attire and accessories.[20] Possessing these beauty assets does not guarantee journalists wealth but does increase their likelihood of having access to the privileges and opportunities afforded to on-air personalities.

News organizations, like employers in many industries, tend to reward individuals who embody social privileges. Workers whose gender, race, ethnicity, or body type do not "conform to an aspirational aesthetic" may be overlooked for employment or limited to "nonvisible," lower-status positions.[21] The following sections examine how this aspirational aesthetic in television news has impacted journalists in various identity groups.

Race and Ethnicity

Journalists of color who do not embody White beauty standards historically have been at a disadvantage. Early on, television lacked racial and ethnic diversity. That changed incrementally beginning in the late 1960s when stations, bowing to public pressure to better reflect their communities and in an effort to attract minority audiences, hired more journalists of color.[22] These journalists felt pressure to "fit into an established [newsroom] culture that was not expected to bend to accommodate them." They were expected to "mimic Whites not only in their behavior and attitudes, but also in appearance."[23]

In the 1970s, some television stations sought "the beautiful ethnic"—journalists who were prized for their looks and were chosen to represent an ethnic group with a large local presence. These "ethnic slots" were filled by candidates whose backgrounds were easily identifiable to viewers.[24] In the decades that followed, stations sought to reap the benefits of diverse on-air representation without the perceived risks. Adams, the consultant/agent, recalls a news director once telling her, "I need someone Hispanic who doesn't sound Hispanic." Adams hears that type of request less often now. However, several interviewees shared examples of tokenism. "What I hear from [newsroom leaders] is, 'We don't have enough Brown people or Black people' or 'We need to get somebody who's Asian,'" says broadcast consultant and talent coach Valerie Geller. "Then they start looking in that talent pool for the prettiest people, who get a chance to audition."[25]

Diversity in local television news has improved incrementally but has not kept pace with the U.S. minority population. One study found that Asian Americans are particularly underrepresented.[26] Other research shows that while Hispanics remain underrepresented among anchors, television stations serving racially diverse populations largely reflect that diversity on air, representing progress in physical representation.[27]

Yet in one important respect, diversity remains limited. The publicity-photo study found that journalists with light skin predominated, even among Black and Hispanic talent, prompting researchers to write that "on-air journalists reflect a disproportionate representation of Whiteness."[28] Having light skin makes Black journalists "palatable" to news directors and increases their chances of getting hired, Libby Lewis found in her book on race in television news.[29] Prejudice or discrimination against individuals with darker skin, known as colorism, is common throughout the industry. In Spanish-language media, managers often prefer "Caucasian-passing types" with fair skin, according to television journalist Javier E. Gómez.[30] Typically at these stations, the majority of on-air journalists are Mexican, says former television executive Hugo Balta.[31] A well-established Hispanic journalist warned Gómez to expect problems finding a prominent on-air position because he looked "obviously Caribbean" and the norm was to look "obviously Mexican."[32]

Physical Features and Body Types

That journalist also pointed out that Gómez has small eyes. "I was told, 'People in broadcasting need to have big eyes that can be seen clearly by the camera.'" She listed other perceived physical flaws. "None of them were things I could do anything about other than having plastic surgery," Gómez says. After hearing this "heartbreaking" feedback, he stopped pursuing on-air positions in commercial broadcasting. By contrast, broadcast journalist Antoinette Lattouf repeatedly heard that she has "acceptable features." She benefited from being attractive by Western standards. "People say to me, 'Even though you're Lebanese, you aren't too ethnic looking,' as though my Arabness is diluted because I've agreed to work in an environment that's traditionally people of Anglo backgrounds."[33]

In image-conscious industries like television, applicants thought to have attractive physical features and body types have long received hiring preference. Television news may have been most appearance driven in the 1950s, when local stations often seemed more concerned with on-air journalists' looks than their journalistic credentials.[34] The "grey-haired, avuncular image," once the primary model for newscasters, yielded to a more youthful look in the 1970s. Stations had a "near-obsessive" preoccupation with finding young, attractive anchors.[35] For decades, news was delivered almost exclusively by "beautiful faces" as managers prioritized attractive anchors who could draw large audiences.[36] Those who are youthful looking, slender, and have faces with classical "masculinity or femininity appeal" historically have been viewed as possessing natural beauty assets.[37] Those deemed unsuitable for television may hear feedback about their small eyes, large nose, crooked teeth, or other supposed beauty deficits.

Prejudice against those whose appearance is considered unattractive or contrary to social norms and cultural standards is known as lookism. Judging others based on physical appearance can lead to stigmatization, which can be followed by unequal treatment and exclusionary behavior.[38] Black women in television news commonly perceive that they are not hired or promoted because of their weight, according to Tucker, the television journalist who once led the National Association of Black Journalists. Evidence from the publicity-photo study supports this concern; few women in that study were classified as overweight.[39] Says Nyorkor, the television journalist: "I always knew that because of the way I looked—I was not a size six—that I had to report better, write better, and sound better than everyone else."[40]

Journalists with physical anomalies have found it difficult to break into the profession. When Bree Walker was an aspiring television journalist, she was classically beautiful, with blonde hair and a slender build. But because she had fused fingers, a television executive said he could not hire her as an anchor because her hands would disturb viewers during their dinner hour. Walker eventually became an anchor but hid her hands until later in her career, when she went public about her condition.[41]

Journalists may be counseled to have cosmetic surgery to fix their perceived physical flaws, although Geller, the consultant and talent coach, says that is now less common.[42] In a case that received press attention, a television news manager advised an intern to get his ears pinned back because they were "a big distraction." The intern got plastic surgery for his ears and a chin implant, later telling a reporter, "The vanity of TV news is something people should understand before getting in the business."[43]

Gender Double Standards

The importance of looks is itself gendered, sociologist Ashley Mears has observed. Women invest more in their looks and are held more rigidly to heteronormative beauty standards.[44] These standards historically have been set by men. A 2000 survey of local news anchors found that the most common professional barrier for women, but not men, was overemphasis on physical appearance. Male anchors in the survey acknowledged that women's looks faced more scrutiny.[45] Nearly two decades later, researchers found that female journalists continue to be more scrutinized than men and more often criticized for their physical attributes.[46] Criticism is often in public view, such as when a British television critic and a longtime television executive described a TV presenter as "too ugly for television."[47]

Christine Craft says she never had any doubts that she was attractive enough for television.[48] Betty Furness, an actress, spokeswoman, and television journalist, once told Craft that she was "pretty enough, not too pretty"—which, in Furness's view, was ideal.[49] Women in television news are expected to be attractive, but not so much so that others claim that they are trading on their looks or that attractiveness is the sole reason for their success.[50]

Craft's looks were a source of contention. As her book title, *Too Old, Too Ugly, and Not Deferential to Men*, suggests, while she was an anchor in Kansas City, she received persistent criticism about her appearance.[51] When she accepted the job, Craft warned her news director that appearance was not her top priority and that she would not be coerced into a makeover.[52] Soon after she started, the news director praised her for being "credible and authoritative." But he and others in management also pointed out her perceived physical deficiencies, including a "squarish jaw" and "somewhat uneven eyes." Craft was "puzzled by the emphasis on things I could not change short of major plastic surgery" and noted the station's double standards. "The men could be balding, jowly, bespectacled, even fat . . . yet the women had to be flawless."[53]

Craft said the news director cited negative audience reaction to her appearance as among the reasons for removing her as coanchor. She left the station shortly afterward and sued for (among other things) age and sex discrimination, alleging a pattern of "hounding" female journalists about their appearance. She won several trials but lost on appeal. Craft believes that her lawsuits, begun in the 1980s, benefited female journalists and those vulnerable to discrimination and made consultants more careful about the degree of change they suggest for on-air talent.[54] Yet appearance double standards remain. As Craft wrote in 2019, "If the male anchors can be a decade older than the women and still be on the air—jowls, balding pates and all—then we have not come nearly far enough."[55]

Head Coverings

Television journalists traditionally have avoided head coverings that draw attention to their religious affiliation or ethnic identity. Several who challenged this norm have received pushback. A professor who worked in television news told Noor Tagouri that she could not be objective while wearing a hijab. "He meant that any story I did, my identity would play a factor." That same professor asked, "Can't you just take off your hijab on camera?" to which she responded, "No, it doesn't work that way." Tagouri expected resistance. It is one reason why she started college early, at age sixteen, to get a head start on what she assumed would be a slow-developing career. "I thought, 'I'm going to give myself two years of rejection.' I didn't want to fall behind, so I needed that buffer time."[56]

Tagouri was motivated to become the first U.S. anchor/host in commercial television to wear a hijab. In college, she had broadcast internships and excelled in school while traveling the world as a public speaker. She was a news producer and later took an on-air job in the Washington, DC, bureau of a Canadian television network. Even though her experience in the newsroom was generally positive, Tagouri experienced harassment in the field. She and her main videographer, a Black woman with dreadlocks, jokingly called themselves the "best worst team" because people often inappropriately commented on their appearance.

Tagouri's on-air career stalled. She heard from hiring managers that they did not think their viewers were ready for a journalist who wears a hijab. Her response was, "How will they be ready until we show them they need to be?" The managers were not persuaded. "In local news, people are too afraid," she says. "We're constantly catering to a status quo that needs to change." Tagouri stopped pursuing work in traditional television news. She started a consulting and production company dedicated to telling diverse stories and created a podcast in partnership with iHeartMedia that, among other topics, examines misrepresentations of Muslims in U.S. media.

Early in her career, radio journalist Mariam Sobh sent tapes to dozens of local television stations but received few responses. Even when she was interviewed, she felt regarded as "more of a curiosity" than a serious candidate. Sobh resorted to submitting headshots and tapes without her hijab. An agent who had ignored her previous inquiry responded, telling Sobh, "Thank God you took that thing off. . . . Now you look like the girl next door." Yet the agent still showed no interest in representing her. Even with plenty of industry connections, Sobh had no luck getting an on-air television job. She stayed in radio, later tried podcasting, and eventually became a communications strategist.[57]

A journalist Sobh mentored finally broke the barrier that Sobh faced. Tahera Rahman's career began much like Sobh's. Unable to find an on-air television job, she settled for one in radio. Thereafter, Rahman took a different path. She was a television producer in the Quad Cities, a small market on the Illinois-Iowa border. She tried unsuccessfully to get an on-air position at that station. An assignment editor told her that the community was not ready for a journalist wearing a hijab. Despite her years of experience, Rahman once lost out to someone straight out of college. "That hurt the most because I was like, 'What else can I do?' I felt like I had exhausted everything and maybe it just wasn't meant to be." After one late shift, she called her mom on her way home. "I had to pull over. I was crying on the side of the road, right by cornfields. That was the low point."[58]

Encouraged by her mom to persist, Rahman finally got an on-air reporting job at the Quad Cities station. In 2018, she became the first full-time hijabi Muslim newscaster on mainstream U.S. news. She was overwhelmed by press requests to interview her but accepted many of them out of a sense of pride and duty. "It's important to celebrate achievements when they come," she says, "so that other people know that it's taken so long for this to happen and that's not okay." She also wanted to show young journalists of color that this door could open for them, too. Rahman had a security detail when reporting from the field and her news director regularly checked on her well-being. She also felt supported at her next job, a station in Austin, Texas. But she still feels there is more work to be done to increase representation. "Just because I got hired at one station in one market doesn't mean the next one will come easy. There will always be a barrier."[59] Sobh was thrilled for Rahman and hoped to see a ripple effect, with more hijabi reporters or anchors hired. But thus far, change has come very slowly.

In Western countries, there are few examples of journalists wearing other types of head coverings. It happened, unexpectedly, at *BBC World News* in 2022 when a producer filled in at the last minute on camera and became the first presenter ever to wear a kippah. However, it is still easier to find stories of journalists being harassed for wearing kippahs in public than stories about them being accepted for wearing them on television.

Attire

The remaining sections focus on a different aspect of appearance: personal style, which can more easily be changed to conform to industry norms. Many who advise television journalists on attire give feedback similar to what Kane, the coach/agent, tells her clients: "Don't give audiences anything to object to and keep it simple." The safest bet is to look conventional, or "somewhat generic," in Kane's words.[60]

Generic attire works in television news, Kane and others say, because it helps on-air talent have broad appeal and avoid becoming a distraction. Conventionally dressed journalists do not "call attention to the storyteller rather than the story," image consultant Barbara Allen-Rosser says. "There's a norm, and it's not the perfect style or perfect color, it's a sense of decorum. It's a sense that you know you're a professional and you're expected to be authoritative." When asked who or what determines that norm, Allen-Rosser responded, "Whatever you see on television in that market."[61]

Television news has never been a place to take fashion risks, says former news director and consultant Craig Allen. Talent learned to "look good but not steal the show," to "dress middle of the road, like the guy next store who would go to church and wear his Sunday best."[62] That is what Middle Majority audiences favored when consultants studied their tastes starting in the 1960s. Viewers praised a female reporter for being "classically stylish rather than clothing fad oriented."[63] One male anchor was lauded for dressing sharply, not in an outlandish or "far out" style.[64]

A television news consultant advised Craft in the early 1980s to pay attention to feedback on her attire because viewers decide whether or not to listen to an anchor—especially a woman—largely based on what colors, fabrics, and styles she uses to create an image of authority.[65] The consultant showed Craft tapes of anchors across the country. "It was uncanny how they all looked the same, talked the same, and wore variations of the same clothes and makeup," Craft wrote. "Chicago looked just like Cleveland, just like Miami, just like Denver."[66] Craft reluctantly agreed to follow a "fashion calendar" approved by consultants that included a mixture of blazers, shirts, blouses, and matching skirts.[67]

Through the early 1990s, female anchors wore "demure jackets, matte lipstick, and tame hairdos."[68] Styles have changed in recent decades, generally becoming less conservative. A 2007 study of television newscasters on FOX, CNN, MSNBC, and one NBC affiliate found that women dressed "suggestively" (e.g., open blouses, tight-fitting skirts) slightly more often than they dressed "demurely."[69] The 2018 publicity-photo study came to a different conclusion. Researchers described most local broadcast journalists as wearing modest attire.[70] The difference in findings warrants explanation. The 2007 study examined appearance during actual newscast performances, likely reflecting the direction of news managers. The still (and stilted) photos in the 2018 study, which were used to promote the station to advertisers as well as to viewers, seem less likely to reflect performance input from news managers.

While dress expectations for women have become less rigid, their look is still heavily managed—particularly if they are in a highly visible role in a big market or at a national station. When Gloria Riviera took an on-air job at ABC News, a wardrobe consultant visited her apartment, looked through her clothes, and identified what she could and could not wear on camera. The network paid for a new wardrobe and a makeover. "It was all cut from the same mold—solid colors, certain hair, certain jewelry."[71] When Lattouf held on-air roles at national stations in Australia, she was told to stick to single-color dresses with a blazer and to refrain from wearing necklaces or large earrings. "If I was showing my shoulder, I would get a message from our lead stylist or the news director telling me my outfit wasn't appropriate and that I needed a consult."[72]

Defining what is appropriate is often a point of contention. Allen-Rosser, the image consultant, finds a sleeveless shirt that exposes a tattoo unsuitable for television because it is likely to distract viewers. Viktoria Capek wore such an outfit on air when she worked at a television station in Arkansas. Encouraged by a colleague to show off the rose tattoo on her upper arm, Capek ran the plan by her news director, who did not object. Shortly after the morning newscast, an anchor texted Capek to say that her outfit looked unprofessional. "Thank you for your consideration," Capek responded, "but I know what I'm doing." The station received audience complaints about the tattoo, but Capek was unmoved. "It's not like I have a middle finger tattooed on my shoulder," she thought. "It's roses. If you're offended, that seems like a you problem."[73] Despite having no personal objections, the news director told Capek to cover up the tattoo for the next newscast. She reluctantly put on a blazer and posted about her experience on TikTok, where she had a large following.

Capek did not dress conventionally by television news standards. Some of her outfits were loose fitting. A talent coach once told her to wear tighter dresses instead of blazers that made her shoulders look square and bulky. "I'll listen to your advice because I always want to know how to get better at something," she told the coach, "but I don't care about appearances."[74] Capek often spoke on social media about being a queer woman in television news who challenged antiquated industry norms. Her TikTok video explaining the tattoo incident attracted immediate attention. Capek's social media followers defended her as inspirational for being true to herself and flooded the station with complaints. She had not wanted to draw more attention to the conflict, but she appreciated the support.

Capek found other ways to challenge norms, for example by wearing suits and other outfits that, by conventional standards, are not considered feminine. Before she left television news, Capek commented that the industry "needs to accept that people are different than they were in the 1950s. We grow and we change and it's common for people to have art on their bodies and a desire to show that off. [Television news] needs to change with the times."[75]

Journalist Jana Shortal describes television appearance norms as "archaic" and the traditional newscaster uniform as "milquetoast" and "not reflective of who we are as people anymore." Early in her career, Shortal wore conservative attire and shoulder-length, dyed-blonde hair. Dressing in "unfeminine" ways seemed taboo. "I was afraid of that exterior part being something that people didn't like," she says, "so I just blended in." Shortal felt pressure to dress like a "straight midwestern woman who is subservient to the male anchor." She was "one way at work and another way not at work" and hated having to be closeted. "We're supposed to be in the truth-telling business and I was a walking lie."[76]

Shortal came out as gay and continued dressing like a traditional television journalist. She finally was given her own news show in 2016. While she was away from the camera preparing, she did not wear her "lady uniform." During rehearsals, Shortal told an executive at her station's parent company who had become used to her off-camera look—T-shirt, pants, and unstraightened hair—that she dreaded having to put on her newscaster uniform again. Suggesting that Shortal no longer cover, the executive casually said, "This show is supposed to be different, so you should be who you are." Shortal went on air wearing a T-shirt and a blazer. "No one beat me up about it after the show, so I kept doing it," she says.[77] Throughout, she felt supported by her station and its parent company.

Shortal no longer had straight, shoulder-length hair; it was curly on top and short on the sides. She wore glasses, colorful jacket-pant combos, and an assortment of ties. Free from dressing in a costume and abiding by restrictive gender norms, Shortal says she was more authentic on air. She observes that appearance norms in journalism are changing. "I'm not sure my story would even attract much attention now—it was a different time back then."[78]

Hair

Norms for hair have been slow to change. A look at television journalists from the shoulders up suggests the existence of ageism and gender and racial double standards. The publicity-photo study found plenty of men but no women with gray hair.[79] Hairstyles were predictably gendered. Men all had short or very short hair; women had mostly medium-length hair.[80] This conventional newscaster hair can be limiting for men but not especially difficult to style, but it is often both restrictive and time consuming for women.

Many Black journalists feel that the straight-hair norm is particularly problematic. It costs them time and money to be camera ready and often leads to hair damage and loss. Some see it as a sign that only White beauty standards are deemed professional. In many work settings, Black women with natural hairstyles are viewed as less professional and are less likely to be recommended for a job interview than Black women with straight hair and White women with curly or straight hair. They also receive negative evaluations when applying for jobs in industries like television news with strong appearance norms.[81] Black female journalists historically have been told to straighten their hair and keep it shoulder length because audiences (implicitly White) find it "neat and tasteful" and more credible than natural hair.[82] Black men's hair is also policed in the workplace; the expectation is that they wear it short or shave it completely.

Black women in local television news have challenged hair norms most publicly. In the early 1970s, Melba Tolliver wore an Afro, her natural hairstyle, on a trip to Washington, DC, to cover a White House wedding ceremony. Tolliver's news director told her that she did not look feminine and should change her hairstyle if she wanted to be seen on camera. She refused, appearing in wedding footage with her natural hair. Tolliver's scheduled appearances the next day were canceled, and when she did not follow orders to straighten her hair, she was temporarily taken off air. Support from viewers quelled station leaders' fears of a backlash and Tolliver was allowed back on television. A rival station she later worked for promoted her natural hairstyle to audiences.[83]

A decade later, Dorothy Reed was suspended for wearing cornrows. Reed's news director found her hairstyle unattractive and distracting and told her to get rid of the cornrows. She refused, viewing the ultimatum as a sign of racism. Reed appealed to the public, telling the press that this constituted "White male-dominated management deciding how I should look as an acceptable Black woman." Hundreds marched on her behalf in the days before her situation was resolved. Reed was compensated for her suspension time and was allowed to wear braids without beads. The station did not renew her contract, and Reed never sought another television news job, feeling that she had essentially been blackballed.[84]

In recent years, Black journalists have had mixed results challenging hair norms. Early in Brittany Noble's career, she straightened her hair so frequently that she remembers thinking, "I'm going to burn my hair out—it will all be gone." She also tried wearing expensive sew-ins and wigs because she "didn't want [stations] to know that my hair wasn't perfect and didn't do what it's supposed to do."[85] Noble resented having to spend so much time and money on hairstyling, but she saw no other option. "I was desperate and I'd do anything to get my foot in the door. When I had a job, I was just doing what I had to do to keep it." Noble was so focused on "manipulating myself to look just like [her White colleagues]" that she questioned whether she was attractive enough for television. "I remember telling my friend, 'I've never been the ugly girl.' She said, 'Brittany, you're not the ugly girl, you're the Black girl.'"[86]

Noble had perfected the conventional newscaster hairstyle by her fourth local television job. In that way she fit in, but she "felt so different" as the only Black reporter at her station.

Noble says that after having her son, she asked her news director if she could wear her natural hair. Noble says he gave her approval but just weeks later instructed her to stop because she looked unprofessional. "Mississippi viewers need to see a beauty queen," she remembers him saying.[87] Noble returned to straightening her hair. She filed complaints with the station's parent company, citing alleged mistreatment, including being reprimanded for wearing natural hair. She later filed an Equal Employment Opportunity Commission (EEOC) employment discrimination claim. In 2018, she was fired for what her employer described as excessive absenteeism and what Noble felt was retaliation. Neither the EEOC claim nor a later-filed court action was successful. After a long hiatus from local television news, in 2023 Noble started at a new station and no longer sported straight hair.

Other journalists have publicly celebrated successfully challenging restrictive hair norms. "Years ago I was told to take a clip out of my newsreel because I was wearing braids," journalist Treasure Roberts tweeted. "The news director told me I wouldn't get a job with braids. I left the clip in and landed a job in the industry. Now, I'm wearing them on air for the first time. Braids are professional."[88] After years of being told to maintain a "professional image" that excluded natural hair, journalist Kaci Jones wrote on Twitter that "for the first time in my career I'm wearing braids on air. I'm so happy to be a part of an industry wide shift challenging and refusing 'beauty norms' that stem from White supremacy."[89]

Nyorkor and Miller also celebrated their milestones after years of covering. Nyorkor was used to hiding her natural hair. She began using hair relaxer before she was ten years old and used it religiously early in her on-air career, a process that led to hair thinning and eventual hair loss. She sometimes wore a weave to hide her braids. At a conference Nyorkor attended, fellow journalists gave her rave reviews on her natural hair. When she ran out of time to straighten it after the trip, she went on air with a natural look. She expected a reprimand but instead heard praise from an assistant news director, which she found "very freeing." After that, she stopped straightening her hair. Nyorkor started with her hair in buns and Afro puffs and worked up to a full Afro. "The night before I did it, I had a lot of anxiety because I don't want my hair to be a distraction. But the feedback from viewers was phenomenal."[90]

Miller also waited a long time before wearing natural hair at work. Growing up in humid Houston, she found braids easier to manage. She would change her hairstyle when she applied for jobs. She wore weaves, wigs, and extensions as a reporter and anchor. One time when her hairdresser was unavailable, an anchor friend helped her braid cornrows. Miller spent the weekend crocheting a curly Afro. "I wasn't trying to make a statement, but I thought it looked good," she says. After debuting the style on television, a manager messaged her saying, "I wish you would have told me before you went on air." As Miller recalls, "The message wasn't 'I don't like your hair' but it was understood. That's when it became clear that I didn't own my style; I didn't own who I was on TV."[91]

Even though she found it demoralizing, Miller became conditioned to seek permission before changing her hairstyle. She did that as a reporter in Cincinnati until managers said she could style her hair how she wanted. Miller wore braids on air. She says that when managers encouraged her to continue, a mental load was lifted. Her news director suggested that she write a commentary about her experience, which she did. "I'm so blessed to work for a management team that embraces what makes their on-air talent different. . . . Braids are professional," she wrote.[92]

Miller said that for Black women in television, "there's still some confusion over what's expected and it's hard to know whether natural hair might hurt our job chances." Nyorkor used to hedge her bets by making two different demo reels—one with straight hair and one with curly hair—and advised young journalists to do the same. "Those days are over," she says. "Now I tell them, 'As long as you did a good story, put it on your reel.'"[93] At the National Association of Black Journalists conference, where many broadcast journalists come to network, Nyorkor says that women no longer feel obliged to wear straight hair. She was proud to be in a photograph that was widely shared online of dozens of women at that conference showing off their natural styles.

Nyorkor and Miller have mixed feelings about receiving attention for challenging long-standing norms. "People say I was at the front end of this wave and helped pave the way for others, which makes me feel good," Nyorkor says.[94] She is ready for natural hair on television news to become so normalized that it is not newsworthy. Miller agrees. "I'm happy there's light shed on this issue, but I hope for the day when stories like mine aren't headline makers."[95]

Summary

Television journalists have long been expected to look consistent and conventional. The aspirational aesthetic—which includes light skin, a slender physique, classically attractive features, short to mid-length straight hair, and fashionable but somewhat conservative attire—has been slow to change. Some observers see signs of progress. "There was more of a homogenized look 20 years ago, and that's no longer the case," says Geller, the consultant and talent coach.[96]

Whether journalists have succeeded in challenging appearance norms has depended on the news market and their station leadership. Consistency, in many respects, is still expected, although perhaps less so for some attributes, such as hair, in some newsrooms. As more journalists deviate from the conventional look, those from historically marginalized groups may feel less pressure to cover. That many still feel obliged to seek approval from managers to diverge from the norm suggests that more progress is needed.

6

"Accentless" Speech
and Attractive Voices

• •

(Performing on Television—Part II)

Viktoria Capek grew up hearing that she had a "golden voice." The Georgia native spoke clearly and without the often stigmatized southern accent. She received praise for sounding like a prototypical newscaster. "People said I would be a great fit for broadcast journalism because I have a really nice mid-Atlantic accent."[1] Jill Olmsted feels she benefited from growing up in Minneapolis. "I think because I didn't have a Boston accent or a southern twang it helped me in my broadcast career."[2] Tanya Ott considers herself a "vocal lottery winner" because she spent her formative years in Iowa. "I had a very flat midwestern accent, which when I started my career was what people wanted."[3]

Broadcast journalists tend to sound midwestern, mid-Atlantic, or geographically unidentifiable. Many project well, enunciate, speak slowly and smoothly, and have an "exaggerated lilt."[4] They are expected to speak General American, known also as Standard American English, broadcast English, or network English.

General American has long been considered a neutral, accentless variety of spoken American English.[5] However, it is *not* neutral. Neutrality implies not taking sides or not having strongly marked characteristics or features. General American privileges ways of speaking associated with educated White Americans.[6] Because standard speech is "arbitrarily assumed to reflect the highly educated members of a society, a similarly arbitrary definition pegs other social dialects as nonstandard."[7] As Deion Broxton's story illustrates, journalists from historically marginalized groups often hide regional accents and other dialect attributes (e.g., grammar, vocabulary) that mark them as outsiders.

The existence of accentless speech is a fallacy. "We all speak with an accent," says speech-language pathologist Cathy Runnels."[8] General American is accented but hard to place geographically, although many associate it with the Midwest.[9] "There's nothing objectively good or bad about an accent; it's all about social connotation," explains linguist Rob Drummond.[10] Audiences are conditioned to view familiar newscaster accents as natural and authoritative, and underrepresented ones as inferior and unprofessional. Yet nearly a century ago, new broadcast speech practices did not come naturally to most journalists; they had to learn them.[11]

This chapter details how General American became the broadcast news standard, why it remains so, and how standardized broadcast speech became the norm outside the United States. I explore the perceived advantages of sounding placeless and unclassifiable. I examine why accents, dialects, and vocal attributes that are common in the general population are rarely heard on television news. Finally, I address how journalists from historically marginalized groups have challenged restrictive norms and have attempted to redefine what sounds authoritative.

A "Neutral" Accent from Everywhere but Nowhere

Watch local news across the United States and it becomes apparent that many newscasters sound alike. Television journalists do not have homogeneous backgrounds, but they learn to adhere to institutional norms.[12] While some norms have changed, General American remains the gold standard in television news.

There are practical reasons for this. Many on-air journalists begin in small television markets and work their way up. They must be adaptable and geographically mobile. To achieve big-market ambitions, they must appeal to hiring managers and news audiences who live in different regions and have diverse tastes. Sounding geographically ambiguous can be an asset. "The more neutral your voice can sound, the wider you'll be able to go," voice coach Sally Prosser tells television journalists.[13] "Not being able to detect where someone is from is very important," says consultant/agent Dana Adams. "The idea is you have to appeal to a mass audience."[14] Audiences want to identify with the storyteller, agent Liz Hart tells clients. "The more generic [your speech] is, the easier it is for them to identify with you."[15] Textbook authors give similar advice. Great communicators can have accents, but the safest bet is to adopt standard broadcast speech.[16] Many journalists internalize that message. "You don't want to be in Louisiana and sound like a New Yorker," anchor Jeannette Reyes said in a viral TikTok video. "The 'neutral' accent makes you sound like you're from everywhere but nowhere."[17]

General American is viewed as broadly palatable and unobjectionable. When Dan Rather began in broadcasting, he tried to hide his Texas accent and sound midwestern after he was told that the latter was the least identifiable and most acceptable way of speaking.[18] Many, including Reyes, believe it is also the clearest and, to viewers, the most authoritative. "As it was explained to me, the midwestern accent is easy for everyone to understand," says former broadcast journalist Don Champion. "I took that at face value and went after trying to adopt it."[19]

Setting Speech Standards

General American was not always the broadcast news standard. In radio's early days, there was little standardization. Provided that journalists sounded well educated, regional dialects were permitted.[20] That changed when stations sought to unite the country around a "correct" form of speech with uniform pronunciation standards. As a journal article from the 1930s explained, radio "offers a standardization which freely admits certain outstanding localisms and regionalisms, crystalizing some, absorbing others," thus developing "distinctly American speech."[21]

In the early twentieth century, many public figures who lived on the East Coast spoke with the British-influenced transatlantic accent. While some viewed that accent as sophisticated, others thought it sounded "artificial and affected" and preferred "pure" midwestern speech.[22] Sounding vaguely midwestern became the norm in broadcast news due largely to an influential pronunciation expert from Ohio. John Samuel Kenyon was not the first scholar to reference General American, but he was arguably the most prominent. Kenyon, a linguist and English professor, authored several guides to American English pronunciation. Acknowledging that no official standard existed, he implicitly endorsed how he and other northeast Ohioans spoke as the model.[23] Some linguists, however, dispute that General American ever reflected how people in Ohio—or in any region—actually talked.

Broadcasting companies adopted Kenyon's guidelines in their speech and language manuals, such as the *NBC Handbook of Pronunciation*. An NBC executive promoted the ideal as "decent American pronunciation, affected as little as possible by localisms."[24] Stations established diction and pronunciation courses for announcers and newscasters, sending some to the Midwest to eliminate unwanted regional accents.[25] Radio broadcasters received awards for speech precision and exemplifying proper General American English.[26]

Efforts to promote uniformity in pronunciation were largely successful. Standardized speech became the norm on radio and eventually on television, which originally featured regional accents before becoming increasingly homogenized.[27] Through their on-air performances, journalists contributed to the standardization of spoken language.[28]

The BBC and Received Pronunciation

The British Broadcasting Corporation (BBC) also attempted to standardize broadcast speech and promote its adoption in the general population. When the BBC began in the early 1920s, no preferred accent or policy on proper pronunciation existed. Some stations aired regional accents, although presenters often gravitated toward Received Pronunciation (RP), a social dialect associated with the educated, urban upper class.[29]

Seeking to "fix" English pronunciation and achieve a unified sound, BBC executives turned to Welsh phonetician Arthur Lloyd James to create in-house speech standards. James, a founding member of the BBC's advisory committee on spoken English, acknowledged the importance of linguistic diversity. However, he felt that the BBC needed to select one speech model as "correct" and promote that standard nationwide in order to have a clear identity.[30] James endorsed RP, which, like General American, was regarded as neutral because it allowed presenters to mask their regional identity.[31] James helped institutionalize RP through his work with the BBC. He produced booklets on broadcast English (also called BBC English) and created broadcasts designed to educate the public about proper pronunciation.

The BBC wanted presenters to sound alike and downplay their individuality. To convey detached impartiality, for a time the public service broadcaster did not identify on-air journalists by name.[32] That policy was short lived, however, and the broader effort to encourage homogeneity proved difficult.[33] The BBC abandoned a single standard accent policy and mandatory pronunciations of common words.[34] Some consider the attempt to standardize and regulate speech a failure, especially at local stations, where journalists from different social classes spoke with diverse accents. But BBC English remained a fixture on national stations and throughout the UK.

Standardization in Other Performance Fields

Performers in other fields also learn standardized forms of "good speech." In theater, that standard has long been World English, which prominent speech trainer and acting consultant Edith Skinner popularized and described as "Good American Speech" in her 1942 book *Speak with Distinction*. This "neutral" form is unmistakably highbrow but difficult to place; it vaguely resembles RP and the transatlantic accent. Generations of actors have learned World English, also called American Stage Speech, in theater classes and training sessions.[35]

Beginning in earnest in the early 2000s, speech trainers advocated dropping Skinner's work as the standard. Several published essays rejected her view of World English as neutral and called the speech training tradition elitist. A young actor from an ethnic or racial minority group would conclude that their speech is not good, one professor wrote. "Good," he argued, is "mired . . . in a model of class, ethnic, and racial hierarchy that is irrelevant to the acting of classical texts and repellent to the sensibilities of most theater artists." The notion of "American" is also spurious, he wrote, because no Americans spoke this way unless they were educated to do so.[36]

World English, Received Pronunciation, and General American endured to varying degrees because they were endorsed by influential institutions and individuals. These speech standards became closely associated with a professional role (e.g., anchor, actor) and came to be perceived as natural despite not resembling the way most audience members spoke.

Speech Forms that Are Largely Absent in TV News

Accents and other aspects of dialect that are common in parts of the United States are underrepresented or entirely absent in television news. Journalists from racial and ethnic minority groups and from geographic areas where people are stereotyped as sounding uneducated often feel pressure to adjust their speech to align with institutional norms.

Race and Ethnicity

Aside from having a deep voice, little else about how Broxton spoke when he began in broadcast news was considered an asset. He sometimes left the *s* off plural words, dropped consonants, and omitted syllables ("Flor-da" rather than "Flor-i-da"). Broxton spent months trying to fix these perceived problems so he would fit in, which he did when he began his first on-air job in Montana. His memorable, unscripted response to spotting bison, "Oh no, I ain't messin' with you," was not the way viewers were used to hearing him. That line was changed to "Oh no, not messing with you" when it was used on a National Park Service wildlife safety poster.

Journalists from communities of color are used to having their grammar and pronunciation corrected. Many are told to avoid colloquial language and slang and are criticized for sounding too casual or urban, which Broxton considers code for too Black. Those who advise journalists about proper speech often do so without directly referencing race or ethnicity. Reflecting standard advice given in broadcast textbooks, one author advised the use of "educated" pronunciations and usages. "Saying 'dese' instead of 'these' can reflect a nonstandard social dialect, as can loose pronunciation. 'Whatcha gonna do' is not acceptable speech for a newscaster."[37] Many coaches and consultants agree. "There are situations where [managers] say, 'Hey, I understand that's colloquial slang, but we'd like you to say it in proper English,'" says talent coach/agent Carolyn Kane. "That's important to follow."[38]

Broxton has mixed feelings about uniform pronunciation but says that it is reasonable to ask journalists to avoid slang and use correct grammar. Yet he is bothered by the perception that his speech when he began in journalism sounded unintelligent and lazy. That is a common critique of those who use African American Vernacular English, a dialect associated with the urban Black working and middle classes.[39] Historically, as White immigrants spread throughout cities and adopted the local dialect, Black community members remained geographically and linguistically isolated. They often moved into racially segregated neighborhoods, maintaining speech patterns from the South and developing their own distinctive vernacular.[40] These speech patterns were unwelcome in primarily White professional settings. Speaking properly, many thought, just required sufficient effort.[41]

That sentiment was—and arguably remains—prevalent in broadcast newsrooms. Managers told television journalist Libby Lewis that "the midwestern (read White) speech pattern is preferable." Her takeaway: Black journalists seeking to advance in television news must adopt signifiers of Whiteness.[42] Dorothy Tucker was told to "work on" words that she pronounced like southerners do. Tucker never heard directly that she sounded too Black, but that seemed implicit in her colleague's comment that she mispronounced the word "asked."[43] Runnels, the speech-language pathologist who worked with Broxton, says that some Black journalists have "minor articulation issues that are reacted to in a very major way" and that the response from managers is "more intense than the severity warrants," perhaps indicating bias.[44]

While working in management at English-language television stations, Hugo Balta observed "overt bias" against journalists with Spanish accents. It was not a blanket dislike of accents. "[Managers] would reject someone who had a 'Spanish' accent but embrace someone with a British accent." His view of this was that "you're OK hiring someone who represents a miniscule percentage of the population nationally, let alone in your local market, but you're unwilling to hire someone who represents the second-most-popular spoken language in the country?"[45] This inconsistency also perplexes Kane, who says that "hearing a Latin accent is more American than hearing a British accent on TV."[46]

Even as the Spanish-speaking population in the United States has burgeoned, it remains uncommon in many local television markets to hear journalists with Spanish accents. Journalists are often told that foreign or ethnic accents are distracting and impair clear communication. Yet many accents are slight and comprehension is not a valid concern. As Balta observed, manager bias—and fear of viewer bias—is a likelier explanation for this advice.

Balta says that as a result, many journalists feel the need to "neutralize" their Spanish accent. Javier E. Gómez attempted that for years. Despite extensive on-air experience, good industry connections, and repeated feedback that he had talent, he got few job interviews, in part, he thinks, due to his still-discernable accent. Gómez was hired by a public, educational, government-access cable television network and felt accepted for how he spoke. After years of trying to "assume a persona that felt like an act" when applying for on-air jobs in commercial news, he decided "this had to stop" and no longer applied to such stations.[47]

Vanessa Ruiz had a smoother start to her career. She landed jobs in Miami and Los Angeles and heard no objections to her on-air delivery. But soon after becoming an evening news anchor in Phoenix, viewers began complaining about how she rolled her *r*'s, pronounced certain letter combinations, and otherwise showed bilingualism. Ruiz refused to follow the long-standing practice of anglicizing city and street names of Spanish origin. "I'm very proud of who I am and where I come from," says Ruiz, who is of Colombian descent. "My first language was Spanish. I can't say certain words in a way that's not authentic to the language skills I have used practically since birth."[48]

Ruiz shared that message with viewers when she addressed their criticisms on the evening news. Her station posted the video of her remarks and *BuzzFeed* wrote about it, proclaiming that Ruiz "Just Shut Down the Haters Who Criticized Her for Her Accent." After the article went viral, Ruiz received supportive messages, but audience criticism also intensified. "I tune in to watch the news and a newscaster, not a mariachi," read one social media response. "Go back to your country," others exclaimed. "If you're going to come here, speak the way we speak." (Ruiz was born in Miami.) Ruiz had not expected—or wanted—the attention. "I was new to the city and my job. I'm used to reporting the news, not becoming the news." But for days she was. In retrospect, Ruiz wishes that managers would have helped her craft a written response instead of relying on her to write and deliver that message on air. She felt unsupported by some colleagues as she dealt with the public fallout. After a short time at the station, she left for a job in academia.

Spanish-speaking journalists commonly encounter these types of scenarios. Like Gómez, they may find it difficult to get high-profile jobs due to a perceptible accent. Or, like Ruiz, they may work their way up but face criticism for choosing to use authentic Spanish pronunciations when they have the ability to sound "accentless." Some who advise on-air talent voiced concerns about such pronunciations becoming a distraction. "If you have someone who's a Spanish-speaking journalist but their English is perfect, there's no accent, but when they get to their name or certain words it's suddenly a very strong accent, it can go a little overboard,"[49] says Adams, the broadcast consultant/agent.

Accents are also a hot topic in Spanish-language media. U.S. stations with a national audience have long favored a standard form of Spanish that lacks identifiable regional characteristics—the equivalent of General American speech.[50] The ideal in many markets is Mexican Spanish. Puerto Rican, Dominican, and Cuban accents are rarely heard outside markets where those populations are substantial.[51] Because cable networks increasingly try to reach Latino viewers with English-language programming, Latino journalists with a strong command of English are in demand.[52]

Native English speakers are in high demand outside the United States. For instance, despite the fact that Montreal is located in a French-speaking Canadian province where Anglophones are the minority, most on-air journalists there are Anglophones, not Francophones, according to radio journalist Gretel Kahn. She says that it is rare to hear Francophone accents on the Canadian Broadcasting Corporation.[53]

Regionalisms and Social Class

Regional pronunciations and expressions, commonly known as regionalisms, can be signifiers of social class. In U.S. cities, accents associated with working-class neighborhoods that historically have been home to immigrants are often considered uneducated and unprofessional. It is rare to hear newscasters, even in local markets, who sound like they are from South Boston or the Bronx. Southern accents, which are often considered blue collar and are derided as uncultured, are also underrepresented in television news. "Y'all does not cut it over the microphone," a textbook author wrote. "Southern announcers, like their cohorts everywhere, are expected to speak in a clear, generic fashion without discernable regional tint or coloration."[54]

Yet in some cases, a regional accent can be an asset. A television host with a southern accent says that viewers in her southern market were excited to hear someone who sounded like them. Audience enthusiasm for the accent disappeared when she took a job outside that region.[55] Journalists who cover college football, which has a large southern fan base, say that their southern accent gives them regional credibility and distinguishes them from other commentators.[56] One caveat: those journalists are all White. In many cases, people of color do not benefit similarly from having a regional accent.

Outside the United States, newscasters also feel pressure to cover up regional, working-class accents. When Lattouf started work at a commercial television station in Sydney, Australia, a voice and elocution coach tried to "get the Western Sydney out of my accent."[57] People in her area commonly are told that they sound uneducated and are taught to emulate those from posher East Sydney. Other groups, including Indigenous Australians, who often come from less-wealthy areas, are also asked to assimilate to an East Sydney accent, the basis for the television standard of General Australian. To address the pressure that journalists feel to hide disfavored regional, socioeconomic, and cultural accents, Lattouf cofounded Media Diversity Australia, an organization that seeks to increase cultural and linguistic diversity in Australia's news media. This nonprofit advocates for the Australian media to look and sound like what is arguably the most multicultural nation on earth.

In the UK, where half of workers believe a regional accent and working-class background are obstacles to workplace progression, journalists who do not sound elite often get left behind.[58] Lucrece Grehoua grew up in East London around friends with limited professional opportunities, in part because they spoke Multicultural London English (MLE), a dialect associated with working-class, racially and ethnically diverse neighborhoods. At school, where she was around mostly White classmates, Grehoua sometimes felt "stupid" when she used MLE.

So she learned to code switch and continued doing so when she entered predominantly White UK newsrooms.[59]

Grehoua observed that almost all newscasters used RP or a "looser" and less posh version of that accent called Estuary English. Even though she was accustomed to practicing code switching at her workplace, she still felt like an imposter at times. When Grehoua voiced an audio documentary for BBC Radio on linguistic discrimination, even though she felt self-conscious because she worried that listeners "would not understand a Millennial coming in speaking like I do," she used MLE to make a point about lack of vocal diversity. After the documentary aired, many of her colleagues revealed that they too covered up regional accents and dialects. Despite receiving positive feedback, Grehoua left mainstream British media because she was "tired of trying to be something that I'm not."[60]

Instead of covering, some UK journalists defend their perceived speech differences. Sky News political editor Beth Rigby has received many complaints that she sounds uneducated because she incorrectly pronounces words ending in g. Television viewers hacked her Wikipedia page to include a section with the heading "severe speech impediment." Poking fun at herself, she responded on Twitter: "Someone has been kind enough to update my Wikipedia page. I don't know what they're talkin about.'"[61] Other journalists defended Rigby, accusing viewers of "snobbery" for attacking her speech. As they pointed out, Rigby does not have an impediment but rather a speech pattern that is common in Estuary English.[62]

Some observers see progress as more types of accents are heard on British broadcasting stations. Drummond agrees, with an important caveat. "Among the most prominent voices on the BBC and other stations, there is still an overrepresentation of RP. It's a newer version of the same standard accent—very White, very middle class, very London." In the UK and elsewhere, diverse forms of speech are still limited.

Attributes of Anchor Voice and Delivery

Many vocal attributes we associate with newscasters have nothing to do with accent or dialect. Anchor voice, as it is commonly known, refers to qualities such as rate, pitch, and cadence. What is viewed as the broadcast standard has remained consistent for some attributes and evolved considerably for others. A notable example of the latter is tone and style of presentation.

From Voice of God to Conversational

In the early days of broadcasting, newsreaders were taught to "punch their copy" by speaking loudly and enunciating carefully. This reduced the likelihood of noise in communication, which was common with primitive radio technology. This exaggerated style was adopted by radio broadcasters as the standard. By the time television emerged, broadcasting technology had improved, yet newscasters—many of whom began in radio—still sounded in many ways like their radio peers. With deep voices and a formal delivery that made them sound like the voice of God presenting the news from on high, Walter Cronkite and his contemporaries became the standard in television news.[63]

Broadcast journalists eventually moved away from that style and tone. Sounding conversational became—and remains—the standard. Journalists are taught to project the image of a "real person rather than a disembodied voice or a talking head," to exude warmth and intimacy, and to speak to many people but sound like you are talking to each person individually.[64] Journalists tend to sound different than the general public. They inflect more intentionally. Their elocution is better. Some sound more stilted. But compared to journalists from previous eras, they speak less formally and try to sound more natural.

Yet perceptions of what sounds natural may differ. "You might think you *are* being conversational and then someone says you aren't," says voice coach Jessica Hansen.[65] "People across races and ethnicities have different styles of communication," says voice coach Tanya Ott. "Their idea of casual, conversational style may be vastly different from someone else's."[66] Differences in expectations can cause friction between those who run a newsroom and the journalists who are its most frequently heard voices.

Gender and Voice

News stations historically have valued warm, rich-sounding, deep voices.[67] Broadcasters were involved in early decisions that benefited male presenters. Radio signals were intentionally set to a range that favored those who spoke in a lower pitch. Microphones were also geared toward deeper voices. Station directors and other broadcasting industry leaders suggested that most women's voices were not compatible with crude radio technology.[68] The author of an influential broadcast training handbook wrote that the transmission and reception of radio is "not as kindly to a woman's speaking voice as it is to that of a man." He noted that a woman's voice "approaching the range of that of the male proves more pleasing over the radio than that of her sister whose tones are of a higher pitch." Most women are not trained speakers, he wrote, and may lack "pleasing voices, good enunciation, and other qualities contributing to good microphone appearance."[69]

An enduring claim is that women with high-pitched voices cannot become successful broadcast performers.[70] Even as radio technology improved, women's voices were still often deemed too shrill and nasal to be aesthetically pleasing and too thin and weak to be authoritative. Some broadcast voicing handbooks assert that low-pitched voices are inherently more pleasant. Eliminate harsh or shrill sounds, authors of one book advise, and speak at or near the lowest pitch level that is comfortable.[71] A more nuanced assessment from other authors is that a range of voices are acceptable, but a deeper-sounding voice is advantageous, especially for women.[72]

Voice coaches often advise female journalists against speaking in an unnaturally low register for a prolonged period because it can lead to muscle tension and damaged vocal folds, the tissue that extends from the larynx and is used to produce the voice. According to Hansen, speaking in a low register can also be counterproductive because "if women are trying to sound deeper, they are usually pushing their voices down into the gutter and cutting off half of their tone, which makes them sound less authoritative."[73] There is evidence that listeners accept female newscasters who use their natural pitch and that lower variability in pitch correlates more closely with perceived news presenter credibility than low frequency of pitch.[74]

Yet women often feel pressure to speak in a lower pitch. When television news colleagues told Gloria Riviera that she would sound more authoritative if her voice was not as high pitched, she felt compelled to take their advice.[75] When she was in her twenties, Lattouf, the Australian broadcast journalist, also heard that her voice lacked authority. In one memorable exchange, a female producer praised a package she did on sex trafficking in Syria but said that it was hard to take the subject matter seriously because she sounded like a girl. At that point in her career, Lattouf felt obligated to take the advice. "I thought if I lowered my voice register and sounded more like a man or a woman 10 years older than me, people might take my work more seriously."[76]

Sexual Orientation and Voice

Some men are told they do not sound authoritative because their voice is not stereotypically masculine. One of many gender-normative expectations in broadcasting is that men should have deep, powerful voices.[77] Dating back decades, high-profile television anchors have been lauded for exuding masculine authority and gravitas.[78] Although the modern-day male anchor sounds tonally less like the voice of God, it is still expected that his voice be resonant and that he create a commanding presence. When male journalists are told that their voice sounds weak, the implicit message is that they do not sound masculine.

In some cases, this is a comment on their sexual orientation. Gay journalists often hear that their voice sounds too "queeny" or "effeminate." Those terms are used to describe upspeak, singsong, sibilant *s*'s, and other characteristics of stereotypically gay-sounding voices. Because judgments about sexual orientation based on voice can prompt group-based discrimination, some speakers try to cover up vocal characteristics perceived as undesirable.[79] The 2014 documentary *Do I Sound Gay?* follows journalist David Thorpe as he seeks the help of voice coaches and speech therapists in transforming his voice into what he deems a more "standard-sounding, nondescript" male voice.[80] In that documentary, out television journalist Don Lemon reveals that early in his career, he was self-conscious about his voice sounding gay.

So was Harrison Hove. While he was at his first television job, he contacted a talent agent in the hope of moving up to a larger market. The agent showed no interest in representing Hove, telling him that his voice "isn't bad" but was "just not strong and authoritative," coded language that was familiar to Hove. "I don't necessarily think it was a knock against my sexual orientation, but it was easy for me to internalize because one of my weak areas was my voice. Growing up, you get teased for various reasons, and gay voice is one of them." Hove says that during his career, "being gay wasn't a dealbreaker, but being the wrong kind of gay was. If you weren't the masculine, all-American, apple pie kind of gay, then you were too gay." He tried to sound stereotypically masculine at the start of his career by artificially deepening his voice. It was one of several ways he "tried to be someone else."[81]

Champion, the former television journalist, says that news executives never explicitly said he sounded too gay, but they told him to change his voice and presence using coded language to make that clear. They complained that he was "queening out" during live shots and needed to "butch it up," "speak with more oomph," and "be harder." "I understood that to mean be more masculine," Champion says. It was not the first time a colleague drew attention to his demeanor. At a previous job, a station mentor (who is also gay) advised him to "tone down" his hand gestures."[82]

Champion's voice coach had difficulty deciphering what exactly the news executives wanted him to change. Champion spoke to another gay reporter at his New York station who had heard similar critiques about his voice. The reporter tried, essentially, to sound less gay and suggested that Champion do the same. "Part of me was like, 'I'm not doing that. That's not who I am and how I got here, so why would I change to appease someone who clearly has bias in his heart?'" But Champion was a freelancer living in an expensive city. He needed the work. "You get to a big market and you don't want to lose that. The comments I heard were demeaning and made me feel awful. To have your livelihood at stake because of them is terrible, but I felt like I didn't have a choice." So Champion did his best to cover. Feeling harassed and discriminated against in other ways, he left the station and quit broadcast journalism.

Hart, Champion's former agent, warned him before he took the New York job that his bosses might be unsupportive and even hostile. "I knew those managers. I was sickened by what he went through. But I have not had a lot of clients go through an experience like that." Adams, the agent/consultant, says that in her experience, gay journalists feel less pressure than they once did to "fake it" by altering their voice, delivery, or demeanor to meet normative expectations. Yet the problem has not been resolved universally.

Disability and Expectations of Fluency

Broadcast journalists are judged on their delivery as much as on their voice and are expected to be fluent communicators. That means speaking flawlessly and without hesitation. "Good" voices historically have signified healthy bodies, and it has been incumbent on journalists to avoid sounding even minimally disabled.[83]

Employers and educators who evaluated journalists for a study agreed that speech impediments and vocal tics are "faults" that may lead listeners to question a person's suitability for broadcasting.[84] On-air performers with fluency difficulties are often considered ineffective communicators.[85] Repeated stumbling, some news directors contend, creates the impression that journalists are ill prepared or uncertain, which can hurt their credibility.[86] Speech disabilities are thought to be distracting and aesthetically unpleasing.[87] As disability advocates have noted, it is rare to hear stutters, lisps, or anything else on air that makes journalists "sound disabled."[88]

Although this chapter focuses on television, several examples from radio are relevant. Diane Rehm's health problems started just as her self-titled public radio show was set to become nationally syndicated. First, her voice quivered. On bad days it shook uncontrollably. She had tightness in her throat and struggled to speak. She was embarrassed by how she sounded and considered her voice problems to be a sign of failure. Worried that her career was over, Rehm took a leave of absence from her show. When she was diagnosed with spasmodic dysphonia, a condition that affects the muscles that control speech, she wondered what would come next. To her relief, audiences had grown accustomed to her voice patterns and managers wanted her to continue.[89] She remained in public radio for decades and later moved into podcasting.

Jamie Dupree spent decades on Capitol Hill filing radio reports for Cox Media Group. Listeners across the country heard his smooth baritone voice. In 2016, he fell ill and began to have trouble speaking. Eventually, he was unable to say more than a few words at a time. He was diagnosed with a neurological disorder called oromandibular dystonia. The self-proclaimed "radio guy who can't talk" found workarounds. He wrote interview questions and held them up for sources to read. He used text-to-speech technology that took clips from his prior recordings to create an automated voice, known as Jamie Dupree 2.0. Though it sounded artificial, it helped Dupree stay on air for a short time.[90]

In broadcast news, Rehm and Dupree are more the exception than the rule. Had their speech disabilities developed earlier in their career, before they had built up goodwill and earned listeners' trust, they likely would not have had the opportunities they did.

Opportunities are also limited for journalists who stutter, a speech disorder characterized by repetition of sounds, syllables, or words; prolongation of sounds; and interruptions in speech. "You don't see stutterers on TV," magazine journalist John Hendrickson wrote in his autobiographical book on stuttering. "If anything, the people you see on TV have spent years honing their skills to specifically *not* stutter on air."[91] People who stutter may even be considered unfit for print positions because of a common perception that stuttering is wrongness of speech. One hiring manager gave a journalist who stutters all indications that he was set to hire him before deciding against it.[92] The reason he gave was that the job required semi-regular television appearances. The implication was that the news outlet was not comfortable with someone who stutters as its public representative.[93]

Broadcast journalists who stutter said that colleagues often questioned their competency before they proved themselves professionally. Feeling self-conscious about their speech, some journalists avoided extended conversations in the newsroom, which led others to question their intelligence or level of engagement. An on-air journalist says that early in his career he was given only "run-of-the-mill" assignments, which he connected to his stutter or his efforts to disguise it. This journalist was given more substantial assignments only after demonstrating his ability over time.[94]

People with disabilities are commonly viewed as requiring attention and accommodations that slow productivity and create resentment among colleagues.[95] Yet when managers gave journalists who stutter basic accommodations, the journalists found ways to fulfill their job duties without being disruptive. Several shared their stutter-management strategies. To prepare for a live newscast, one host reads scripts aloud three times off air. A television journalist anticipates every conversation he is likely to have that day and plans his questions and responses. Such strategies may not work during breaking news and live interviews, when journalists cannot plan or practice for situations that may arise. Given those constraints, journalists who stutter often try to avoid unscripted scenarios.

Some journalists who stutter have had successful broadcast careers. For others, stuttering has slowed their career trajectory and limited their opportunities. Journalists who are able to manage their stutter so it is barely perceptible or undetectable typically have the most options.

When journalists with perceptible speech differences succeed, they tend to attract attention. Barbara Walters was known for breaking journalism gender barriers, interviewing world leaders and A-list celebrities on television specials, and creating and cohosting *The View*. But on *Saturday Night Live* in the 1970s, she was caricatured as "Baba Wawa" in comedian Gilda Radner's recurring sketches that poked fun of Walters's difficulty pronouncing *r*'s and *l*'s. Even before *Saturday Night Live*, Walters knew what others thought of her speech. While at *The Today Show*, an NBC producer, perceiving that Walters had a problem, sent her to a speech coach to fix her pronunciation. As Walters wrote in her autobiography, lazy *r*'s are common among people who grew up in Boston. Walters understood the need to sound like a standard newscaster but thought the speech pattern the specialist prescribed sounded "phony and stilted." She soon went back to her "natural way of speaking" but avoided sentences with too many *r*'s.[96]

In the *Saturday Night Live* portrayal, Radner exaggerated Walters's speech differences, pronouncing all of her *r*'s as *w*'s and butchering other pronunciations. At first, Walters found the portrayal "extremely upsetting" but acknowledged that audiences found it "hysterically funny." She lamented being called

Baba Wawa behind her back—and sometimes to her face. "Because I was so depressed at the time," Walters wrote, "I felt they were laughing at me rather than laughing at Gilda's characterization of me."[97] However, Walters later embraced the portrayal, commenting that "it's good to be made fun of" because "that means you're slightly famous."[98] She complimented Radner on the impression when they met in person, and years later went on *Saturday Night Live*, joking that it was an honor to "see my groundbreaking career in journalism reduced to a cartoon character with a ridiculous voice."[99] Walters eventually wrote of her speech issues, "I've all but conquered the problem."[100]

Summary

Many television journalists feel compelled to fix perceived problems with their vocal delivery and hide aspects of their identity. They are expected to speak without stumbling. Opportunities are greatest for those who sound "accentless" and have "golden" voices. Broadcast news forms are familiar but they are not neutral. They reflect the tastes of those who held power and influence in the early days of broadcasting. Decisions about what sounds well educated, authoritative, and aesthetically pleasing have favored—and continue to favor—those from dominant groups. In many cases, journalists from historically marginalized groups have found it difficult to challenge voice and speech norms. Efforts to draw attention to the negative impact of covering on journalists have been less organized in television than in public radio, the focus of chapter 7.

7

The Enduring
#PubRadioVoice

• •

(Performing on Radio)

Public radio began reckoning with its lack of vocal diversity before 2015. But in January that year, typically private conversations about code switching and institutional Whiteness went public in an unprecedented way. Most notably, #PubRadioVoice briefly trended during a Twitter chat hosted by *Code Switch*, NPR's race and culture podcast. Some of public radio's most recognizable voices discussed their experiences with covering ("Sitting in host chair for first time I channeled White voice from Midwest and lost my own," said Lulu Garcia-Navarro)[1], listeners' mistaken assumptions about journalists' race ("People usually don't react to my voice they react to their Google image search," said Audie Cornish)[2], and the limitations of mission statements ("If an org is telling you they believe in diversity but don't invest in it, what's that belief worth?," asked Al Letson).[3] The featured guest, who wrote the manifesto that sparked this dialogue, was not a high-profile NPR host or a local radio personality. He was a devoted public radio listener who had just produced his first narrative audio story.

A college professor and hip-hop artist, Chenjerai Kumanyika was no stranger to performance. But in his manifesto, he shares that during an audio production workshop, he struggled to imagine his voice, which had been shaped by "Black, cultural patterns of speech and oratory," as the narrator of a nonfiction radio profile.[4] While he edited his script, Kumanyika, who is Black, realized that he was imagining another voice as narrator—one that sounded White. That voice was a cross between two giants in narrative audio, Roman Mars (founder of the podcast collective Radiotopia and host and creator of the podcast *99% Invisible*) and Sarah Koenig (longtime *This American Life* producer and host and executive producer of the podcast *Serial*).

Kumanyika reflects on why he felt the need to sound like someone else when narrating. "Without being directly told, people like me learn that our way of speaking isn't professional. And you start to imitate the standard or even hide the distinctive features of your own voice."[5] Turning the focus to public radio and its affiliated podcasts, Kumanyika writes that journalists of various ethnicities, genders, and other identity categories code switch to be consistent with culturally dominant White styles of speech and narration. He notes that "a narrow range of public radio and podcast host voices and speech patterns have become extremely common. . . . There is a whole range of vocal styles that are common in the African American, Latino, Asian American, and Native American cultures but rarely heard from hosts."[6]

Kumanyika concludes that public radio generally has not lived up to its promise to sound as diverse as America. In this chapter, I examine whether those who have worked at NPR or its independent, locally owned and operated member stations think that there is, or ever was, a dominant public radio voice. I explore how and from whom journalists get feedback on their vocal delivery, what advice journalists receive, and why some flatten or suppress distinguishing vocal characteristics. First, I review decisions made a century ago that restricted diversity in radio and consider how, as Kumanyika observed, public radio became a speech community with its own norms and forms of aesthetic capital.[7]

Limiting Access to the Airwaves

Radio in the early 1920s was vocally diverse with thousands of stations featuring a range of on-air performers. Historians describe this period as both democratic and chaotic. With easy access to the airwaves, amateur radio flourished. Racial minority groups—most notably Black Americans—were heavily involved as performers and station operators. Yet some influential listeners complained about signal interference and felt that regulation would help radio become professionalized with programming that was "clean and fit" for common consumption.[8]

Congress responded with the Radio Act of 1927, which gave the newly created Federal Radio Commission authority to regulate radio. The agency granted and denied radio licenses, giving preferential treatment to White station owners while mostly shutting out racial minorities.[9] The commission assigned the most powerful broadcast frequencies to stations such as NBC and CBS and gave the least desirable frequencies to smaller, underresourced stations. As a result, many people of color lost their platform and the public airwaves became less diverse.[10]

The Federal Radio Commission and its successor, the Federal Communications Commission, permitted the evolution of a system that was racially exclusionary in ownership, hiring practices, and news content, Juan González and Joseph Torres write in *News for All the People: The Epic Story of Race and the American Media*.[11] After Congress passed the Radio Act of 1927, it took the federal government roughly two decades to award licenses and desirable frequencies to stations that aired diverse voices and roughly half a century to adopt a policy that promoted minority ownership of broadcast stations.

The stations that were reserved for noncommercial radio were "primarily owned by White-dominant universities and were all managed by White men who drew from their predominantly White student body to recruit radio trainees," sociologist Laura Garbes writes. "The demographic makeup of noncommercial radio producers between World War II and the formation of the NPR system was predominantly White and male."[12]

NPR's Not-So-Blank Slate

The Public Broadcasting Act of 1967 paved the way for NPR, which was established three years later to produce, acquire, and distribute programming to dozens of member stations across the country. Acknowledging that radio did not reflect America's diversity, NPR's founders and employees espoused service to diverse publics.[13] They hoped to start with a blank slate, in the words of NPR's first employee, Jack Mitchell. Yet that "blank slate" was a White one, Garbes argues. Although NPR was new, the public broadcasting field was already institutionalized.

Those involved in NPR's founding and early operations were socialized into a White habitus—a world view that Whiteness constitutes normality—leading them to adopt the racially exclusionary practices of the noncommercial radio field.[14] According to Garbes's research, NPR's founders set technical standards that prevented many non-White radio stations from qualifying for membership. Founders and managers recruited through informal networks, drawing from nondiverse candidate pools that led to a White-dominant workforce. In programming decisions, NPR modeled itself on existing legitimated paradigms. The form and content of NPR's early programming mirrored programming that appeared in the White-dominant field of educational radio, where many station employees worked before NPR.[15]

The two men perhaps most responsible for shaping NPR's sound were Mitchell, the first producer of flagship show *All Things Considered*, and Bill Siemering, NPR's first programming director. Siemering wanted NPR's tone to be different from commercial news, which he felt sounded too "preachy" and "stilted."[16] He pointed to the traditional White male voice of authority as "exactly how we don't want to sound."[17] Siemering envisioned hosts speaking conversationally, the way they talked to their friends, in "regular voices, as regular people, not announcers."[18] NPR, he declared, would have national appeal without sounding bland. It would speak with many voices and dialects so the country could hear itself reflected.[19]

All Things Considered was a chance to set that tone. Cohost Susan Stamberg stood out for several reasons. Most notably, she was the first woman in her role at a national nightly news program. Also, she did not talk like a typical radio host. Some NPR board members in the Midwest felt that Stamberg sounded "too New York." But Mitchell and Siemering liked the authenticity of her voice. When Siemering told Stamberg not to alter the way she spoke, she was relieved to no longer have to put on a "man-sounding voice."[20]

If NPR sounded more like America than its competitors, it was largely due to its "founding mothers"—Stamberg, Nina Totenberg, Linda Wertheimer, and Cokie Roberts, all of whom were in prominent on-air roles. Throughout the 1970s and 1980s, *All Things Considered* sought out voices that, like Stamberg's, had regional or foreign inflections.[21] That included contributors from across the country who produced radio essays with "idiosyncratic accents."[22] NPR's flagship shows featured some forms of vocal diversity. As the organization became more mainstream in subsequent decades, so did its voices, prompting internal complaints that NPR did not sound racially or ethnically diverse.[23] As NPR's ombudsman concluded in 2005, "When it comes to aural diversity, NPR sounds . . . not very diverse at all."[24]

Outsiders have made similar observations. NPR's idea of diversity is recruiting Black personalities and asking them to assimilate to the liberal, White, boomer mentality that dominates *All Things Considered*, a magazine journalist once wrote.[25] Latinx voices have long been marginalized, Christopher Chávez argues in *The Sound of Exclusion: NPR and the Latinx Public*. By employing Standard American English, in which regionally and ethnically marked features are suppressed, NPR reifies existing social hierarchies. These practices, Chávez notes, are disconnected from the organization's mission and are increasingly out of sync with a country that is becoming more ethnically, culturally, and linguistically diverse.[26] Chávez argues that despite its pretense of informality, NPR's speaking style is an idealized dialect that is "not really spoken anywhere" but instead is acquired through professional training and favors those from wealthier, more highly educated backgrounds.[27]

"NPR-ness" and Public Radio Voice

What is the speaking style Chávez refers to? Is there a signature NPR or public radio voice? Jessica Hansen does not think so. She worked with many on-air journalists as NPR's in-house voice coach. "None of them sound the same to me," Hansen says. "[NPR] doesn't want people to sound the same. We want a diverse-sounding cast of characters. We want different dialects and colloquialisms. We want people who sound like they're from places all over the world."[28] That was

Hansen's message for Huo Jingnan when they met for a voice coaching session. Hansen encouraged her to sound "relaxed and natural."[29]

While journalists at NPR and its member stations certainly do not sound homogeneous, many convey "NPR-ness." As author and former radio journalist Michael P. McCauley writes in his book on NPR's evolution, programs—and their hosts—gain legitimacy when they are similar in content and tone to *All Things Considered* and *Morning Edition*, which appeal to public radio's core listeners.[30] In the narrative genre, journalists signal NPR-ness through performances that call to mind seminal public radio programs such as *This American Life* and *Radiolab*.

NPR-ness was captured most comedically by Ana Gasteyer and Molly Shannon of *Saturday Night Live*. In their iconic 1998 sketch, known as "Schweddy Balls," the cast members play cohosts of the fictitious NPR show *The Delicious Dish*. Alongside guest Alec Baldwin, they speak slowly and softly in warm, monotone voices to discuss savory holiday food, using double entendres laced with sexual innuendo. While Gasteyer and Shannon's performance is an exaggeration (no NPR host is *that* monotone), it is immediately recognizable as a spoof of the iconic public radio voice and delivery.

Journalists' descriptions of the archetypal public radio personality tend to be more sober: "a tenured professor reading you a bedtime story—a story that includes a lot of market reports"; someone who sounds like "mellow, middle-aged, upper-income Whites from the urban Northeast or Midwest."[31] NPR sounds liberal, one scholar contends, because of its flexible notion of gender roles reflected in journalists' voices. Women's voices are uncommonly low and often lack pitch variance; men tend to speak in higher-than-normal pitches.[32] Most public radio journalists could teach a master class in elocution. They have good diction and pause in the right places.[33] They end sentences with emphatic inflection.[34] Their delivery is soothing, like warm milk, tea, or coffee, as Kumanyika and others noted during the #PubRadioVoice Twitter chat.

Challenging #PubRadioVoice

In his 2015 manifesto, Kumanyika refers to public radio hosts as "informed, interesting, gentle friends" who keep him company as he cooks and commutes.[35] Yet those friends do not speak the way he and his friends do. Kumanyika describes the experience of listening to public radio as "going to someone else's house who is living in a different world than me and listening to them talk about their lives. They're talking about things I care about, but their cultural references, the way they're speaking, it's clear I'm a guest here."[36]

That feeling was inescapable as Kumanyika attended a Transom workshop for beginning audio producers. As he worked on his script for a profile story, he realized he was writing in a voice that was not his own. He grew self-conscious about instinctive code switching in certain conversational contexts. Kumanyika the hip-hop artist had a very different vocal delivery than Kumanyika the journalist, who was unable to show off his oratorical skills. As he notes in the manifesto, "When the vocal patterns of a narrow range of ethnicities quietly becomes the standard sound of a genre, we're missing out on essential cultural information."[37]

Listening to his narration for the profile, Kumanyika felt that he sounded lackluster. He voiced that concern to Rob Rosenthal, the workshop trainer. "When Chenjerai looked at me and said, 'I don't sound like myself when I'm reading,' I said to him, 'well, how do you want to sound?' He said, 'I want to sound like Chenjerai,' and I understood him immediately—of course he should sound like himself."[38] Rosenthal describes that moment as a "lightning strike." He had worked for many years in community radio, where "everyone gets a microphone" and stations generally sound as diverse as their community. Yet Rosenthal says he ended up teaching "a public radio sort of thing" in workshops. "In public radio, there has historically been a unifying sound. I didn't think about it because I was that unifying sound. So long as I didn't have my Cape Cod accent, I fit in, because I'm White, male, college educated, middle class or upper-middle class. I'm the classic NPR audience member. I adopted that understanding of what voice should sound like without even realizing it." Rosenthal says that he had rarely thought about voicing in terms of race, gender, or class until his conversation with Kumanyika. "That's when I realized that I need to be thinking differently about this when I help people do [voicing]. I became more keenly aware of not trespassing on someone's individuality."[39]

Rosenthal and his Transom colleagues wanted Kumanyika to revoice parts of his profile so he would feel better about the final product and so they could highlight how much better radio sounds when a narrator writes and talks in a voice that feels natural. Kumanyika redid the narration and, at Rosenthal's invitation, wrote about his experience. His manifesto includes audio from before and after the redo. The differences are stark. Kumanyika sounds far more comfortable in the rerecorded version. He is conversational in his own way. His voice is deeper and at times more excitable. "I feel more centered," he writes. "I sound like myself, rather than sounding like myself pretending to be a public radio host."[40]

Prominent public radio journalists embraced the manifesto and shared it widely on social media. Dozens of industry veterans commented on it online. NPR journalists coached Kumanyika as he recorded an audio version of the manifesto. He went on public radio programs to discuss public radio voice and code switching. He was a guest on the first podcast episode of *Code Switch* and was cited in a later episode that then-interns Huo Jingnan and Khalon Richard pitched and helped report. Kumanyika's call to action inspired the #PubRadioVoice Twitter chat, which gave journalists the space to share personal anecdotes and discuss systemic problems. "It's not just race," an NPR journalist wrote. "Class, education, faith, experience.... So often we don't sound anything like America."[41]

Journalists had expressed these concerns before. In Kumanyika's manifesto, they found, in his words, a "central text"—a reason to publicly reengage in conversations about vocal diversity. "People were already struggling with these issues," Kumanyika says. "As an outsider, I was able to say things that people on the inside maybe did not feel comfortable speaking about freely."[42] Alison MacAdam, a former NPR producer, senior editor, and trainer, remembers how she and her colleagues responded. "We weren't like, 'wow, oh my gosh, there's a public radio voice.' It was like, 'wow, this guy, he just named it so well and at the right moment.' It was a really important conversation to put in front of people who have the power to make change."[43]

Standardization and Room for Variation?

Public radio program directors and other newsroom leaders have that power. During scheduled airchecks, they review aspects of journalists' on-air performance—such as reading copy, having lightly scripted conversations, ad-libbing, handling transitions between station breaks, and running pledge drives.

Airchecks, which once were standard practice in radio, have become less common as program directors' responsibilities have expanded.[44] But these reviews remain important, according to Steve Olson, a former news director, program director, president of the Public Radio Program Directors Association, and director of program services at NPR. A station's sound defines its identity. Airchecks allow managers to reinforce that identity, which Olson and others refer to as "stationality." As he explains, "Everything that comes out of the speakers, it should be consistent so that anytime one of my audience members tunes in, it sounds like the same station to them."[45] In Olson's view, everyone's announcing style should match the overall sound of the station. "This doesn't mean there isn't room for a variety of accents, vocal tones, or even delivery speed," he wrote in the trade publication *Current*. "But the way announcers handle break elements, use call letters or branding slogans, or allow time to lapse before speaking at the end of a musical piece—these are techniques that should be standardized."[46]

Olson distinguishes between standardizing how journalists handle technical aspects of their job, which he considers critical to strengthening stationality, and standardizing journalists' vocal delivery, which he deems unnecessary. "Announcers aren't going to have the same voice because everyone is different," he says. "Airchecks aren't about changing [local anchors] to sound like some announcer who's sitting in Washington, DC, or getting rid of their accent. It's not about encouraging conformity; it's about sounding professional."[47]

Olson's views are not universally shared by managers. Radio journalist Diana Opong recalls a program director "nitpicking what I said and how I said it" and coaching everyone who spoke on air to sound alike. Opong found this frustrating because "you cannot aircheck an entire group of people against the same standard when everyone talks differently."[48] Participants in the #PubRadioVoice

Twitter chat voiced similar frustrations, with one host commenting, "Having my delivery so meticulously managed is literally the one thing I don't like about doing radio."[49]

Catherine Stifter says she was "never told as an NPR trainer to try to get people to sound a certain way." When she sat in on voice coaching sessions at NPR member stations, she never heard producers or editors articulate how public radio journalists should talk. Nor did she hear them instruct on-air talent to imitate a specific host. What she heard instead were subtle nudges. "They would say things like, 'No, that's not it. Let's do it again' or 'Try it a different way.' Sometimes, having people imitate me, I would say, 'Try this way. Let's emphasize different words here.'"[50] Those giving feedback often made clear what they wanted to hear without having to be explicit. "Journalists hear a lot of, 'Oh, you need to inflect your voice like this and put the emphasis here, but, oh, no, don't change your voice," says public media executive Gabrielle Jones. "But what you're telling them is to change their voice." Often, this is done without an explanation of why. "Who says we should inflect there? Who says that's the way people talk?"[51]

Some who coach journalists use euphemisms to describe perceived problems. Opong was told she needed to sound warmer, which she took to mean "safe and welcoming" and "as unthreatening as possible." She was told to slow down. "Within my culture, it's normal to speak quickly. That comment stuck with me."[52] Celeste Headlee, the former public radio journalist, heard similar feedback from colleagues. "They would never say you sound too urban. They would say things like, 'You sound young, you sound rushed, you sound panicked, you sound too casual.' They used all these other framings until you got it. Once you'd been in for a few years, you knew what sound they were looking for."[53]

Station leaders wanted journalists to have "an American accent that can't be placed," Headlee says. "They wanted you to sound very calm and measured. And me, a Black Jew from Los Angeles, I don't sound calm or measured most of the time. . . . It's this implicit racism where they don't realize what they're asking is for us to sound like we're White." Headlee wrote her own widely shared and endorsed manifesto: "An Anti-Racist Future: A Vision and Plan for the Transformation of Public Media." One of many problems she identified was that "Black on-air talent are told their dialect and speaking voices do not fit the public radio prototype."[54]

Flattening Vocal Attributes to Sound "Neutral"

As a public radio host, Headlee did such a convincing impression of *All Things Considered* host Melissa Block that her friends did not recognize her on air. Criticized by colleagues for sounding too young, Headlee spoke in an unnaturally deep voice despite the known health risks of doing so. She talked slowly and formally. "Once I mastered imitating the public radio sound, I don't think it sounded authentically like me anymore."[55] Kumanyika barely recognized himself when he listened to his original profile story because his voice "sounded too high and all the rounded corners of slang are squared off." He felt that he had "flattened" the interesting aspects of his voice.[56] Although there is no truly "neutral" voice, some in public radio try to "make their voices—and themselves—invisible," NPR's Linda Holmes tweeted during the #PubRadio-Voice chat.[57] Many do what Kumanyika first did—flatten their voice and modify their delivery to hide aspects of their identity.

When Stephanie Foo worked in public radio, colleagues told her to tone down her delivery. "I spoke like any normal Millennial. But they would make me dial it back and be much more flat and unaffected. They would always say, 'We're trying to make you sound like yourself. This is how you sound like yourself.' And I was thinking, 'Am I completely disassociated when I'm here in the office? Is that what you think sounds like me? Because this doesn't sound like me at all—it sounds like a zombie version of me.'"[58]

Dmae Lo Roberts tried to sound relaxed and be conversational when she narrated pieces for NPR. As a freelancer, she felt the need to please editors, who could spike a story they deemed to be poorly narrated. Some advised her to deepen her voice to sound more authoritative. It felt inauthentic, but she was used to performing a character as a theater artist. She assumed that she had mastered the voice until an editor told her that she sounded "too sexy" and needed to tone it down. "I wasn't trying to sound sexual or sensual or anything, but there was a certain kind of voice they would accept and it was a very narrow margin."[59]

NPR's Tamara Keith spent years trying not to sound like a young woman from California with an occasional southern twang before realizing her mistake. "My stories didn't sound right because they didn't match up to the voice I heard in my head when I was writing them," she wrote. "The thing that was missing from my reporting was me."[60] Once Keith stopped trying to hide aspects of her identity, she felt that her voicing improved. Sam Sanders was at NPR for years before he started to write how he spoke in real life. At first, he says editors tried to subtly whitewash his voice by removing vernacular and colloquialisms from his scripts that felt unique to him.[61] NPR's former ombudsman heard many such complaints from journalists of color who felt pressure to sound less like themselves.[62] Some cite this as among the reasons why the organization has struggled to retain high-profile talent.[63]

Journalists in the cases mentioned above initially tried to flatten or hide distinguishing vocal attributes but eventually found that untenable. Gisele Regatão never considered that form of covering to be a viable option. She grew up in Brazil, moved to the United States in her mid-twenties, and never shed her Portuguese accent. Regatão sometimes stresses a syllable or pronounces a word in a way that stands out, although it is unclear to many people where she is from. An accent that she considers mild has, at times, prevented her from getting on air.

Regatão spent much of her early career as a producer and also did reporting. While working at an NPR member station, she conducted interviews for a story but did not end up voicing it because her managing editor thought she sounded unprofessional. Regatão knew her accent was the reason why. Years later, after Regatão had voiced stories for public radio programs, she pitched a story to NPR about a Brazilian artist. She says an editor there told her he liked the story idea but warned her that producers might take issue with her accent.

Regatão proceeded anyway with the reporting and the editor coached her while she voiced the story. Weeks later when it still had not aired, she wrote the editor asking for an explanation. He said her accent was a contributing factor. "I was livid," Regatão says. "We all know accent bias exists because we don't hear those voices on the air. But nobody had ever said to me directly before, 'your accent is the problem.' I couldn't believe I was being told this in an e-mail."[64] This experience motivated Regatão to write an article in the *Columbia Journalism Review* about accent bias in broadcasting. NPR executives she interviewed apologized for how she was treated, called the producers' response antithetical to the organization's values, and reiterated that NPR is open to voices of the world. Regatão pushed back, citing the lack of hosts and reporters with accents. "Allowing certain people on air is about gatekeeping," she says. "By saying your voice doesn't belong, [NPR] is signaling that this kind of accent is not professional or authoritative."[65]

Summary

The experiences of journalists highlighted in this chapter illustrate that NPR and its member stations still have a long way to go to truly reflect America's diversity. Rosenthal says when he listens, he does not hear a cross-section of America. Headlee hears more diverse voices than she used to on NPR. But to her, the flagship shows still sound White and vocal diversity is lacking at many local stations.

Some industry insiders and observers point to signs of progress—specifically, prominent on-air talent who have accents or "non-traditional" radio voices. Many referenced NPR's Ayesha Rascoe, one of several women of color to become host of a flagship news program in 2022. Her executive producer told the news outlet *The 19th* that Rascoe is "a definite change in direction" for NPR and "exactly the kind of voice" the organization wants to bring on the air—someone who "sounds like herself . . . a Black woman from Durham, North Carolina."[66]

Voice coach Viki Merrick says that when she asked a manager at the public radio program *Marketplace* whether she could tell reporters to sound like themselves, the response was "absolutely."[67] The notion that radio journalists should all speak in one voice or sound like they are from one part of the country is antiquated, says Goldstein of the Public Media Content Collective. "I don't think that's been true for a while in public radio. We want that sense of place."[68]

MacAdam, the former NPR producer, senior editor, and trainer, cites this measure of progress: "If you talk to young reporters now and say, 'whose voice do you hear in your head when you try and deliver a script or are talking off the cuff?' you're probably not going to hear [longtime *All Things Considered* host] Robert Siegel." It is likelier to be someone like Rascoe or a podcast host who has never tried to perform public radio voice. Chapter 8 explores why, like Kumanyika, many journalists have taken advantage of opportunities in podcasting to experiment with form and challenge broadcasting norms.

8

Semi-Performative
and Vocally Diverse

• •

(Performing on Podcasts)

Listen to journalists talk on radio and podcasts and their versatility as performers becomes clear. When Diana Opong goes on air as a reporter or announcer, she tends to speak formally because "it's ingrained in me that I'm supposed to sound proper." When she guest hosts *Life Kit*, NPR's advice podcast, she tells herself to relax. "I can't be super proper while talking to guests if I want to sound conversational."[1] Shereen Marisol Meraji also instinctively alters her presentation depending on the context. "I am well aware that I sound different on our podcast than I do when I'm reporting a story for *All Things Considered*," she told her cohost on a 2018 *Code Switch* episode. "I'm totally much more myself with you and much more formal on *All Things Considered*."[2] Huo Jingnan's NPR colleagues tell her that they try to sound more casual on podcasts than on radio. "You can hear it in their cadence," she says.[3]

Podcasts lend themselves to what journalist Nicholas Quah describes as a "semi-performative" speaking style—a slightly elevated, more performed version of everyday conversation.[4] Compared to radio, podcast formats tend to be less rigid, leaving room for unscripted banter. Intros, interviews, even ad reads are typically looser. Many podcasts sound less produced, although some in the narrative genre sound slicker than almost anything on radio. In Opong's experience, podcast hosts and guests tend to be more diverse. "*Life Kit* allows for people with different voices to come on and be themselves."[5]

Podcasting has a shocking amount of diversity, as longtime podcast creator and strategist Eric Nuzum observes in his book about audio storytelling. Creators who work independently, in newsrooms, and at production companies all experiment. On the other hand, he writes, there is a tremendous amount of sameness. One way to break the cycle of sameness is to have a unique voice.[6] Even as podcasting has become more professionalized, it remains open to many voices and no one type of voice has become dominant. Sample shows in a variety of genres and that becomes evident. Or consider just one category, like current events podcasts hosted by journalists. Plenty of shows share DNA with *The Daily*, but daily news podcast hosts have diverse speaking styles. No one tells listeners what else they need to know today quite like Michael Barbaro, who does so (in his words) in a "weirdly inflected way."[7] *Code Switch* is one of many podcasts about race and culture, but the dialogue between cohosts and guests helps set the show apart.

Diversity of form is part of podcasting's appeal to audiences and creators. Listeners expect podcasters to sound authentic, not like polished newscasters. They are used to hearing idiosyncratic voices, distinctive accents, colloquialisms, and slang. Many want hosts to get personal and let their personalities show. Podcasters like the freedom to perform in different ways. Some are new to hosting and want to find their voice. Others are transitioning from broadcasting and want a new platform to express themselves.

The podcast industry is vocally diverse. It also reflects America's diversity in other ways. Roughly half of podcast creators are non-White and many come from lower- and middle-income groups, a 2022 survey found. Yet the industry skews young and remains male-dominated.[8] Concerns about diversity, equity, and inclusion have been well documented. Most notably, in 2021, journalists of color at Gimlet, a narrative podcasting company acquired by Spotify, accused managers of creating a toxic work environment where their perspectives were trivialized. Staffers felt that White, upper-middle-class public radio veterans with similar tastes in audio held disproportionate power.[9] Several years earlier, Chenjerai Kumanyika told the *Columbia Journalism Review* that while he had positive experiences working with editors, pitching to popular podcasts produced by Gimlet or NPR inevitably meant going through White gatekeepers.[10] That article ("Why Are #PodcastsSoWhite?") highlighted a range of problems throughout the industry, including a lack of high-profile opportunities for podcasters of color (particularly those who did not have media profiles) and a lack of investment in promoting shows with Black hosts.[11]

The barriers to entering podcasting are low, but achieving sufficient popularity to attract meaningful revenue is difficult. Established production companies with significant resources have struggled to find sizable audiences for some shows, which suggests that their rapid expansion into podcasting may have saturated the market. Independent creators without the same level of financial backing have even more trouble breaking through. Layoffs throughout the industry have become commonplace and content production has slowed. One report showed that the number of new shows dropped by nearly 80 percent from 2020 to 2022.[12] Yet there are still signs of hope. A 2022 survey found that podcasting accounts for roughly one-fourth of all spoken-word audio consumption and that nearly 20 percent of U.S. residents over age thirteen listen to a podcast every day. Time spent with podcasts has steadily increased.[13]

Podcasting remains attractive to journalists because of the low entry costs, the growth possibilities, and the ability to experiment. Those who start a new show or create a new company may not begin with an entirely blank slate, but they are less constrained by audience expectations and are better positioned to challenge conventions than colleagues who work in more established parts of the news business, where long-standing norms influence how journalists perform.

This chapter examines how podcasting has created opportunities for journalists who have traditionally been underrepresented in news. It explores how organizations that produce podcasts set expectations that in many cases discourage covering and how hosts from diverse backgrounds negotiate their performances. I begin by exploring how early podcasters helped redefine what sounds authoritative by normalizing nontraditional broadcast voices and a casual, conversational style that has since seeped into other mediums.

Nontraditional Voices and a Semi-Performative Style

In the early 2000s, before podcasting became a big business, few gatekeepers existed and the landscape was largely democratic.[14] Podcasters generally fell into two groups: radio professionals (often from public radio) and amateurs without on-air experience, according to Evo Terra, an early podcaster, author, and podcast strategist. The radio professionals typically sounded polished; the amateurs did not. A large contingent came to podcasting from blogging and embraced its DIY ethos. Amateurs generally did not try to emulate professional radio announcers, Terra says. "We all wanted, for lack of a better word, our authentic voice to come through."[15]

Early podcasters rarely had anyone micromanaging their performance. "It was very shaggy and casual—people just trying stuff out," says Quah, who covers the podcast industry. "There was a feeling that this isn't top to bottom, it's peer to peer."[16] In the beginning, "it seemed like anything went—it was a free-for-all," says voice coach and radio producer Viki Merrick. Hosts relished their autonomy. "There was this sense of, 'You can't tell us how to talk.'"[17] The prototypical podcast voice was "the opposite of guarded," Merrick told the *New York Times*. "It was 'let it rip.'"[18]

More than in other mediums, experimentation has long been the norm in podcasting. That is especially true for independent creators who tend to have the most autonomy and the least pressure to amass large audiences. Mariam Sobh started a comedy news podcast after a long career in radio news. "In radio, it's like they're scared to take risks," she says. "In podcasting, you're taking risks all the time and seeing what works."[19] Journalists who lead podcasting efforts at established institutions also have been given freedom to experiment. When Nuzum had that role at NPR in the mid 2000s, few executives paid close attention at first to podcasts. That allowed Nuzum and colleagues to develop niche programming that sounded less buttoned up than radio. They encouraged hosts to "loosen up some of the dogmatic yet baseless assumptions of how someone needed to sound on NPR." The cohosts of a video game podcast were "completely unpolished," Nuzum says. "But they knew their stuff and could speak with authority and authenticity, and that's what mattered."[20]

Authenticity has long been considered one of podcasting's defining characteristics.[21] Podcast hosts generally do not try to appeal to a broad, middle- to upper-class audience by faking an announcer voice or attempting to sound accentless, like they are from everywhere but nowhere. More commonly, they try to earn listeners' trust by showcasing their unique voice from somewhere that reveals something about their identity. Nuzum tells aspiring podcasters, "You don't have to have a refined announcer voice that comes with years of practice. With the democratization of media, listeners expect to hear people who sound like them."[22]

Voice coaches and consultants often convey a similar message. "In the podcasting world, we are typically quite accepting about voices," Terra says. "You're probably not going to get a lot of hate mail because you don't have a perfect radio voice when you start a podcast."[23] Coaches may intervene when they hear voices they do not consider technically sound, but they often discourage clients from covering up distinguishing vocal features. "The listener wants to relate to you," voice coach and podcast strategist Mary Chan tells aspiring hosts. "If they have your accent, if they hear themselves reflected, they are going to love your show that much more. People are seeking out voices that sound like theirs."[24]

Terra hears more types of listeners reflected now than he did when he started in podcasting. "There are more ethnic and non-White voices; people who clearly don't sound like me, a cisgender White man in his fifties. 'There's something different about this voice,' I find myself thinking, and it's not at all distracting." Another observable difference is that shows generally sound more professional than they once did. "Not necessarily more polished and produced like radio," Terra says, "but hosts who are better with their own voices."[25] Even as podcasting has become less DIY and as more people with highly trained voices become podcast hosts, Terra assures clients there is still a place in the industry for people without broadcasting experience—the amateurs who helped normalize the "unfiltered natural voice."[26]

"Natural" and "conversational" are words that are often associated with podcasting. "There's no question that podcasting champions a looser writing and delivery style," says story editor, trainer, and editorial consultant Alison

MacAdam. "It's a younger and more diverse industry than broadcasting. You have people at the microphone and behind the scenes who have different standards [than those in radio] of what normal speech is."[27] Many podcast hosts speak informally and with minimal self-editing. The casual tone they set encourages guests to open up and give unrehearsed answers instead of carefully worded sound bites. Conversations generally sound unscripted, even when there is a script or an extended outline.

Put another way, podcasters often perform backstage talk in frontstage settings. They want listeners to think of what they are hearing as the kind of honest, unfiltered conversation that takes place when the cameras and microphones are off and no one feels pressure to perform. But podcasters are engaged in impression management, as they would be in any frontstage setting. They aim for believable performances, which Goffman referred to as a sincere approach to acting out social roles.[28] Many hosts believe that their act—the impression of reality they stage—is an expression of their true identity. They need others to believe this too.

Podcasters often perceive that sounding authentic and believable attracts listeners. "When you listen to a podcast, it's all about how much you trust that person," host Mary Harris said during a podcasting festival panel. "It's a different relationship than you have with radio or television or other media in your life. It's plugged into your ear; you're listening during an intimate moment, letting the podcast into your life." That is freeing from the host's perspective, Harris said, because "you can really be yourself."[29] Podcasting is considered the most intimate medium in part because the host invites the listener into their life, sharing personal stories and insights. Even though they likely will never meet—the hallmark of a one-way parasocial relationship—the listener assumes they know the "real" host. "The podcasters I listen to, I feel like they are being themselves," says Kim Fox, a professor who teaches podcasting. "If I saw them in the street, I expect that's exactly who I would get."[30]

Hosts who come to podcasting from other mediums often must adjust to these expectations. Gloria Riviera spent most of her career in television news. During COVID-19, she started *No One Is Coming to Save Us*, a limited series podcast about America's broken childcare system. She narrated the first episode using her well-rehearsed, seemingly neutral television reporter voice. Producers wanted less detachment and more emotional resonance for an episode about women without access to affordable childcare. Riviera was not used to that kind of performance. To get into the right frame of mind, she listened again to the women's stories and considered her connection to them. She then rerecorded her narration, which sounded more sincere. "I realized that being yourself is encouraged. It's OK to be honest about what you're thinking, share intimate personal experiences, mess up, and be wide-eyed. That's how we are in real life, and that's what makes for a successful podcast."[31]

Varied Backgrounds, Different Traditions

In Gustavo Arellano's view, the best podcast hosts sound "completely natural." That is how he tried to sound when hosting *The Times*, a daily news podcast from the *Los Angeles Times* that ended in 2023. Arellano had previously dabbled in radio. He hosted a show on a Los Angeles station and did public radio commentaries. But he never considered himself to be *of* radio. Before coming to the *Los Angeles Times* as a columnist, Arellano had spent most of his career cultivating a unique writing voice at an alternative weekly newspaper. He was editor of Orange County's *OC Weekly* and was best known for his satirical syndicated column, "¡Ask a Mexican!," which he eventually turned into a book.

Because Arellano did not go through the traditional radio pipeline, he had never been through an aircheck or received formal voice coaching. He had never seen a report on how listeners perceived his presentation or felt the need to unlearn vocal habits. Many other podcast hosts find themselves in the same position of working in podcasting without having trained in broadcasting. Podcasters, with their varied backgrounds, often sound unlike those who trained in journalism schools and broadcast newsrooms.

Arellano sounds nothing like a smooth-talking television anchor or a soothing radio host. His vocal delivery stands out. He speaks with an upward inflection, and not just at the end of sentences. He is a notorious fast talker. He occasionally stammers and thinks out loud, using the Spanish phrase *"como se dice"* when searching for words. "People have always tried to slow me down, but I don't want to be slowed down,"[32] he says. The few times he tried that when he was on radio, he felt that he sounded like a zombie.

Arellano unapologetically mispronounces words. Take the word "accept." "I've pronounced it as 'assept' my entire life," Arrelano says. When producers at *The Times* corrected him at first and suggested a retake, he resisted. "We all mispronounce words, especially if you're a child of an immigrant. Spanish was my first language. I've been English-dominant since I was a child, but I still have certain ways of staying stuff that I think makes me more interesting as a host." When Arellano introduced himself on the podcast, he used the Spanish pronunciation. "[Listeners] sometimes get mad and say, 'Why can't you use the English pronunciation?' I say, 'I'm going to pronounce it how it's supposed to be pronounced.'" Arellano often used Spanglish on the podcast. "I hear a lot of, 'Stop trying to push this on us' or 'It's cool that you're mixing in Spanish.' My response is, 'I'm not trying to be clever—it's just how I speak. I don't play a Mexican American for anyone. I'm a product of my life. If you don't like who I am, that's on you, not me.'"[33]

Arellano did not see any reason to emulate prominent radio personalities (he finds public radio voice dull). He did not want his show to be confused with *The Daily*, produced by the *New York Times*. The *Los Angeles Times* has been around for nearly 150 years, but it only recently made a serious push into podcasting.

Because of that, Arellano did not have to challenge long-standing institutional norms about what sounds professional. This gave him more leeway in terms of how he performed as host.

Some podcasters have backgrounds that are even less traditional than Arellano's. While some may not consider themselves to be journalists in the traditional sense, they do acts of journalism. Many have no prior background in news and have never learned to write in a journalistic style. Objectivity and neutrality often are of peripheral importance to their work. They may find the warm coffee voice stifling, the television newscaster voice antiquated, and other vocal forms more attractive.

Shannon Cason's experience is illustrative. He studied advertising, not journalism. He listened to radio but preferred comedy and sports talk to NPR. Before getting into podcasting, he was a writer and performer. He made appearances on *The Moth* and *TEDx* and became a regular storyteller on the acclaimed radio program and podcast *Snap Judgment*. As a performer, Cason drew inspiration from hip-hop. "In that world, originality is key—having a unique style and voice; not following the trend of whatever voices you hear," Cason says.[34] He wanted to carry that into podcasting.

Cason hosts the independently distributed podcast *Shannon Cason's Homemade*. When Chicago public radio station WBEZ began distributing the show after dozens of episodes, Cason was not interested in adjusting his speaking style for a new audience. "The classic radio voice has always bothered me. I figured if I was listening to this show, I would want to hear my authentic voice. And if it didn't work out, it probably wasn't a good fit." WBEZ producers liked the fit— they praised the way Cason spoke with a rhythm and cadence unlike many in public radio. They did not refer him to a voice coach or ask him to alter his delivery. Cason has hosted several other shows. His speaking style may limit his opportunities in podcasting, but he does not view code switching as an option. "That's the choice I've made. I don't want to go to work and do a news segment in a voice that's not mine."[35]

Kumanyika no longer has a voice in his head telling him to sound like someone else when narrating stories. Since writing his manifesto on public radio voice, he has been involved in several podcast projects, most notably as cocreator and cohost of Gimlet's Civil War history podcast *Uncivil*. He has found a writing style that matches his storytelling voice and a performance style that feels true to his background as a hip-hop artist, which reflects important aspects of his personality.[36] When editors and producers hear him speaking in a different voice, they remind him that "this doesn't really sound like you."[37]

Like Kumanyika, Saidu Tejan-Thomas Jr. has a performance background outside journalism. He did acting and slam poetry before getting into podcasting. After interning on *Uncivil* and working on other Gimlet podcasts, he cocreated and hosted *Resistance*, a podcast featuring stories from the front lines of the movement for Black lives. The *New York Times* described the show as "dominated by a medley of young, Black voices." Tejan-Thomas told the *Times* that he tries to approximate his natural speaking style, which he hopes Black listeners recognize as someone they know or grew up with.[38]

A Space of Their Own

Maxie C. Jackson III wants public radio to be—and sound—more diverse. The longtime public radio executive has recruited with that aim. But he knows that journalists of color have plenty of other options. "When I was trying to build a roster of African American talent for podcasts, I was told that the people I was going after don't need to come to public radio. If you don't feel like you belong or that you're welcomed into a media environment, you go elsewhere. A lot of folks are choosing to create their own space."[39]

Those types of spaces have existed in some form for many years. Black-owned radio stations like WURD Radio in Philadelphia play an important role in the media ecosystem. In the early 2000s, when Sara M. Lomax's father bought the station, she observed that elsewhere in the market, Black journalists "basically had to sound White to be on radio." When Lomax, a journalist and media entrepreneur, took over for her father, she expanded programming and kept the station's tradition of airing diverse voices not heard elsewhere on local radio. At a Black-owned station, Lomax says, "every cultural reference doesn't need to be explained" and hosts don't feel the need to code switch.[40] WURD is part of URL Media, a network that Lomax cofounded to support existing Black- and Brown-owned media organizations.

Although Black-owned radio stations are on the decline, Black-owned podcast networks—and individual podcasts with Black hosts—are ascendant. Many shows feature insight into and discussion of African American lived experiences and lifestyles, "capturing the Black vernacular in organic settings," Fox and coauthors write in their study about Black podcasting. "This informal mode of discourse is reminiscent of the early days of Black radio, which amplified the sentiments of the community."[41] Hosts often strive to have "conversations that Black people have when White people aren't in the room," as one show's tagline stated.[42]

Code Switch has featured many such conversations. The podcast aims to "reflect to the broader, mostly White NPR audience what the rest of the country actually looks and sounds like," says Juleyka Lantigua, a former senior producer and editor. "It was a conscious decision not to try to massage away distinctive features of how people spoke." Yet during her short stint at NPR in the late 2010s, Lantigua worried that the podcast industry was developing some of radio's bad habits—most notably, being too East Coast–centric and not reflecting the country's diversity. "I thought, 'Ok, we can't make that mistake again in podcasting or we're going to miss out.'"[43]

Lantigua saw a particular need for podcasts that are aimed at young Latinas, who had largely been ignored despite their population growth and their tendency to be early adopters of technology. Her company, LWC Studios, targets that listenership with shows about topics such as the challenges adult children of immigrant parents face and the professional successes of trailblazing Latinas. LWC is one of a growing number of women-owned podcast networks whose shows are primarily hosted by women of color. On LWC's flagship podcast *70 Million*, host Mitzi Miller reports on how people across the U.S. are addressing the role of jails in their backyards. One of the reasons Miller was chosen as host is that she embodied the listener Lantigua imagined for the podcast and the entire network: "the child of immigrants, raised in an urban environment, with a college degree, and a digital native."[44]

Another podcast production studio that aims to amplify the work of young journalists of color is LAist Studios, a division of Southern California Public Radio. Quah's podcast about the podcast industry, *Servant of Pod*, was an LAist production until the show ended in 2021. He describes his voice as "atypical" in part because he grew up in Malaysia and learned English as a second language and because he speaks quickly. When he started the show, Quah did not feel pressure to change his vocal delivery. "I figured I would just roll with it, have fun and be myself, and see where it went."[45]

Podcasting has been a boon to people with disabilities, whose voices are rarely heard in mainstream media. Scholar Beth Haller notes that disability podcasts benefit both nondisabled audiences, who learn about the lived experience of disability, and disabled people who access them and can feel empowered by voices from their community.[46] Disability rights advocate Alice Wong has been outspoken about the need for more disabled voices in radio and podcasting. In 2017, she started the *Disability Visibility* podcast, which featured conversations on politics, culture, and media with disabled people. Wong, who was born with spinal muscular atrophy, began using an assistive device later in life to help her breathe. As a first-time podcaster, she says her voice was not "smooth or easily understandable" and the rhythms of her speech were "not natural." Yet she "grew to embrace this difference," and listeners around the world embraced the podcast.[47] After 100 episodes, Wong ended the podcast in 2021. Another prominent voice in the disability community is Thomas Reid, who hosts and produces *Reid My Mind*, a podcast that introduces listeners to people impacted by all degrees of blindness and disability.

Podcasting also has enabled people who stutter to have a space of their own. *StutterTalk*, which began in 2007, is the first and longest-running podcast on stuttering. The program features both people who stutter and researchers and speech-language pathologists. Maya Chupkov, a stuttering advocate and a person who stutters, started the podcast *Proud Stutter* in 2021 to change societal norms around stuttering and the disability community. Specifically, her goal is to "bring justice to those who stutter and are constantly misunderstood by society" and to "raise awareness that stuttering is just a different way of speaking, where the very idea of 'normal' speech is undone."[48]

How Podcasting Has Influenced Radio

The influence of podcasting on radio is undeniable. When Nuzum worked at NPR in the mid 2000s, he was struck by how his colleagues responded to hearing new podcasts. Journalists who only appeared on radio were intrigued by how raw podcasts sounded by comparison and how much fun hosts seemed to be having in this new medium. "They would come up and say, 'Whoa, I can't believe podcasts are sounding like this.' I said, 'Why can't you sound like this on radio? Who's stopping you?'"[49]

Decades later, public radio journalists sound somewhat more like podcasters. When Quah listens to public radio, he hears journalists speaking more casually than they once did. Hosts of NPR's flagship programs, for instance, tend to sound a bit looser, closer to how journalists talk on the semi-scripted *NPR Politics Podcast*. Former public radio journalist Tanya Ott observes that "there's a much more conversational approach now on radio, and I think podcasting is the driving factor. People are really starting to value voices that stand out rather than the vanilla sound."[50]

Radio also has had an unmistakable influence on podcasting. Many podcasters grew up on commercial talk radio. Others were heavily influenced by prominent public radio programs. In narrative podcasting, the imprints of *This American Life* are everywhere. Shows are commonly written in a similar style, and hosts often sound similar to Ira Glass. The Glass/*This American Life* aesthetic has become even more dominant since 2014, the year that *Serial*, a podcast from the creators of *This American Life*, debuted and became a smash hit.

In recent years, many public radio journalists have migrated to podcasting. Some now host prominent shows or run large production companies. As a result, elements of public radio have carried over to the newer medium, although many differences remain.

Summary

Podcasting differs from radio in ways that have enabled hosts to speak in a manner that better reflects their identity or that simply better aligns with their performance inclinations. Many creators are not affiliated with major media organizations. Even organizations that produce podcasts may not impose institutional norms that restrict diverse forms of self-presentation. Therefore, podcasters often feel little or no pressure to cover. The relatively low barriers to podcasting have enabled many to enter the medium, resulting in a wide variety of voices and perspectives.

Podcasting has served as something of a laboratory for fleshing out characteristics of audio news that appeal to a broad range of potential listeners to an extent that legacy radio has not allowed. The impact of this experiment is summarized in this 2021 Nielsen report:

> How and how often different identity groups show up in content—and where within the storyline or subject—matters. . . . As people look for content to accurately articulate and illustrate their lived experience, there are a burgeoning number of options, especially when you consider audio platforms. Importantly, for diverse audiences, podcast content is resonating and an important medium.[51]

In short, podcasting has demonstrated the appeal of hosts with diverse backgrounds and presentation styles.

Part 3

**Laws and
Suggested Actions**

· ·

9

Legal Protections and Their Limits

●●●●●●●●●●●●●●●●●●●●●

Journalists who believe that media employer actions have improperly created pressure for them to cover may have some legal protection. Although a comprehensive analysis of applicable law and forums for seeking remedies is beyond the scope of this book, this chapter provides an overview of the existing legal framework for such laws as well as notable limits in their application.[1]

Adverse treatment of employees with respect to appearance or speech may be viewed as unfair, unwise, and unnecessary. Yet to a significant extent, such discrimination is legal. Although no federal law explicitly prohibits this type of employment-related discrimination and very few state or local jurisdictions do so, requiring members of protected groups to cover can, in some circumstances, violate antidiscrimination laws. The employment-at-will doctrine is a useful starting point for analysis.

Employment-at-Will Doctrine and Its Exceptions

Employment is presumptively at will, terminable by either the employee or the employer at any time with or without cause, unless limited by statute, other law, public policy, an agreement, or a binding promise. Through legislation, only Montana and Washington, DC, have changed this long-standing common-law presumption.[2] Public policy exceptions to the employment-at-will doctrine, which most states have, prohibit firings in response to actions employees take to vindicate other important rights, to refuse an employer's request to break the law, or to report employer wrongdoing to the government or the media.[3]

Employment contracts or union contracts can have enforceable protections, including those related to termination. The majority of states recognize an implied contract exception to the employment-at-will doctrine when, even absent an express written employment agreement, an employer makes oral or written representations to employees about job security or procedures for taking adverse employment actions.[4] For example, an employer may be bound by policy statements or directives in employee manuals or elsewhere that create a reasonable expectation of limits on the employer's power to terminate the employment relationship (e.g., by describing job duties, work rules, and conditions of termination). However, employers can avoid being so bound by stating clearly that their policies do not create contractual rights and that these policies can be modified or revoked at any time.[5] Because courts have often held at-will employees' reliance on their employer's policies to be unreasonable, this protection has proved to be an unreliable basis for fighting job termination.[6]

Eleven states recognize a covenant of good faith and fair dealing exception to the employment-at-will doctrine. These exceptions subject employer personnel decisions to a "just cause" standard or prohibit bad faith or malicious terminations.[7] Some legislation provides limits on employer flexibility in treatment of employees that may in some instances apply to employer pressure to cover.

Statutes Governing Employer Treatment of Employees

Certain groups have protected status from discrimination in employment under law, which limits employer discretion. Federal law protects employees from discrimination based on race, ethnicity, sex, sexual orientation, religion, age, and disability. State and local laws may provide additional protections for these categories.

Federal Antidiscrimination Laws

This section reviews federal laws with provisions related to employment discrimination. The first, Title VII of the Civil Rights Act of 1964, makes it unlawful to discriminate against any individual with respect to compensation, terms, conditions, or privileges of employment because of such individual's race, color, religion, sex, or national origin.[8] In 2020, the Supreme Court held that Title VII also covers discrimination based on sexual orientation and gender identity.[9] Employment policies and practices that are subject to scrutiny can include recruiting, hiring, promoting, transferring, training, disciplining, discharging, assigning work, measuring performance, and providing benefits. Discrimination claims under Title VII may be based on disparate treatment (intentional discrimination) or disparate impact (which need not be intentional). Intentional discrimination occurs when an employment decision is affected by the person's status as a protected group member. This can include conscious or unconscious stereotypes about the abilities, traits, or performance of individuals of certain groups. A "neutral" job policy that disproportionately excludes protected group members and that is not job related and necessary to the operation of the business would be considered to have a disparate impact.

An employer may discriminate on the basis of religion, sex, national origin, or age (but not race) if it can establish that a bona fide occupational qualification (BFOQ) is reasonably necessary to the normal operation of that particular business or enterprise.[10] To qualify as a BFOQ, the discriminatory job qualification must "affect an employee's ability to do the job" and must "relate to the 'essence' or to the 'central mission of the employer's business.'"[11] An employer must prove that (1) a direct and closely related relationship exists between the employee's or applicant's protected status and their ability to perform the job, (2) the essence or goal of the business actually requires the characteristic (good-faith belief of business necessity is not sufficient), (3) there are no less discriminatory means that would serve the same purpose, and (4) the employer actually considered the attribute when making the hiring decision.[12]

Some courts have deemed customer preference to be a BFOQ but have rarely allowed discrimination based solely on this.[13] One legal scholar states flatly that Title VII prohibits basing employment decisions on bigoted customer preferences regardless of economic impact, such as a loss of customers.[14] The U.S. Equal Employment Opportunity Commission, which is responsible for enforcing Title VII, instructs that basing employment decisions on the racial preferences of clients, customers, or coworkers constitutes intentional race discrimination.[15]

Employer policies that appear to be neutral but cause a disparate impact may be improper if they are motivated by a discriminatory bias unless the employer can establish a business necessity for the policy.[16]

The second federal law related to employment discrimination is the Age Discrimination in Employment Act of 1967, which prohibits age discrimination within the employment relationship against people who are age forty or older.[17] The BFOQ defense is available to employers under this law.[18]

The third federal law is the Americans with Disabilities Act of 1990, which requires employers to offer reasonable accommodations to employees with disabilities unless doing so would impose a significant difficulty or expense.[19] The Americans with Disabilities Act does not have a BFOQ defense. However, employers may defend the use of a qualification standard that screens out an individual on the basis of disability by showing that the standard is job related and is consistent with business necessity if they can show that the standard accurately measures the individual's ability to perform the position's essential functions.[20]

Application of federal antidiscrimination laws to covering demands. Courts often have determined that antidiscrimination laws do not protect employees from employer demands to cover. In his book *Covering: The Hidden Assault on Our*

Civil Rights, Kenji Yoshino notes that courts commonly distinguish between an individual's *status* and an individual's *conduct* (or between *being* and *doing*), disfavoring employer actions based on the former but upholding them if based on the latter. Drawing this distinction can result in protection against discrimination for "being a member of a protected group, but not [for] doing things associated with the group."[21] Courts are prone to protect against discrimination based on the *immutable* but not the *mutable* aspects of one's identity. For example, ancestry, skin color, or natural hair texture may be considered protected immutable attributes, but not an employee's refusal to minimize or hide a mutable characteristic associated with an identity group. Put another way, courts may protect the "unchosen but not the chosen aspects" of one's identity, such as the choice to be a mother or wearing hair in a cornrow style deemed to be an "easily changed characteristic."[22]

Federal antidiscrimination laws also have been applied to accent-based and appearance-based employment actions.

Accent-based discrimination. While Title VII does not mention accents, courts recognize that it may prohibit discrimination based on accent when shown to be the functional equivalent of national origin. However, employers may require employees to have sufficient communication skills. Therefore, accent-based discrimination claims are largely unsuccessful when communication is important to job function or performance and intelligibility is a concern.[23] In one case, a White applicant for a job involving recorded public announcements was selected over an Asian applicant who spoke accented English. The discrimination claim failed. Citing speech experts' testimony that "standard English is that used by radio and TV announcers" and "standard English pronunciation should be used by radio broadcasters," the court noted that "the White applicant was selected because he had better diction, better enunciation, better pronunciation, better cadence, better intonation, better voice clarity, and better understandability."[24]

While courts have largely rejected customer preference defenses in other types of Title VII suits, such defenses have been more often accepted in accent cases. Judgments about speech intelligibility and pleasantness can be negatively affected by prejudice or by unconsciously held assumptions. Comprehension, therefore, can be a function of the listener's attitude.[25] When evaluating speech, people are susceptible to cultural stereotypes they have absorbed that lead them to evaluate "low-status" accents as foreign and unintelligible and "high-status" accents as clear and competent.[26] "Like many employers, courts rely on their own subjective assessments in accent discrimination cases, making possible the intrusion of cultural and speech stereotypes upon their judgment."[27] Citing courts' tendency to accept employers' (often false) assumptions about a person's intelligibility uncritically and often without empirical foundation, and linguistic evidence that it is relatively easy for motivated listeners to make comprehension adjustments, legal scholars have argued that customer preference should not be accepted as a defense without evidence that listeners experience difficulty with and avoid listening to an employee's speech.[28]

Research shows that listeners who belong to the linguistically normative group rate accented speakers less favorably than "standard" speakers.[29] People tend to find information delivered in a foreign accent less believable than information presented in a native accent. This tendency may exist independently of any prejudice they have.[30] Multicultural upbringing and experience has been shown to positively affect attitudes toward accented speech.[31] Yet even short exposure to an accent improves listener processing of it, which can reduce bias. Ensuring exposure to foreign accents can reduce discrimination against nonnative speakers.[32]

Appearance-based discrimination. No federal civil rights law explicitly prohibits discrimination based on appearance.[33] Under Title VII, appearance is not given protected status. Consequently, it is not necessarily illegal to discriminate based on appearance, for example by hiring only attractive people. Individuals seeking redress must attempt to link their appearance to one of the protected categories of Title VII, the ADEA, or the ADA.[34] Title VII prohibits unwarranted appearance polices based on physical traits linked to race or that reflect racial identification or religious belief. Courts have most readily found race-related appearance policies to constitute race discrimination.[35] For example, courts have tied height and facial hair to a class protected under Title VII.[36] Title VII also prohibits requirements about grooming, dress, and appearance that are based on gender stereotypes. The Supreme Court held that gender stereotypes cannot be the sole basis for discrimination against a woman with masculine traits.[37] Employers may even find it difficult to justify gender-neutral policies that have requirements that unequally burden genders.[38]

Members of a group protected under Title VII may face barriers to successfully challenging employer pressure to cover based on appearance under the primary liability theories of disparate treatment and disparate impact. An employee must show that the disparate treatment generally imposes an unequal burden to conform to an employer's standards. Appearance policies or demands often involve unconscious biases. This makes it difficult to prove intent to discriminate, "which usually requires conscious bias or purposeful discrimination."[39] Disparate impact does not require proof of intent to discriminate. However, discrimination can be difficult to show absent a sufficient number of employees from the protected group—which newsrooms may lack—or if other group members comply with the appearance requirement imposed.[40]

As previously noted, antidiscrimination law more strongly protects an individual's immutable characteristics. The more personal and changeable a characteristic is, the less it is deemed entitled to civil rights protection due to its mutability. This applies to aspects of physical appearance that can be readily changed, such as hairstyle or attire.[41]

Appearance policies that serve to discriminate based on age can be challenged under the ADEA if it can be proved that the employer thought that a claimant aged forty or over "looked too old."[42] Appearance policies that work to discriminate based on disability can be challenged under the ADA.[43] The ADA protects people who can effectively do their jobs (with or without a reasonable accommodation) if their employer's action was motivated by a perceived disability, even if it is not an actual one.[44] For example, this might include someone with a cosmetic disfigurement.[45] The ADA also covers an employer's false opinions based on appearance that relate to an employee's ability to do his or her job.[46] However, redress based on aspects of physical appearance has been described as limited.[47]

Courts have narrowly applied the business necessity exception as a justification for employer actions in appearance-based cases, for example by limiting its use to endeavors such as modeling. Courts rarely allow appearance-based discrimination when it is motivated solely by customer preference.[48]

State and Local Antidiscrimination Laws

Most states have some type of antidiscrimination law that may protect employees to an extent that is similar to or greater than federal law. Some state and local jurisdictions have passed laws prohibiting discrimination based on various aspects of personal appearance. Michigan directly prohibits discrimination based on appearance.[49] The Washington State Supreme Court has held that obesity is always an impairment under the Washington Law Against Discrimination.[50] The District of Columbia Human Rights Act directly prohibits employment discrimination based on personal appearance unless it is related to a business necessity or a reasonable business purpose.[51] Santa Cruz and San Francisco prohibit discrimination based on weight and Urbana, Illinois, and Madison, Wisconsin, prohibit discrimination based on aspects of personal appearance.[52] Although these local statutes seem to have some potential to address concerns about appearance discrimination, their impact has been limited. There has reportedly been little or no enforcement of such legislation, and only a limited number of complaints about appearance discrimination in the workplace have been made in those jurisdictions.[53]

Federal legislation called the Creating a Respectful and Open World for Natural Hair Act (CROWN Act) has been proposed, but not enacted, to prohibit discrimination based on "race-based hairstyles" by extending statutory protection to hair texture and styles such as braids, locks, twists, and knots in the workplace and public schools. As of this writing, about twenty-three states have passed the CROWN Act or legislation inspired by it, although not all of these laws apply to the workplace.[54]

Future Direction of the Law

Legal experts generally acknowledge the need for statutory protection against employment-related discrimination on the basis of voice and appearance, particularly when characteristics are immutable. Legal scholar Heather R. James writes that federal antidiscrimination law addresses the unfair reality that "people make decisions based on exterior stereotypes and frequently form opinions supported solely by prejudices.... Even employers evaluate individuals on the basis of erroneous characteristics."[55] Members of federally protected groups receive legal protection because employment discrimination based on immutable characteristics has historically been proven to be unjust and irrational.[56] Legal scholar Frank J. Cavico and his coauthors recognize that workplace appearance standards often affirm societal stereotypes and biases toward attractiveness, undercut more pertinent accomplishments, and devalue diversity by requiring conformity to White, heterosexual norms.[57]

Yet some scholars question the likelihood or propriety of expanding legal protections. James favors allowing employers to enforce standards relating to mutable aspects of appearance "because employee appearance affects both the image and success of public and private employers," in part because there is a common objective standard of what people generally find attractive.[58] Cavico notes that in some instances, appearance—particularly attractiveness—can be changed and is "fundamentally a cultural creation." He doubts that any law could significantly reduce appearance discrimination because people are naturally attracted to what they consider beautiful.[59]

Neither James nor Cavico favors explicit legal protections for appearance attributes such as attractiveness because of the difficulty of defining who falls within a protected class (unlike groups covered by existing federal laws) and the likelihood of inconsistent results in the adjudication of compliance.[60] James adds that giving protected status for appearance would make proving a discriminatory motive, which is already difficult under current law, even more complicated "because the importance of beauty is so ingrained in American culture" that "employers may discriminate subconsciously."[61] Both legal scholars accept economists' views that employees whose appearance is appealing or consistent with an employer's brand (when appearance is essential to the brand) is a material employer benefit that is substantially related to the functions of the job.[62] Economist Robert J. Barro has suggested that a worker's physical appearance, to the extent that this characteristic is valued by customers and coworkers, is "as legitimate a job qualification as intelligence, dexterity, job experience, and personality."[63] Cavico concludes that where the law fails to protect all workers from appearance discrimination, it is best to encourage employers to lead by example with "forward-thinking written policies" that protect workers.[64]

Yoshino views the court-imposed immutability doctrine as an ill-advised limitation on applying civil rights protection in order to prevent the subordination of traditional civil rights group members to dominant-group norms though covering demands. He argues that "if civil rights law fails to protect [marginalized] groups against coerced conformity, it will have stopped short of its end [goal]."[65] Yoshino prefers adoption of what he terms a "group-based accommodation model." In this model, instead of courts merely asking whether employees can comply with the demand to conform, employers must justify the need for compliance and prove their inability to accommodate employee attributes as they are. However, out of what Yoshino describes as a need to "temper passion with realism," he notes that courts are unlikely to do this and advocates for "reason-forcing conversations" outside the courts.[66] Such conversations involve an individual confronted with demands to cover asking their employer why this is deemed necessary and the employer considering whether tolerance is warranted.

I leave it to legal experts to debate the merits and likelihood of legislation to protect against undue pressure to cover. While legal protections are important, regardless of whether and how they change, reducing the pressure to cover ultimately requires action by those who advise, train, and manage journalists. The final chapter addresses what types of action would promote this outcome.

10

How Change Happens

• •

Previous chapters examined the cost of covering and how journalists have challenged restrictive institutional norms. Many interviewees have been instrumental in raising awareness of inequities and advocating for change. Some change has already occurred. Although the pressure to conform still exists, a person entering the profession now may have more agency over their self-presentation than they would have had in previous decades. "We've come a long way in a short period of time," says Harrison Hove, a journalism educator and former broadcast journalist. "There's a greater understanding that your strongest news team reflects your entire community instead of just the heteronormative, White, middle-class community." Hove says students with accents, nontraditional broadcast voices, and appearance attributes that "would have been dealbreakers twenty years ago" are now able to find employment.[1]

However, some are deterred from entering the industry, struggle to find on-air work, or have trouble advancing in their career. Whether those who perform on air feel accepted, sense that they must ask permission to be themselves, or hide aspects of their identity largely depends on where they work. Some newsroom leaders still narrowly perceive what looks good and sounds right. As a result, professors and performance advisers have a complicated message to convey to aspiring and early career journalists about industry expectations.

There is still work to do to make newsrooms more diverse and inclusive. While actions taken by individuals affected by covering are important, they will not achieve this goal alone. Change happens when institutional leaders commit to addressing inequities and get buy-in from employees. It happens when influential figures outside the newsroom support and advocate for journalists and challenge norms they consider outdated and unjust.

This chapter explores how educators, performance advisers, and newsroom leaders can promote further progress. I share recommendations from those who have worked to address problems. I also suggest a protocol for assessing the legitimacy of reasons for asking an individual to change aspects of their self-presentation. Finally, I identify obstacles to implementing changes and consider how those who advise about or manage journalists' performance can help remove those barriers by reimagining their roles and rethinking their understanding of audiences.

The Role of Educators and Suggested Action

Journalism educators strive to prepare students for the workforce. Many who teach broadcasting and podcasting draw on their industry experience—and the experiences of former students—when giving advice. They describe what might distract audiences and what has proven to appeal to newsroom managers. Seeking to be pragmatic, educators prepare student journalists for the type of feedback they may receive about their self-presentation.

Instead of just reflecting the industry as they believe it exists, educators should consider how it *should* operate and also serve as advocates. "We as educators have a responsibility not only to support students but also to bring about change in the industry," says Vanessa Ruiz, a former television journalist who more recently has taught journalism, directed a journalism school's diversity initiatives, and worked to advance educational attainment for students.[2] Advocacy can mean supporting students' decisions to present in ways that feel genuine, discouraging covering, and pushing those who recruit and hire students to have justifiable performance expectations.

Effectively combining pragmatism and advocacy can be challenging. Educators must candidly—and accurately—describe existing employer expectations to students. Yet their understanding of newsroom culture and manager preferences may be limited if they only worked in a few news markets and it may be outdated if they left broadcasting a long time ago. Without knowledge and consideration of how expectations have changed, guidance on self-presentation may be unnecessarily constraining. Presenting an inaccurate portrayal of the industry helps perpetuate restrictive norms.

Even if educators are well informed about current industry expectations, they may be tempted to self-censor, particularly when they are unprepared to discuss social identity or are uncomfortable with commenting on a person's appearance or vocal delivery. They may be concerned that students will feel unfairly targeted and view comments as microaggressions. Even if constructive feedback is justified, it can shake a student's self-confidence. These sensitive conversations, which often are implicitly or explicitly about race, gender, or sexual orientation, may be most productive if conducted privately. This allows for an open discussion and avoids a situation where a student may draw unwarranted negative conclusions by comparing feedback they have received to feedback classmates have received. The educators I interviewed felt that too much focus on self-presentation can be counterproductive but that ignoring it is also unhelpful. Journalists told me that they generally felt unprepared when they had heard nothing while in college about voice and appearance.

Ruiz says that those who feel equipped to discuss self-presentation should consider how they approach such conversations and frame their feedback carefully. "You have to be truthful and transparent about the challenges, but that conversation should include all the impactful, important things students can do with journalism." At her university, upper-level students who work in a campus newsroom learn about professional self-presentation during a bootcamp that happens early in the semester. Topics include hair, makeup, attire (e.g., wearing well-fitting clothing; avoiding distracting patterns), and accessories (e.g., avoiding noisy jewelry). "Within that," Ruiz told students when she ran sessions, "let's work with who you are, your identity, and your personality, so you can still be you and be professional." Ruiz says that some students would request individual consultations after this feedback.[3]

Before having such meetings, some educators ask students in their broadcasting and podcasting courses to observe how professional journalists present themselves. When doing so, it is important for professors to show examples from a diverse pool of news programs, highlight diverse forms of self-presentation, and make clear that expectations differ within the industry. They should avoid blanket statements about what looks and sounds professional. Proclamations about who has a "good voice for radio/podcasting" or the "right look for television" may unintentionally dissuade students from pursuing on-air work.

Students tend to be most receptive to feedback from professors who have earned their trust, Hove says. He often waits for students to approach him with questions or concerns but will initiate the conversation when he deems it beneficial. Hove likes to start with a supportive message, telling students, "I respect the uniqueness in you."[4] Kris Vera-Phillips has a similar approach. She advises students and young journalists on their self-presentation as a mentor with the Asian American Journalists Association. Her goal is to get aspiring journalists to "value who they are and where they come from." She tells people she mentors, "What you have to say and how you say it matters. Newsrooms shoot themselves in the foot when they don't recognize and value that." She reminds journalists entering small markets with little diversity that "you may be going to a market that isn't representative of you, but you offer a specific voice, a unique perspective, so you're bringing something new to the table."[5]

Vera-Phillips then delivers a reality check to "prepare students for the real world," specifically "the pushback they may get on their appearance or voice." She warns them: "When people bring you on because you're a diverse hire, recognize that they'll try to polish you up for a specific look and sound."[6] Hove tells students that when applying for jobs and working in newsrooms, feedback on their self-presentation "will be all over the place." His advice is that "you need to hear the feedback, but you may not have to internalize the feedback."

Before Hove tells students what they might hear, he identifies whether he is assuming the role of a recruiter, a news director, or an agent. "The feedback I'm giving you is through a different lens than myself," he explains. "It reflects the industry standard, not my opinion."[7] Even when commenting from the perspective of others without endorsing the feedback, educators must determine what they are comfortable saying. Ruiz never comments on anyone's body. "I'd like to think [newsroom managers] are aware that's inappropriate."[8] Hove is comfortable advising students about attire—particularly if what they wear on camera is overly casual or revealing. He does not comment on students' natural hairstyles or other forms of identity expression because "that's the uniqueness of America, and we should embrace that."[9]

When professors warn students about what others may say, they should explain the likely rationale. Hove notes that agents and other advisers want clients to be "as broadly employable as possible in order to appeal to the masses." This often leads advisers to tell aspiring journalists to tone down their outfits and "be somewhat vanilla."[10] Journalists might also hear that they need to reduce their accent to improve clarity and listener comprehension. Educators should state whether they consider this advice and rationale to be legitimate, provide other potential reasons for such comments (e.g., implicit bias or fear of alienating audiences), and tell students how, if at all, expectations have evolved throughout the industry.

Educators should be as specific as possible about how students can make changes to their self-presentation, particularly vocal delivery. This requires educators to be aware of gaps in their knowledge and learn more about speech and language and how the voice works or engage experts to guest teach such topics. A colleague who specializes in voicing visits my podcasting course to provide technical training. If I am unable to answer student questions about voice and speech/language, I advise them outside class to consult with a specialist.

In addition to giving students the information they need to decide how to present themselves, educators should empower them to do so. Ruiz gave an example of what she might tell a student with a visible piercing. "If you decide this is part of who you are and you aren't changing it, great, but know that in some TV markets, this is something that could play a role in whether a news director hires you or not."[11] After Hove tells students what others may say about how to look broadly appealing, he often continues by advising that "there's also an appeal to being different, so it's up to you to figure out which one is you and what you're OK with."[12] Vera-Phillips advises aspiring and early career journalists to determine how much they are willing to compromise to advance. "If in your gut you're moving too far away from who you are, you have to consider whether this is the right place to be," she says.[13] Increasingly, journalists can find newsrooms where they feel accepted—a message that some educators I interviewed try to convey to students.

Beyond the classroom, educators should speak out against antiquated norms just as theater professors did decades ago when they denounced the teaching of World English, the supposedly neutral speech standard that many viewed as elitist. Professors who have ties to the news industry should encourage newsroom leaders to be open to hiring journalists who present in diverse ways.

Journalism studies scholars are well suited to further study issues related to journalists' self-presentation, contemporary audience demographics and preferences, and the impact of covering on individuals and society. Educators should routinely include up-to-date information about these topics in journalism curricula, in professional publications, and at conferences and should refer to such research when interfacing with newsroom leaders. Credible, current data of this type can reduce barriers to change that are based on incorrect and outdated assumptions.

The Role of Performance Advisers and Suggested Action

Performance advisers have varied job titles and duties. Their objectives may differ depending on what they advise about, whom they advise, and whether a journalist or an employer hires them. Yet interviews revealed similarities in how voice coaches, image consultants, talent agents, and other advisers approach their work. Many are broadcast news veterans who use their industry experience and connections to advise journalists about how newsroom leaders evaluate talent. They often position themselves as audience representatives to assess whether journalists sound compelling and clear, whether any aspect of their self-presentation is distracting, and how well they likely would fare in various media markets. Some advisers serve as intermediaries by helping newsroom leaders and talent understand each other's needs and concerns and by advising both sides about any action required.

Performance advisers tend to be pragmatic. They consider norms and preferences in specific newsrooms and news markets. Pragmatism can entail considering what will make a journalist broadly employable or the best possible fit for a specific position. Tanya Ott advises young journalists seeking broad employability to sound like themselves but warns them that doing so "might limit your job opportunities if you're applying to stations that are run by people who aren't as welcoming to a lot of different voices."[14] Several consultants and agents shared that message with clients when advising them about their appearance, particularly their hair. Although many advisers observed an increase in welcoming newsroom environments, they felt that it was necessary to caution journalists about the range of potential responses in order to help them make informed choices.

Like educators, performance advisers also should help journalists advocate for themselves. Journalists often feel an urgent need to fix perceived problems. But many advisers endorse first asking performers how they want to present themselves before focusing on a fix. "I love the question, 'Have you given thought to who you want to be behind the microphone?,'" says Rob Rosenthal.[15] Then, during voice coaching sessions, he asks, "How are you feeling as you read this? Does it feel right to you; does it feel *like* you?" Dara Allen asks female journalists who have been advised to deepen their voices, "What do you want for yourself?"[16] For an episode of NPR's *Code Switch*, Khalon Richard asked voice coaches about their approach to advising journalists. "Some said, 'I want you to focus on meeting your goals and sounding the way you want to sound,' whereas others seemed focused on teaching them the 'right way of speaking,'" which she found disheartening. "We should never tell anyone the way they speak is wrong."[17] Radio journalist Diana Opong shares that view. "You can't give vocal tips to everybody and hope that they'll all sound the same. Instead, ask the person, 'What do you want to work on? How do you want to sound better?'"[18] Asking about self-perceptions and goals signals that these are important considerations and indicates that the adviser will, when appropriate, support journalists' decisions not to change their self-presentation.

To help journalists productively process criticism, performance advisers should filter negative comments they receive about clients' presentation and help them keep perspective on audience disapproval. Dana Adams wants clients to be aware of news directors' responses to their demo reels but is selective about what she shares. She prioritizes recurring comments and instead of repeating "brutal" feedback verbatim, she reframes it to be constructive.[19] Advisers commonly encourage journalists not to overreact to criticism. Jessica Hansen asked journalists she coached at NPR to consider the source. "Most of the time, people take on feedback that isn't important. If some listener wrote in, there are probably many others who think they sound great. If it's [a complaint] they hear consistently and it's in their head or if it's feedback from their manager, I tell them, 'Let's figure this out.'"[20]

Performance advisers should push newsroom leaders to clearly articulate their concerns about journalists' self-presentation. They should also help journalists communicate their interests and intentions to their managers. "I want [clients] to advocate for themselves," Cathy Runnels says. "Broadcasters often hear some vague reference about a problem and then don't know how to respond."[21] With her clients' permission, Runnels speaks with their managers so she can understand their concerns. She gives clients tangible goals to work toward and helps them direct their conversation with managers. "I teach them how to go back to their bosses and say, 'Here's what I'm working on and I'd like feedback.'" Particularly when advisers are hired by a news organization, they should ask newsroom leaders to explain how their organization sets and enforces performance expectations and how their concern about a journalist's self-presentation fits within those expectations.

Advisers should consider how their personal preferences—and their assumptions about audience preferences—may affect their judgment. Many say that they set aside what appeals to them and instead focus on whether the average audience member will hear a journalist clearly, perceive their appearance positively, and stay focused on their message. Some principles of self-presentation are widely accepted (e.g., journalists should not sound monotone or wear intricate patterns). Yet there are no objective standards for judging what is unclear or distracting. The role of audience representative involves subjective assessments about appearance and vocal delivery. The adviser's background is consequential. It may affect who they imagine as the average audience member and how they perceive accents, hair, and other aspects of self-presentation. Some journalists I interviewed identified a need for more performance advisers from diverse backgrounds.

When advisers suggest that clients cover to serve their short-term professional interest, this can reinforce restrictive norms. Interviews indicate that many advisers understand the harmful impact of covering and increasingly view it as unnecessary given increased acceptance of diverse forms of self-presentation.

The Role of Newsroom Leaders and Suggested Action

Newsroom leaders often are in a position to most directly affect whether journalists feel pressure to cover. During recruitment they signal what looks and sounds professional, and when hiring they make choices about aesthetic fit. They set expectations for new hires, conduct performance reviews, and suggest changes to journalists' self-presentation. News managers may favor forms of self-presentation that they find attractive and authoritative. By accepting more diversity of form—particularly forms that reflect the actual and potential diversity of an audience—managers help foster a more inclusive newsroom culture.

Top-level managers who shape newsroom culture at U.S. broadcast stations remain overwhelmingly White and male. This needs to change so that news organizations better reflect their local community and the country's diversity. "When you have people who come from different experiences having the power to make decisions that affect people's lives, that's when you're going to see a big difference," Ruiz says. Chenjerai Kumanyika observes that "who is in power can have implications for how people perform and how 'professional' is defined."[22]

Having diverse newsroom leaders increases a news organization's likelihood of having diverse on-air talent. A 2022 study found that news teams are significantly more diverse at stations with minorities in leadership positions.[23] Journalists I interviewed said that organizations must go beyond putting journalists of color on air; they must actively support them, sometimes despite negative audience comments. Such support requires diverse leadership, says Sara M. Lomax, who started URL Media to support diversity in media ownership.[24]

Many journalists also point to the need for increased diversity among producers, who may set the agenda for news programs and advise journalists on self-presentation. "When you have producers who are cut from the same mold, who come from the same college or community that's not diverse, you end up erasing stories that matter to diverse audiences," says Vera-Phillips, a former producer. Ariana Martinez, who has worked in a variety of production roles, notes that producers and others involved in editing are gatekeepers whose cultural and social experiences can affect whether speech characteristics such as accents, pronunciation, and stuttering are aired. Producers cut tape, Martinez says, "deciding what matters and what parts of a story are worth telling."[25] Former public radio journalist Stephanie Foo says that producers can "direct [speakers] to sound less homogeneous and choose tracks that are less homogeneous."[26] Increasing diversity among producers can also have a downstream effect; in public radio, many later assume on-air roles.

Newsroom leaders should ensure that every part of the hiring process avoids unnecessarily discouraging journalists from applying for or accepting jobs. Job advertisements should include clear performance expectations that list only the desired candidate attributes (verbal communication or appearance) that have been vetted for actual necessity and avoid using coded language that may inadvertently signal bias, especially with respect to vocal delivery. The skills employers seek should be tied to the specific job tasks that require them. Job postings should state that any verbal skills or attributes sought, including intelligibility, will be fairly evaluated with a nonprejudiced listener in mind and that reasonable task adaptations or other accommodations will be considered when assessing candidates' abilities to perform to a satisfactory standard.[27] Such specificity and assurances enable potential applicants to assess their ability to perform the stated job requirements, understand which skills they may be able to improve to meet expectations, and identify reasonable task accommodations that could enable them to do so. Applicants can therefore prepare from the outset to inform potential employers of specific adaptations or accommodations needed, available strategies for using their strengths to compensate for weaknesses, and plans for personal growth—and feel more comfortable doing so.

These considerations for communicating performance expectations and the possibility of accommodations also apply to the job interview process and to performance reviews. When meeting with new hires, in particular, managers should proactively identify their own interests and expectations and ask journalists how they wish to present themselves. Managers at television news stations should discuss expectations about consistency of appearance, especially with regard to hair. Journalists I interviewed said they were unclear about expectations in some cases and whether they needed to seek permission to change their hairstyle. Managers should justify why consistency is important. If employers can convincingly explain the reasoning behind their expectations, employees may be less likely to feel targeted for disparate treatment. Such conversations also may help managers recognize when pressure to cover can have a harmful impact on journalists.

Before asking journalists to change an aspect of their self-presentation, managers should ensure that the reasons for doing so are not based on outdated practices, unconfirmed current assumptions, personal aesthetic preferences, or bias. They should weigh the benefits of the requested change against the potential harmful impacts of covering. Because managers so directly impact on-the-job pressure to cover, I propose a specific protocol they can use to weigh these considerations. The following steps should contribute to a lessening of undue pressure on journalists to cover:

(1) If the requested change is intended to achieve adherence to job performance standards, identify each standard at issue and critically assess how necessary it is.

(2) If the change is based in part on audience demographics or preferences, make sure that the rationale reflects established facts rather than unconfirmed assumptions. Assumptions about audience preferences often lack empirical foundation. For example, they often reflect false beliefs about listeners' inability to comprehend certain accents. Evidence suggests that comprehension adjustments are relatively easy for motivated listeners.[28]

(3) If the change is intended to avoid a loss of revenue due to audience attrition, realistically assess the existence and materiality of the expected adverse effect. Such claims, at a minimum, should be supported by some evidence that a journalist's presentation is the reason for attrition. Anecdotal audience complaints or threats to disengage are unreliable indicators.

(4) Consider if the change sought is based primarily on personal preference or bias. Asking journalists to alter their appearance or vocal delivery for this reason should be subject to particular scrutiny.

(5) Determine if the journalist is a member of a protected civil rights group. If so, determine whether asking for the change is prohibited by law. This should involve consideration of whether the performance trait or attribute for which change is sought is strongly linked to membership in a protected group.

(6) If seeking the change is not proscribed by law, weigh the legitimacy of the reasons for seeking it and the significance of the organization's interests against the significance of any adverse impact on the individual. For this step in particular, it is important that those with diverse backgrounds are involved in making this assessment.

(a) If the significance of the adverse impact on the individual outweighs the significance of the legitimate reasons and interests of the organization, the request to change should not be made.

(b) If the significance of the legitimate reasons and interests of the organization outweighs the adverse impact on the individual, before asking the employee to change their presentation, the organization should further consider the interests of the employee's identity group and the public good. For example, could compliance with the request contribute to members of the group being treated as second-class citizens or serve to reassure dominant groups of their superiority? Could limiting audience exposure to diverse forms of self-presentation contribute to perpetuating audience preferences that result in part from a lack of familiarity or from bias? If the overall interests of the individual, the identity group, and the public outweigh those of the media organization, the request to change should not be made.

(7) If a decision is made to request a change, managers should discuss with the journalist the rationale for doing so, encourage feedback, and be prepared to reconsider the request if the discussion produces information about any considerations (including those listed above) that warrant doing so.

Managers who follow this protocol can help promote the normalization and acceptance of a broad range of appearance attributes and modes of speaking and can potentially attract new audiences. Writing about the importance of diverse public radio hosts, Eric Nuzum notes that "you can't expect new audiences to have a sense of belonging unless they hear themselves in such high-profile positions." Directing his comments to public radio leaders, he writes, "Those who speak represent the listeners your programming will attract, so challenge yourself to make other choices than what's comfortable and familiar."[29]

When Richard, formerly of NPR, did interviews for an episode of *Code Switch*, she commonly heard people say, "I listen to NPR to know how to speak correctly." This affirmed to her that public media "has a responsibility to put more accents on air to normalize them so listeners don't consider them distracting."[30] Radio journalist Elena Rivera says that if public radio is "trying to reach a bigger part of our community, then we need to include people on the radio who don't fit the traditional definition of a good talker."[31]

News organizations should trust that audiences will accept diverse ways of presenting when the content is good and should challenge them to do so. Voice coach Viki Merrick says that listeners may be critical of a journalist's voice at first, but "once the content takes over, if it's interesting, you don't care so much about whatever the heck was distracting you."[32] Broadcast journalism professor Jill Olmsted notes that Ira Glass is "such a masterful storyteller that he connects to listeners even with a very nasal voice."[33] Talent coach and consultant Valerie

Geller's thesis is that "if the story is compelling, the audience doesn't care about a speech impediment, a bad voice, or an accent. But if you haven't engaged me, I'm going to pick at how you look, your accent, or your breathing."[34] Kumanyika believes that when it comes to speech diversity, "listeners have to catch up. We need to educate audiences to listen [to a range of voices and delivery styles] so that we can meet the social justice challenges of our time."[35] For example, instead of attempting to reduce accents, efforts should be directed at modifying people's perspectives on accents.[36] Broadcast journalist Tahera Rahman adds: "I think you don't give your audience enough credit when you just perpetuate the same thing that you do day in and day out. The news should reflect the diversity of our communities and our communities are changing, becoming more diverse, and newsrooms need to adapt."[37]

Some who run newsrooms have adapted. When Hove worked in television news, an executive producer who had been a news director pulled him aside and said, "We hired you because we like you. We want you to be you—that's what we're paying for. Let us deal with any criticism." Hove says that was "the most affirming thing anyone had ever said to me in my career." No longer feeling the need to perform neutrally to hide his sexual orientation, he "built a connection with the audience that I never had in any other job."[38]

Hove's experience illustrates why newsroom leaders should embrace diverse forms of self-presentation and stop perpetuating the myth of performance neutrality. Encouraging journalists to speak with a "neutral" accent, flatten distinctive aspects of their voice, appear unclassifiable, dress conventionally, and maintain a consistent appearance has unjustifiably led many journalists to cover. Those who educate, advise, train, and manage journalists can take steps, such as those outlined in this book, to lessen the problem. If they do so, the news industry will become more inclusive and will better serve the public.

Acknowledgments

I want to recognize and thank the following people for helping make this project a reality: first and foremost, everyone who took part in interviews, particularly the current and former journalists who entrusted me with their stories and contributed key insights. Nicole Solano at Rutgers University Press showed interest in my project early on and guided this first-time book author every step along the way. Kate Babbitt provided excellent copy editing. The reviewers gave outstanding feedback that improved this book immensely.

Towson University offered the semester-long sabbatical that gave me the runway I needed to get this project off the ground. My colleagues at Towson provided moral support, especially Beth Haller, who sparked my interest in media and disability, and Pallavi Guha, who guided me through the publishing process. Joyce Garczynski at Towson, James Baxter and Michael Henry at the University of Maryland, and the team at University of Michigan's Bentley Historical Library gave me invaluable research assistance. The work and guidance of my colleagues at other institutions inspired me and helped shape this book. Michael Koliska, a good friend on whom I leaned heavily, introduced me to important research and helped me sharpen my argument. Jacob L. Nelson and Magda Konieczna provided helpful mentorship.

Friends outside the academy, including Alex Sussman, Ken Sharp, Adam Rittenberg, Adam Smith, and Alex Seeskin, gave support and feedback. My wife, Mara Gandal-Powers, and my two sons, Jonah and Zeke Powers, lifted me up, made me laugh, and gave me space to work a few too many nights and weekends. My in-laws, Jan and Larry Gandal, provided encouragement. My aunt, Carolyn Brown, read several drafts and supported me as always. My mom, Linda Powers, shared timely articles and candid feedback. Finally, my dad, Howard Powers, helped me in innumerable ways throughout this process.

Notes

Introduction

1 Elia Powers, "Seeking 'Skilled, Poised, Fluent' Verbal Communicators: Aesthetic Labor and Signaling in Journalism Job Advertisements," *Newspaper Research Journal* 42, no. 1 (2021): 12–28, https://doi.org/10.1177/0739532921989884.

2 Elia Powers, "The Journalist's Speech: A Phenomenological Study of Stuttering in the Newsroom," *Journalism Studies* 21, no. 9 (2020): 1243–1260, https://doi.org/10.1080/1461670X.2020.1738953.

3 Many interviewees held several roles, which is why this total is greater than the number of participants. For brevity, I will refer to voice/speech coaches as voice coaches when referring to the profession.

4 Michael Quinn Patton, *Qualitative Research & Evaluation Methods*, 3rd ed. (Thousand Oaks, CA: Sage, 2002).

5 Patton, *Qualitative Research*.

6 Jonathan A. Smith, Paul Flowers, and Michael Larkin, *Interpretative Phenomenological Analysis: Theory, Research, and Method* (Thousand Oaks, CA: Sage, 2009).

7 Jonathan A. Smith and Mike Osborn, "Interpretative Phenomenological Analysis as a Useful Methodology for Research on the Lived Experience of Pain," *British Journal of Pain* 9, no. 1 (2015): 41.

8 Smith, Flowers, and Larkin, *Interpretative Phenomenological Analysis*.

Chapter 1 Covering (on) the News

1 Deion Broxton, interview with the author, May 30, 2021.

2 Broxton, interview with the author.

3 Megan Figueroa and Carrie Gillon, "I Ain't Messing with You," *The Vocal Fries Pod*, June 28, 2021, https://vocalfriespod.com/.

4 Cathy Runnels, interview with the author, December 20, 2021.

5 Broxton, interview with the author.

6 Broxton, interview with the author.

7 Deion Broxton (@DeionBroxton), "A year later. I get tired of talking about this video." Twitter, March 25, 2021, https://twitter.com/DeionBroxton/status /1375082165122297859.

8 Broxton, interview with the author.

9 Matt Carlson, *Journalistic Authority* (New York: Columbia University Press, 2017).

10 Kimberly Meltzer, *TV News Anchors and Journalistic Tradition: How Journalists Adapt to Technology* (New York: Peter Lang, 2010).

11 Eduardo Bonilla-Silva, Carla Goar, and David G. Embrick, "When Whites Flock Together: The Social Psychology of White Habitus," *Critical Sociology* 32, no. 2–3 (2006): 229–253.

12 Michael Morris, "Standard White: Dismantling White Normativity," *California Law Review* 104, no. 4 (2016): 952.

13 Bonilla-Silva, Goar, and Embrick, "When Whites Flock Together," 231.

14 Pamela Newkirk, *Within the Veil: Black Journalists, White Media* (New York: New York University Press, 2000), 72.

15 Pamela Newkirk, *Diversity, Inc.: The Failed Promise of a Billion-Dollar Business* (New York: Bold Type Books, 2019).

16 Bob Papper and Keren Henderson, "Minority Representation Increases, but Still Lags General Population," RTDNA, November 16, 2022, https://www.rtdna.org /news/minority-representation-increases-but-still-lags-general-population.

17 Carlos Alamo-Pastrana and William Hoynes, "Racialization of News: Constructing and Challenging Professional Journalism as 'White Media,'" *Humanity & Society* 44, no. 1 (2020), 69.

18 Laura Garbes, "'I Just Don't Hear It': How Whiteness Dilutes Voices of Color at Public Radio Stations," *The American Prospect*, August 18, 2020, https://prospect .org/culture/i-just-dont-hear-it-voices-of-color-npr-public-radio/.

19 Celeste Headlee, "An Anti-Racist Future: A Vision and Plan for the Transformation of Public Media," *Medium*, January 18, 2021, https://celesteheadlee.medium .com/an-anti-racist-future-a-vision-and-plan-for-the-transformation-of-public -media-224149ab37e6.

20 Katherine D. Kinzler, *How You Say It: Why You Talk the Way You Do and What It Says about You* (New York: Houghton Mifflin Harcourt, 2020), x.

21 Kinzler, *How You Say It*.

22 Newkirk, *Within the Veil*.

23 Newkirk, *Within the Veil*, 80.

24 Libby Lewis, *The Myth of Post-Racialism in Television News* (New York: Routledge, 2016), 1.

25 Alamo-Pastrana and Hoynes, "Racialization of News"; Nikki Usher, *News for the Rich, White, and Blue: How Place and Power Distort American Journalism* (New York: Columbia University Press, 2021).

26 Alamo-Pastrana and Hoynes, "Racialization of News"; Garbes, "'I Just Don't Hear It.'"

27 Erving Goffman, *Stigma: Notes on the Management of Spoiled Identity* (New York: Simon & Schuster, 1963).

28 Goffman, *Stigma*.

29 Goffman, *Stigma*.

30 Patrick W. Corrigan and Deepa Rao, "On the Self-Stigma of Mental Illness: Stages, Disclosure, and Strategies for Change," *Canadian Journal of Psychiatry* 57, no. 8 (2012): 464–469.

31 Goffman, *Stigma*.

32 Kenji Yoshino, *Covering: The Hidden Assault on Our Civil Rights* (New York: Random House, 2007), Kindle.

33 Yoshino, *Covering*.

34 Russell K. Robinson, "Uncovering Covering," *Northwestern University Law Review* 101 (2007): 1835.

35 Kenji Yoshino and Christie Smith, "Uncovering Talent: A New Model of Inclusion," Deloitte, last modified December 6, 2013, https://www2.deloitte.com/content/dam/Deloitte/us/Documents/about-deloitte/us-about-deloitte-uncovering-talent-a-new-model-of-inclusion.pdf.

36 Yoshino and Smith, "Uncovering Talent."

37 Yoshino and Smith, "Uncovering Talent."

38 Joanne Stephane, Heather McBride Leef, Sameen Affaf, Kenji Yoshino, and David Glasgow, "Uncovering Culture: A Call to Action for Leaders. *Deloitte and the Meltzer Center for Diversity, Inclusion, and Belonging*. Last modified November 14, 2023, https://www2.deloitte.com/content/dam/Deloitte/us/Documents/about-deloitte/dei/us-uncovering-culture-a-call-to-action-for-leaders.pdf?dl=1.

39 Yoshino and Smith, "Uncovering Talent." The 2023 survey did not include data on different forms of covering.

40 Vanessa Ruiz, interview with the author, June 3, 2021.

41 Yoshino and Smith, "Uncovering Talent."

42 Theodore L. Glasser, "Professionalism and the Derision of Diversity: The Case of the Education of Journalists," *Journal of Communication* 42, no. 2 (1992): 132.

43 John Hendrickson, interview with the author, June 3, 2021.

44 Gretel Kahn, interview with the author, January 14, 2022.

45 Carolyn Kane, interview with the author, January 18, 2022.

46 Hanna Pitkin, *The Concept of Representation* (Berkeley: University of California Press, 1967).

47 Amy Jo Coffey, "Challenging Assumptions about Ownership and Diversity: An Examination of US Local On-Air Television Newsroom Personnel," *Howard Journal of Communications* 24, no. 2 (2013): 277–305.

48 Robert J. Richardson, "Local TV Newsroom Diversity: Race and Gender of Newscasters and Their Managers," *Journal of Broadcasting & Electronic Media* 66, no. 5 (2022): 823–842.

49 Maria Hinojosa (@Maria_Hinojosa), "What concerned me also was so many who said they didn't hear their real voices," Twitter, January 29, 2015, https://x.com/Maria_Hinojosa/status/560944879011115008?.

50 "Stephanie Foo," *Transom Review* 16, no. 1 (2016): 1–7, https://transom.org/wp-content/uploads/2016/05/StephanieFoo_review.pdf.

51 James Hamilton, *All the News that's Fit to Sell: How the Market Transforms Information into News* (Princeton, NJ: Princeton University Press, 2004).

52 Mary Angela Bock, "Smile More: A Subcultural Analysis of the Anchor/Consultant Relationship in Local Television News Operations" (PhD diss., Drake University, 1986).

53 John Hartley, *Understanding News* (New York: Routledge, 2013).

54 Catherine Stifter, interview with the author, June 7, 2021.

55 Sia Nyorkor, interview with the author, January 22, 2022.

56 Broxton, interview with the author.

57 Joe Wertz, interview with the author, June 10, 2021.

58 Viki Merrick, interview with the author, January 14, 2022.

59 Diana Opong, interview with the author, December 21, 2021.
60 Dan Bobkoff, interview with the author, January 17, 2022.
61 Elia Powers, "The Journalist's Speech: A Phenomenological Study of Stuttering in the Newsroom," *Journalism Studies* 21, no. 9 (2020): 1243–1260, https://doi.org/10.1080/1461670X.2020.1738953.

Chapter 2   Performance, Form, and the Myth of Neutrality

1 Jeannette Reyes (@msnewslady), "Even anchors get sick of the anchor voice," TikTok, March 22, 2021, https://www.tiktok.com/@msnewslady/video/6942532268082597125.
2 Jeannette Reyes(@msnewslady), "A mix of Rhode Island . . . plus a little bit of Rosie Perez," TikTok, December 28, 2020, https://www.tiktok.com/@msnewslady/video/6910279401355742470.
3 Viktoria Capek (@viktoriaacapek), "Does a 'news voice' count as a customer service voice?," TikTok, October 30, 2020, https://www.tiktok.com/@viktoriaacapek/video/6889458865449012485.
4 Viktoria Capek, interview with the author, December 15, 2021.
5 Kimberly Meltzer, *TV News Anchors and Journalistic Tradition: How Journalists Adapt to Technology* (New York: Peter Lang, 2010).
6 Stuart Hyde and Dina A. Ibrahim, *Television and Radio Announcing* (New York: Routledge, 2017), 165.
7 Jonathan Kern, *Sound Reporting: The NPR Guide to Audio Journalism and Production* (Chicago: University of Chicago Press, 2012).
8 Meltzer, *TV News Anchors.*
9 Kern, *Sound Reporting.*
10 Erving Goffman, *The Presentation of Self in Everyday Life* (New York: Doubleday, 1959).
11 Renata Sago, interview with the author, December 28, 2021.
12 Dmae Lo Roberts, interview with the author, January 7, 2022.
13 Goffman, *The Presentation of Self in Everyday Life.*
14 Joe Atkinson, "Performance Journalism: A Three-Template Model of Television News," *International Journal of Press/Politics* 16, no. 1 (2011): 102–129.
15 Erving Goffman, *Forms of Talk* (Philadelphia: University of Pennsylvania Press, 1981), 241.
16 Goffman, *Forms of Talk*, 241.
17 Goffman, *Forms of Talk*, 198.
18 Kristoffer Holt, "Authentic Journalism? A Critical Discussion about Existential Authenticity in Journalism Ethics," *Journal of Mass Media Ethics* 27, no. 1 (2012): 3.
19 Mark Deuze, *Media Work* (New York: Wiley, 2007).
20 Deuze, *Media Work.*
21 Paul Horwitz, "Uncovering Identity," *Michigan Law Review* 105, no. 6 (2007): 1283.
22 Deborah Cameron, "Language: Designer Voices," *Critical Quarterly* 43, no. 4 (2004): 81–85.
23 Martin Montgomery, "Defining 'Authentic Talk,'" *Discourse Studies* 3, no. 4 (2001): 397–405.
24 Norman Fairclough, *Discourse and Social Change* (Cambridge, MA: Polity Press, 1992).
25 Montgomery, "Defining 'Authentic Talk."
26 Emily Gasser et al., "Production, Perception, and Communicative Goals of American Newscaster Speech," *Language in Society* 48, no. 2 (2019): 233–259.

27 Rob Rosenthal, interview with the author, December 15, 2021.

28 George Bodarky, interview with the author, June 14, 2021.

29 Capek, interview with the author.

30 Chenjerai Kumanyika, interview with the author, June 23, 2021.

31 Michelle Li, interview with the author, February 23, 2022.

32 Kenji Yoshino, *Covering: The Hidden Assault on Our Civil Rights* (New York: Random House, 2007), Kindle.

33 Patric Raemy, "A Theory of Professional Identity in Journalism: Connecting Discursive Institutionalism, Socialization, and Psychological Resilience Theory," *Communication Theory* 31, no. 4 (2020): 841–861.

34 Goffman, *The Presentation of Self*.

35 Goffman, *The Presentation of Self*.

36 Llewellyn Negrin, *Appearance and Identity: Fashioning the Body in Postmodernity* (New York: Palgrave Macmillan, 2008).

37 Rob Drummond, interview with the author, June 25, 2021.

38 Rosenthal, interview with the author.

39 Liana Van Nostrand, "Sounding Like a Reporter—and a Real Person, Too," *NPR Opinion*, August 7. 2019, https://www.npr.org/sections/publiceditor/2019/08/07/749060986/sounding-like-a-reporter-and-a-real-person-too.

40 Agata Gluszek and John F. Dovidio, "The Way They Speak: A Social Psychological Perspective on the Stigma of Nonnative Accents in Communication," *Personality and Social Psychology Review* 14, no. 2 (2010): 214–237.

41 Allan A. Metcalf, *How We Talk: American Regional English Today* (Boston: Houghton Mifflin Harcourt, 2000).

42 Katherine D. Kinzler, *How You Say It: Why You Talk the Way You Do and What It Says about You* (New York: Houghton Mifflin Harcourt, 2020), xi.

43 Devon W. Carbado and Mitu Gulati, *Acting White? Rethinking Race in "Post-Racial" America* (New York: Oxford University Press, 2013).

44 Russell K. Robinson, "Uncovering Covering," *Northwestern University Law Review* 101 (2007): 1809–1815.

45 Devon W. Carbado and Mitu Gulati, "Working Identity," *Cornell Law Review* 85, no. 5 (2000): 1259–1308.

46 Carbado and Gulati, *Acting White?*

47 Brittany Noble, interview with the author, June 17, 2021.

48 Libby Lewis, *The Myth of Post-Racialism in Television News* (New York: Routledge, 2016), 2.

49 Amina Dunn, "Younger, College-Educated Black Americans Are Most Likely to Feel Need to 'Code-Switch,'" *Pew Research Center*, September 24, 2019, https://www.pewresearch.org/fact-tank/2019/09/24/younger-college-educated-black-americans-are-most-likely-to-feel-need-to-code-switch/.

50 "Chenjerai Kumanyika," *Transom Review* 15, no. 2 (2015), para. 2, https://transom.org/wp-content/uploads/2015/01/Chenjerai-Kumanyika-Review.pdf.

51 Dunn, "Younger, College-Educated Black Americans."

52 Carbado and Gulati, *Acting White?*

53 Tahera Rahman, interview with the author, January 16, 2022.

54 Jorge Valencia, interview with the author, December 22, 2021.

55 Sia Nyorkor, interview with the author, January 22, 2022.

56 Gloria Riviera, interview with the author, January 19, 2022.

57 Li, interview with the author.

58 Li, interview with the author.

59 Li, interview with the author.

60 Brian Montopoli, "All Things Considerate: How NPR Makes Tavis Smiley Sound Like Linda Wertheimer," *Washington Monthly* 35, no. 1/2 (2001), https://washingtonmonthly.com/2001/01/01/all-things-considerate/.

61 Diana Opong, interview with the author, December 21, 2021.

62 Tanya Ott, interview with the author, June 17, 2021.

63 "Chenjerai Kumanyika," para. 19.

64 Kumanyika, interview with the author.

65 Kevin G. Barnhurst and John Nerone, *The Form of News: A History* (New York: Guilford Press, 2002).

66 Theodore L. Glasser, "The Aesthetics of News," *ETC: A Review of General Semantics* 37 (1980): 238–247.

67 Tammy L. Anderson et al., "Aesthetic Capital: A Research Review on Beauty Perks and Penalties," *Sociology Compass* 4, no. 8 (2010): 564–575.

68 Pierre Bourdieu, *The Logic of Practice* (Stanford, CA: Stanford University Press, 1990).

69 Pierre Bourdieu, Distinction: A Social Critique of the Judgement of Taste (Cambridge, MA: Harvard University Press, 2018).

70 Anderson et al., "Aesthetic Capital," 572.

71 Laura Vonk, "Peer Feedback in Aesthetic Labour: Forms, Logics and Responses," *Cultural Sociology* 15, no. 2 (2021), https://doi.org/10.1177/1749975520962368.

72 Bourdieu, *The Logic of Practice.*

73 Chris Warhurst and Dennis Nickson, *Aesthetic Labour* (Thousand Oaks, CA: Sage, 2020).

74 Chris Warhurst and Dennis Nickson, *Looking Good, Sounding Right* (London: Industrial Society, 2001).

75 Chris Warhurst et al., "Aesthetic Labour in Interactive Service Work: Some Case Study Evidence from the 'New' Glasgow," *Service Industries Journal* 20, no. 3 (2000): 1–18.

76 Dennis Nickson et al., "Bringing in the Excluded? Aesthetic Labour, Skills and Training in the 'New' Economy," *Journal of Education and Work* 16, no. 2 (2003): 185–203.

77 Nickson et al., "Bringing in the Excluded?"

78 Kjerstin Elmen-Gruys, "Properly Attired, Hired, or Fired: Aesthetic Labor and Social Inequality" (PhD diss., University of California, Los Angeles, 2014).

79 Deepti Bhargava and Petra Theunissen, "The Future of PR Is 'Fantastic,' 'Friendly' and 'Funny': Occupational Stereotypes and Symbolic Capital in Entry-Level Job Advertisements," *Public Relations Review* 45, no. 4 (2019): article 101822, https://doi.org/10.1016/j.pubrev.2019.101822.

80 Ashley Mears, "Aesthetic Labor for the Sociologies of Work, Gender, and Beauty," *Sociology Compass* 8, no. 12 (2014): 1330–1343.

81 Christine L. Williams and Catherine Connell, "'Looking Good and Sounding Right': Aesthetic Labor and Social Inequality in the Retail Industry," *Work & Occupations* 37, no. 3 (2010): 349–377, https://doi.org/10.1177/073088841037374.

82 Elmen-Gruys, "Properly Attired, Hired, or Fired."

83 Barnhurst and Nerone, *The Form of News.*

84 Barnhurst and Nerone, *The Form of News,* 9.

85 Matt Carlson, *Journalistic Authority* (New York: Columbia University Press, 2017).

86 Marcel Broersma, "Journalism as Performative Discourse: The Importance of Form and Style in Journalism," in *Journalism and Meaning-Making: Reading the Newspaper,* ed. Verica Rupar, 15–35 (New York: Hampton Press, 2010).

87 Carlson, *Journalistic Authority*.

88 Sora Newman, interview with the author, January 10, 2022.

89 Sally Herships, interview with the author, January 11, 2022.

90 Samantha Warhurst et al., "Acoustic Characteristics of Male Commercial and Public Radio Broadcast Voices," *Journal of Voice* 27, no. 5 (2013): e1–7, https://doi .org/10.1016/j.jvoice.2013.04.012.

91 Antoinette Lattouf, interview with the author, August 23, 2021.

92 Paul J. DiMaggio and Walter W. Powell, "The Iron Cage Revisited: Institutional Isomorphism and Collective Rationality in Organizational Fields," *American Sociological Review* 48, no. 2 (1983): 147–160.

93 Barnhurst and Nerone, *The Form of News*, 3.

94 Barnhurst and Nerone, *The Form of News*.

95 Alfredo Cramerotti, *Aesthetic Journalism: How to Inform without Informing* (Bristol, UK: Intellect Books, 2009).

96 Markus Ojala, "Is the Age of Impartial Journalism Over? The Neutrality Principle and Audience (Dis)Trust in Mainstream News," *Journalism Studies* 22, no. 15 (2021): 2042–2060.

97 Sandrine Boudana, "Impartiality Is Not Fair: Toward an Alternative Approach to the Evaluation of Content Bias in News Stories," *Journalism* 17, no. 5 (2016): 600–618.

98 Danielle Deavours, "Written All over Their Faces: Neutrality and Nonverbal Expression in Sandy Hook Coverage," *Electronic News* 14, no. 3 (2020): 123–142.

99 Renita Coleman and H. Denis Wu, "More than Words Alone: Incorporating Broadcasters' Nonverbal Communication into the Stages of Crisis Coverage Theory—Evidence from September 11th," *Journal of Broadcasting & Electronic Media* 50, no. 1 (2006): 1–17.

100 Samuel B. Gould and Sidney Diamond, *Training the Local Announcer* (New York: Longmans, Green and Co., 1950).

101 Reeves Wiedeman, "Ambiguously Genuine," *New Yorker*, November 10, 2013, para. 5, https://www.newyorker.com/magazine/2013/11/18/ambiguously-genuine.

102 Gretel Kahn, interview with the author, January 14, 2022.

103 Metcalf, *How We Talk*.

104 Don Champion, interview with the author, June 3, 2021.

105 Kim Fox, interview with the author, June 21, 2021.

106 Gabrielle Jones, interview with the author, June 17, 2021.

107 Catherine Stifter, interview with the author, June 7, 2021.

108 Stephanie Foo, interview with the author, June 25, 2021.

109 Chenjerai Kumanyika, "Challenging the Whiteness of Public Radio," *Code Switch*, NPR, January 29, 2015, https://www.npr.org/sections/codeswitch/2015/01/29 /382437460/challenging-the-whiteness-of-public-radio.

110 Harrison Hove, interview with the author, August 17, 2023.

111 Ron Powers, *The Newscasters* (New York: St. Martin's Press, 1977).

112 Jack W. Mitchell, *Listener Supported: The Culture and History of Public Radio* (Westport, CT: Praeger, 2005).

113 Lewis, *The Myth of Post-Racialism in Television News*.

114 Lewis, *The Myth of Post-Racialism in Television News*.

115 Lewis Wallace, "Objectivity Is Dead, and I'm OK with It," *Medium*, January 27, 2017, paras. 3–7, https://medium.com/@lewispants/objectivity-is-dead-and-im-okay -with-it-7fd2b4b5c58f.

116 Michael Morris, "Standard White: Dismantling White Normativity," *California Law Review* 104, no. 4 (2016): 949–978.

117 Wesley Lowery, "A Reckoning over Objectivity, Led by Black Journalists," *New York Times*, June 23, 2020, https://www.nytimes.com/2020/06/23/opinion/objectivity-black-journalists-coronavirus.html.

118 Tonya Mosley, "The Neutrality vs. Objectivity Game Ends," Nieman Foundation, January 5, 2020, https://www.niemanlab.org/2020/01/the-neutrality-vs-objectivity-game-ends/.

119 Wallace, "Objectivity Is Dead," paras. 3–7.

120 Lea Hellmueller, Tim P. Vos, and Mark A. Poepsel, "Shifting Journalistic Capital? Transparency and Objectivity in the Twenty-First Century," *Journalism Studies* 14, no. 3 (2013): 287–304.

Chapter 3   Learning How to Perform

1 Deion Broxton, interview with the author, May 30, 2021.

2 Sora Newman, interview with the author, January 10, 2022.

3 Thomas Hanitzsch and Tim P. Vos, "Journalistic Roles and the Struggle over Institutional Identity: The Discursive Constitution of Journalism," *Communication Theory* 27, no. 2 (2017): 115–135, https://doi.org/10.1111/comt.12112.

4 Barbie Zelizer, *Covering the Body: The Kennedy Assassination, the Media, and the Shaping of Collective Memory* (Chicago: University of Chicago Press, 1992).

5 Zelizer, *Covering the Body*.

6 Barbie Zelizer, "Journalists as Interpretive Communities," *Critical Studies in Media Communication* 10, no. 3 (1993): 219–237.

7 Kimberly Meltzer, *TV News Anchors and Journalistic Tradition: How Journalists Adapt to Technology* (New York: Peter Lang, 2010).

8 Wolfgang Donsbach, "Journalism as the New Knowledge Profession and Consequences for Journalism Education," *Journalism* 15, no. 6 (2014): 661–677.

9 Fredric M. Jablin, "Organizational Entry, Assimilation, and Disengagement/Exit," in *The New Handbook of Organizational Communication: Advances in Theory, Research, and Methods*, ed. F. M. Jablin and J. Putnam (Thousand Oaks, CA: Sage, 2001), 732–818.

10 Warren Breed, "Social Control in the Newsroom: A Functional Analysis," *Social Forces* 33, no. 4 (1955): 326–335, https://doi.org/10.2307/2573002.

11 Albert Bandura, *Social Learning Theory* (Englewood Cliffs, NJ: Prentice Hall, 1977).

12 Michael C. Keith, *Broadcast Voice Performance* (Boston: Focal Press, 1989).

13 Don Champion, interview with the author, June 3, 2021.

14 Whitney Miller, interview with the author, February 14, 2022.

15 Sia Nyorkor, interview with the author, January 22, 2022.

16 Diana Opong, interview with the author, December 21, 2021.

17 Noor Tagouri, interview with the author, January 19, 2022.

18 Viktoria Capek, interview with the author, December 15, 2021.

19 Jana Shortal, interview with the author, February 14, 2022.

20 Vanessa Ruiz, interview with the author, June 3, 2021.

21 Antoinette Lattouf, interview with the author, August 23, 2021.

22 Elia Powers, "The Journalist's Speech: A Phenomenological Study of Stuttering in the Newsroom," *Journalism Studies* 21, no. 9 (2020): 1243–1260, https://doi.org/10.1080/1461670X.2020.1738953.

23 Powers, "The Journalist's Speech." Journalists interviewed for this study are not named because they were promised confidentiality.

24 Khalon Richard, interview with the author, March 13, 2023.

25 Huo Jingnan, interview with the author, March 13, 2023.

26 Dorothy Tucker, interview with the author, January 8, 2022.

27 Dana Adams, interview with the author, January 11, 2022.

28 Carolyn Kane, interview with the author, January 18, 2022.

29 Brittany Noble, interview with the author, June 17, 2021.

30 Shortal, interview with the author.

31 Lattouf, interview with the author.

32 Katherine D. Kinzler, *How You Say It: Why You Talk the Way You Do and What It Says about You* (New York: Houghton Mifflin Harcourt, 2020).

33 Sally Prosser, interview with the author, June 7, 2021.

34 Marilyn Pittman, interview with the author, June 21, 2021.

35 George Bodarky, interview with the author, June 14, 2021.

36 Javier E. Gómez, interview with the author, September 1, 2021.

37 Michelle Faust Raghavan, interview with the author, December 17, 2021.

38 Dan Bobkoff, interview with the author, January 17, 2022.

39 Ann Utterback, interview with the author, June 7, 2021.

40 Kerry Thompson and Erin Slomski-Pritz, "50 and Forward: An Anniversary Celebration of NPR," podcast, NPR, April 30, 2021, https://www.npr.org/2021/04/30/991424624/fifty-and-forward-an-anniversary-celebration-of-npr.

41 Terry Gross, "'It Was Just Thrilling': 2 NPR Founders Remember the First Days, 50 Years Ago," excerpt from *Fresh Air*, NPR, April 28, 2021, https://www.npr.org/2021/04/28/991268881/it-was-just-thrilling-2-npr-founders-remember-the-first-days-50-years-ago.

42 "Ira Glass," *Here's the Thing*, podcast episode hosted by Alec Baldwin, WNYC Studios, November 23, 2014, https://www.wnycstudios.org/podcasts/heresthething/episodes/ira-glass-interview.

43 Teddy Wayne, "'NPR' Voice Has Taken over the Airwaves," *New York Times*, October 24, 2015, https://www.nytimes.com/2015/10/25/fashion/npr-voice-has-taken-over-the-airwaves.html.

44 "Ira Glass."

45 Alexis Soloski, "When Podcast Hosts Speak, What Do We Hear?," *New York Times*, February 25, 2021, https://www.nytimes.com/interactive/2021/02/25/arts/podcast-voice-sound.html.

46 Veronica Rueckert, *Outspoken: Why Women's Voices Get Silenced and How to Set Them Free* (New York: HarperCollins, 2019).

47 Kathy Tu, interview with the author, March 14, 2022.

48 Stephanie Foo, interview with the author, June 25, 2021.

49 Juleyka Lantigua, interview with the author, December 17, 2021.

50 Celeste Headlee, interview with the author, June 23, 2021.

51 Broxton, interview with the author.

52 Jenny Wiik, "Internal Boundaries: The Stratification of the Journalistic Collective," in *Boundaries of Journalism*, ed. Matt Carlson and Seth C. Lewis (New York: Routledge, 2015), 118–133.

53 Ann S. Utterback, *Broadcast Voice Handbook: How to Polish Your On-Air Delivery* (Santa Monica, CA: Bonus Books, Inc., 2005).

54 Prosser, interview with the author.

55 Jill Olmsted, interview with the author, June 29, 2021.

56 Wyatt Myskow and Piper Hansen, "Incoming Cronkite Dean Has Alleged History of Racist, Homophobic Comments toward Students," *State Press*, June 5, 2020,

https://www.statepress.com/article/2020/06/spcommunity-incoming-cronkite
-dean-has-alleged-history-of-racist-homophobic-comments-toward-students.

57 Kaitlyn McNab, "Black Newscasters Are Redefining What It Means To 'Look
Professional' On-Air," *Allure*, April 4, 2021, https://www.allure.com/story/black
-news-anchors-braids-natural-hair.

58 Tagouri, interview with the author.

59 Nyorkor, interview with the author.

60 Opong, interview with the author.

61 Powers, "The Journalist's Speech."

62 Tahera Rahman, interview with the author, January 16, 2022.

63 Michelle Li, interview with the author, February 23, 2022.

64 Gómez, interview with the author.

65 Marie Hardin and Ann Preston, "Inclusion of Disability Issues in News Reporting
Textbooks," *Journalism & Mass Communication Educator* 56, no. 2 (2001): 43–54.

66 Alan Stephenson, David Reese and Mary Beadle, *Broadcast Announcing Worktext:
A Media Performance Guide*, 4th ed. (London: Taylor & Francis, 2013).

67 Paul Chantler and Peter Stewart, *Basic Radio Journalism* (London: Routledge,
2013); Stuart Hyde and Dina A. Ibrahim, *Television and Radio Announcing* (New
York: Routledge, 2017).

68 Carl Hausman, Lewis B. O'Donnell, and Philip Benoit, *Announcing: Broadcast
Communicating Today* (Belmont, CA: Wadsworth Publishing, 2000).

69 Hausman, O'Donnell, and Benoit, *Announcing*.

70 Hausman, O'Donnell, and Benoit, *Announcing*.

71 Andrew Boyd, Peter Stewart, and Ray Alexander, *Broadcast Journalism: Techniques
of Radio and Television News*, 6th ed. (New York: Routledge, 2008).

72 Stephenson, Reese and Beadle, *Broadcast Announcing Worktext*.

73 Elia Powers and Beth Haller, "Journalism and Mass Communication Textbook
Representations of Verbal Media Skills: Implications for Students with Speech
Disabilities," *Journal of Media Literacy Education* 9, no. 2 (2017): 58–75.

74 Hyde and Ibrahim, *Television and Radio Announcing*, 57.

75 Stephenson, Reese and Beadle, *Broadcast Announcing Worktext*.

76 Gitte Gravengaard and Lene Rimestad, "Socializing Journalist Trainees in the
Newsroom," *Nordicom Review* 35, no. s1 (2014): 81–96, https://doi.org/10.2478/nor
-2014-0105.

77 Miller, interview with the author.

78 Rahman, interview with the author.

79 Opong, interview with the author.

80 Christopher Chávez, "When One Way of Speaking Dominates, Who Gets to Tell
Their Stories on Public Radio?," *Current*, June 25, 2020, https://current.org/2020
/06/when-one-way-of-speaking-dominates-who-gets-to-tell-their-stories-on-public
-radio/.

81 Gretel Kahn, interview with the author, January 14, 2022.

82 Rob Rosenthal, interview with the author, December 15, 2021.

83 Michael Spence, "Job Market Signaling," in *Uncertainty in Economics: Readings and
Exercises*, edited by Peter A. Diamond and Michael Rothschild (New York:
Academic Press, 1978), 281–306.

84 Deepti Bhargava and Petra Theunissen, "The Future of PR Is 'Fantastic,' 'Friendly'
and 'Funny': Occupational Stereotypes and Symbolic Capital in Entry-Level Job
Advertisements," *Public Relations Review* 45, no. 4 (2019): article 101822, https://doi
.org/10.1016/j.pubrev.2019.101822.

85 Elia Powers, "Seeking 'Skilled, Poised, Fluent' Verbal Communicators: Aesthetic Labor and Signaling in Journalism Job Advertisements," *Newspaper Research Journal* 42, no. 1 (2021): 12–28, https://doi.org/10.1177/0739532921989884.

86 Powers, "The Journalist's Speech."

87 Tagouri, interview with the author.

88 Rahman, interview with the author.

89 Broxton, interview with the author.

90 Broxton, interview with the author.

91 Cathy Runnels, interview with the author, December 20, 2021.

92 Valerie Belair-Gagnon, Avery E. Holton, and Oscar Westlund, "Space for the Liminal," *Media and Communication* 7, no. 4 (2019): 1–7.

93 Andrew Jacobs, "Novice Newscasters Get Voice Therapy," *New York Times*, June 16, 1997, https://www.nytimes.com/1997/06/16/business/novice-newscasters-get-voice -therapy.html.

94 Prosser, interview with the author.

95 Mary Chan, interview with the author, May 30, 2021.

96 Bodarky, interview with the author.

97 Ann S. Utterback, interview with the author, June 7, 2021

98 Prosser, interview with the author.

99 Dara Allen, interview with the author, June 29, 2021.

100 Runnels, interview with the author.

101 Pittman, interview with the author.

102 Bodarky, interview with the author.

103 Utterback, interview with the author.

104 Prosser, interview with the author.

105 Utterback, interview with the author.

106 Pittman, interview with the author.

107 Utterback, interview with the author.

108 Opong, interview with the author.

109 Libby Lewis, *The Myth of Post-Racialism in Television News* (New York: Routledge, 2016).

110 Gabrielle Jones, interview with the author, June 17, 2021.

111 Bodarky, interview with the author.

112 Stifter, interview with the author.

113 Jessica Hansen, interview with the author, June 17, 2021.

114 Pittman, interview with the author.

115 Utterback, interview with the author.

116 Hansen, interview with the author.

117 Ron Powers, *The Newscasters* (New York: St. Martin's Press, 1977), 30.

118 Craig Allen, "Discovering 'Joe Six Pack' Content in Television News: The Hidden History of Audience Research, News Consultants, and the Warner Class Model," *Journal of Broadcasting & Electronic Media* 49, no. 4 (2005): 363–382.

119 Johanna Steinmetz, "'Mr. Magic'—The TV Newscast Doctor," *New York Times*, October 12, 1975, https://www.nytimes.com/1975/10/12/archives/mr-magicthe-tv -newscast-doctor-mr-magicthe-newscast-doctor.html.

120 Craig Allen, *News Is People: The Rise of Local TV News and the Fall of News from New York* (Ames: Iowa State University Press, 2001).

121 Craig Allen, interview with the author, January 10, 2022.

122 Craig Allen, "Consultants: Role in Newsroom," in *The International Encyclopedia of Journalism Studies*, ed. T. P. Vos, F. Hanusch, D. Dimitrakopoulou, M.

Geertsema-Sligh, and A. Sehl (Wiley Online Library, 2019), 1–8, https://onlinelibrary.wiley.com/doi/abs/10.1002/9781118841570.iejs0223.

123 Tucker, interview with the author.

124 Barbara Allen-Rosser, interview with the author, January 26, 2022.

125 Allen-Rosser, interview with the author.

126 Li, interview with the author.

127 Nyorkor, interview with the author.

128 Lou Prato, "TV News Refrain: Talk to My Agent," *American Journalism Review* 18, no. 1 (1996): 56–57.

129 Liz Hart, interview with the author, June 17, 2021.

130 Kane, interview with the author.

131 Adams, interview with the author.

132 Adams, interview with the author.

133 Hart, interview with the author.

134 Kane, interview with the author.

135 Adams, interview with the author.

136 Broxton, interview with the author.

Chapter 4   The Influential Imagined Audience

1 Michelle Li, interview with the author, February 23, 2022.

2 Eric Nuzum, interview with the author, September 22, 2022.

3 Eden Litt, "Knock, Knock. Who's There? The Imagined Audience," *Journal of Broadcasting & Electronic Media* 56, no. 3 (2012): 330–345.

4 Juleyka Lantigua, interview with the author, December 17, 2021.

5 Libby Lewis, *The Myth of Post-Racialism in Television News* (New York: Routledge, 2015), 51.

6 Sherman P. Lawton, *Radio Speech* (Boston: Expression Company, 1932), 13.

7 Dwight DeWerth-Pallmeyer, *The Audience in the News* (New York: Routledge, 2013).

8 Lawton, *Radio Speech*, 14.

9 Litt, "Knock, Knock. Who's There?"

10 Herbert Gans, *Deciding What's News: A Study of CBS Evening News, NBC Nightly News, Newsweek, and Time* (New York: Pantheon Books, 1979); Ien Ang, *Desperately Seeking the Audience* (New York: Routledge, 1991), 48.

11 Jacob L. Nelson, *Imagined Audiences: How Journalists Perceive and Pursue the Public* (New York: Oxford University Press, 2021).

12 Anthony Nadler, *Making the News Popular: Mobilizing U.S. News Audiences* (Champaign: University of Illinois Press, 2016).

13 Nadler, *Making the News Popular*.

14 Sora Newman, interview with the author, January 10, 2022.

15 Rob Rosenthal, interview with the author, December 15, 2021.

16 Steve Olson, "Often Overlooked, Airchecking Is Essential to Keeping Public Radio's Audience," *Current*, April 14, 2016, https://current.org/2016/04/often-overlooked-airchecking-is-essential-to-keeping-public-radios-audience/.

17 Ang, *Desperately Seeking the Audience*, 48.

18 Shawn Shimpach, "Viewing," in *The Handbook of Media Audiences*, ed. Virginia Nightingale (Malden MA: Wiley-Blackwell), 75.

19 Virginia Nightingale, "Introduction," in *The Handbook of Media Audiences*, ed. Virginia Nightingale (Malden, MA: Wiley-Blackwell), 1–16.

20 Mark Coddington, Seth C. Lewis, and Valerie Belair-Gagnon, "The Imagined Audience for News: Where Does a Journalist's Perception of the Audience Come From?," *Journalism Studies* 22, no. 8 (2021): 1028–1046.

21 Joe Atkinson, "Performance Journalism: A Three-Template Model of Television News," *International Journal of Press/Politics* 16, no. 1 (2011): 102–129.

22 Claire Wolfe and Barbara Mitra, "Newsreaders as Eye Candy: The Hidden Agenda of Public Service Broadcasting," *Journalism Education* 1, no. 1 (2012): 92–99.

23 Ang, *Desperately Seeking the Audience*.

24 Ang, *Desperately Seeking the Audience*, 48.

25 Allen, *News Is People*.

26 Allen, *News Is People*.

27 Rick Houlberg, "The Audience Experience with Television News: A Qualitative Study," paper presented at 64th Annual Meeting of the Association for Education in Journalism, East Lansing, MI, August 9–11, 1981, https://eric.ed.gov/?id=ED204756.

28 Craig Allen, "Gender Breakthrough Fit for a Focus Group: The First Women Newscasters and Why They Arrived in Local TV News," *Journal of Media Economics* 8, no. 3 (1995): 154–162.

29 Lloyd Grove, "The Bland Leading the Bland," *Washington Post*, November 6, 1983, https://www.washingtonpost.com/archive/lifestyle/magazine/1983/11/06/the -bland-leading-the-bland/50e8264e-ade1-4a62-b074-4df404bfc53b/.

30 Jerry Jacobs, *Changing Channels: Issues and Realities in Television News* (Mountain View, CA: Mayfield Pub. Co., 1990).

31 Allen, *News Is People*, xiv.

32 Powers, *The Newscasters*.

33 Lee B. Becker, Susan L. Caudill, and Jeffrey W. Fruit, *The Training and Hiring of Journalists* (Norwood, NJ: Ablex Pub. Corp., 1987), 71.

34 Powers, *The Newscasters*, 186.

35 Powers, *The Newscasters*.

36 Allen, "Gender Breakthrough."

37 McHugh and Hoffman, Inc., "A Survey of Viewer Attitudes toward Television in the Austin Media Market: Winter 1979," Box 2, Austin, 1978–1979, McHugh and Hoffman Records, 1957–1999, Bentley Historical Library, University of Michigan, Ann Arbor (collection referred to hereafter as McHugh and Hoffman Records).

38 Allen, *News Is People*.

39 McHugh and Hoffman, "Study of Six Female Newscaster Candidates for WJBK TV's Detroit Late-Evening TV News Program," 1976, Box 2, Detroit, 1964-1979, McHugh and Hoffman Records.

40 Christine Craft, *Too Old, Too Ugly, and Not Deferential to Men* (Rocklin, CA: Prima Pub. and Communications, 1988), 66.

41 Craft, *Too Old, Too Ugly*, 66.

42 McHugh and Hoffman, "Television in the Greater Columbus Area," 1968, Box 4, Columbus, 1978–1968, McHugh and Hoffman Records.

43 McHugh and Hoffman, "Viewer Attitudes toward Chicago Television—Feb–March 71," 1971, Box 5, Chicago (cont'd.), 1963–1970, McHugh and Hoffman Records.

44 Robert E. Balon, Joseph C. Philport, and Charles F. Beadle, "How Sex and Race Affect Perceptions of Newscasters," *Journalism Quarterly* 55, no. 1 (1978): 160–164.

45 McHugh and Hoffman, "Viewer Attitudes toward Baltimore Televison," 1977, Box 2, Baltimore, 1968-1979, McHugh and Hoffman Records.

46 McHugh and Hoffman, "Viewer Attitudes toward Houston Television—Spring 1977," 1977, Box 11, Houston (cont.), 1964–1979, McHugh and Hoffman Records.

47 Gordon L. Patzer, "Source Credibility as a Function of Communicator Physical Attractiveness," *Journal of Business Research* 11, no. 2 (1983): 229–241.

48 Allen, *News Is People.*

49 Craig Allen, interview with the author, June 29, 2021.

50 McHugh and Hoffman, "Viewer attitudes toward Baltimore Televison," 1974, Box 2, Baltimore, 1968-1979, McHugh and Hoffman Records.

51 Keith Sanders and Michael Pritchett, "Some Influences of Appearance on Television Newscaster Appeal," *Journal of Broadcasting & Electronic Media* 15, no. 3 (1971): 293–302.

52 Kevin L. Hutchinson, "The Effects of Newscaster Gender and Vocal Quality on Perceptions of Homophily and Interpersonal Attraction," *Journal of Broadcasting & Electronic Media* 26, no. 1 (1982): 457–467.

53 McHugh and Hoffman, "Viewer Attitudes toward Houston Television."

54 McHugh and Hoffman, "Television in Greater New York: A Study in Viewer Attitudes—Early Winter 1964–5," 1965, Box 16, New York, 1963–1975, McHugh and Hoffman Records.

55 McHugh and Hoffman, "Essential Findings and Specific Recommendations for WBAL-TV," 1967, Box 2, Baltimore, 1968–1979, McHugh and Hoffman Records.

56 McHugh and Hoffman, "Attitudes toward Buffalo TV and Station Public Service Imagery—Fall 1971," 1971, Box 2, Buffalo, 1965–1978, McHugh and Hoffman Records.

57 McHugh and Hoffman, "Viewer Attitudes toward Houston television."

58 McHugh and Hoffman, "Viewer Attitudes toward New Haven-Hartford TV," 1979, Box 10, Hartford—New Haven, 1978–1979, McHugh and Hoffman Records.

59 McHugh and Hoffman, "Images of Memphis Television Stations, Newscasts and Newscast Personalities," 1973, Box 13, Memphis, 1976–1979, McHugh and Hoffman Records.

60 McHugh and Hoffman, "Viewer Attitudes toward Chicago Television."

61 McHugh and Hoffman, "Viewer Attitudes toward Chicago Television"; McHugh and Hoffman, "Viewer Attitudes toward Houston Television."

62 McHugh and Hoffman, "Viewer Attitudes toward Houston Television."

63 Balon, Philport, and Beadle, "Sex and Race Affect Perceptions of Newscasters."

64 Allen, *News Is People.*

65 McHugh and Hoffman, "Television in Greater New York."

66 Nissen et al., "Prosodic Elements for Content Delivery in Broadcast Journalism: A Quantitative Study of Vocal Pitch," *Electronic News* 14, no. 2 (2020): 63–77. This study also found that male broadcasters speak at higher mean pitch levels than men in the general population.

67 Hutchinson, "The Effects of Newscaster Gender."

68 Vernon Stone, "Attitudes toward Television Newswomen," *Journal of Broadcasting* 18, no. 1 (1973): 49–62.

69 McHugh and Hoffman, "Viewer Attitudes toward Baltimore Televison."

70 McHugh and Hoffman, "Viewer Attitudes toward Television in the Austin Media Market."

71 McHugh and Hoffman, "Viewer Attitudes toward Maury Povich and Valerie Coleman KGO-TV 5 P.M. Newscast," 1979, Box 22, San Francisco, 1969–1979 McHugh and Hoffman Records.

72 McHugh and Hoffman, "Viewer Attitudes toward Maury Povich and Valerie Coleman"; McHugh and Hoffman, "Viewer Attitudes toward Chicago Television."

73 McHugh and Hoffman, "Viewer attitudes toward Washington D.C. Television," 1973, McHugh and Hoffman Records.

74 McHugh and Hoffman, "Viewer Attitudes toward Television in the Austin Media Market."

75 McHugh and Hoffman, "Viewer Attitudes toward New Haven-Hartford TV."

76 McHugh and Hoffman, "Viewer Attitudes toward Houston television."

77 Houlberg, "The Audience Experience with Television News."

78 William L. Cathcart, "Viewer Needs and Desires in Television Newscasters," *Journal of Broadcasting & Electronic Media* 14, no. 1 (1969): 55–62.

79 Judee K. Burgoon, "Attributes of the Newscaster's Voice as Predictors of His Credibility," *Journalism Quarterly* 55, no. 2 (1978): 276–300.

80 Zijian Harrison Gong and James Eppler, "Exploring the Impact of Delivery Mistakes, Gender, and Empathic Concern on Source and Message Credibility," *Journalism Practice* 16, no. 8 (2022): 1653–1672.

81 Samantha Warhurst, Patricia McCabe, and Catherine Madill, "What Makes a Good Voice for Radio: Perceptions of Radio Employers and Educators," *Journal of Voice* 27, no. 2 (2013): 217–224.

82 Allen, interview with the author.

83 Michael Barthel, Elizabeth Grieco, and Elisa Shearer. "Older Americans, Black Adults and Americans with Less Education More Interested in Local News," Pew Research Center, August 14, 2019, https://www.pewresearch.org/journalism/2019 /08/14/older-americans-black-adults-and-americans-with-less-education-more -interested-in-local-news/; Katerina Eva Matsa, "Fewer Americans Rely on TV News; What Type They Watch Varies by Who They Are," Pew Research Center, January 5, 2018, https://www.pewresearch.org/short-reads/2018/01/05/fewer -americans-rely-on-tv-news-what-type-they-watch-varies-by-who-they-are/.

84 Maria Brann and Kimberly Leezer Himes, "Perceived Credibility of Male versus Female Television Newscasters," *Communication Research Reports* 27, no. 3 (2010): 243–252.

85 David Weibel, Bartholomäus Wissmath, and Rudolf Groner, "How Gender and Age Affect Newscasters' Credibility—An Investigation in Switzerland," *Journal of Broadcasting & Electronic Media* 52, no. 3 (2008): 481.

86 Barbara Mitra, Mike Webb, and Claire Wolfe, "Audience Responses to the Physical Appearance of Television Newsreaders," *Participations Journal of Audience & Reception Studies* 11, no. 2 (2014): 47–52; Wolfe and Mitra, "Newsreaders as Eye Candy."

87 Mitra, Webb, and Wolfe, "Audience Responses to Physical Appearance."

88 Mitra, Webb, and Wolfe, "Audience Responses to Physical Appearance"; Wolfe and Mitra, "Newsreaders as Eye Candy."

89 Maria Elizabeth Grabe and Lelia Samson, "Sexual Cues Emanating from the Anchorette Chair: Implications for Perceived Professionalism, Fitness for Beat, and Memory for News," *Communication Research* 38, no. 4 (2011): 471–496.

90 Mitchell V. Charnley, *News by Radio* (New York: Macmillan Co., 1948), 41.

91 Steve Olson, interview with the author, September 8, 2022.

92 Alan G. Stavitsky, "'Guys in Suits with Charts': Audience Research in US Public Radio," *Journal of Broadcasting & Electronic Media* 39, no. 2 (1995): 177–189.

93 Stavitsky, "Guys in Suits with Charts."

94 Stavitsky, "Guys in Suits with Charts."

95 Jack W. Mitchell, *Listener Supported: The Culture and History of Public Radio* (Westport, CT: Praeger, 2005).

96 Michael P. McCauley, *NPR: The Trials and Triumphs of National Public Radio* (New York: Columbia University Press, 2005), 99.

97 Abby Goldstein, interview with the author, September 13, 2022.

98 Nuzum, interview with the author.

99 Edward Schumacher-Matos, "Black, Latino, Asian and White: Diversity at NPR," NPR, April 10, 2012, https://www.npr.org/sections/publiceditor/2012/04/10 /150367888/black-latino-asian-and-white-diversity-at-npr.

100 Elahe Izadi, "Why Your Favorite New NPR Show Might Sound a Lot Like a Podcast," *Washington Post*, May 3, 2021, https://www.washingtonpost.com/lifestyle /media/npr-50th-anniversary-podcast-audience/2021/05/03/af0d49a0-a8fa-11eb -8d25-7b30e74923ea_story.html.

101 Maxie Jackson III, interview with the author, January 18, 2022.

102 Tyler Falk, "Drop in Younger Listeners Makes Dent in NPR News Audience," *Current*, October 16, 2015, https://current.org/2015/10/drop-in-younger-listeners -makes-dent-in-npr-news-audience/.

103 Nuzum, interview with the author.

104 Goldstein, interview with the author.

105 Olson, interview with the author.

106 Eric Nuzum, "To Serve Diverse Audiences, You Can't Walk the Walk Until You Know Where You Stand," *Current*, March 10, 2022, https://current.org/2022/03/to -serve-diverse-audiences-you-cant-walk-the-walk-until-you-know-where-you-stand/.

107 Khalon Richard, interview with the author, March 13, 2023.

108 Celeste Headlee, interview with the author, June 23, 2021.

109 Renata Sago, interview with the author, December 28, 2021.

110 Laura Garbes, "'I Just Don't Hear It': How Whiteness Dilutes Voices of Color at Public Radio Stations," *The American Prospect*, August 18, 2020, https://prospect .org/culture/i-just-dont-hear-it-voices-of-color-npr-public-radio/.

111 Garbes, "'I Just Don't Hear It.'"

112 Kris Vera-Phillips, interview with the author, August 15, 2023.

113 Chenjerai Kumanyika, interview with the author, June 23, 2021.

114 Nuzum, interview with the author.

115 John Baugh, "Linguistic Profiling," in *Black Linguistics: Language, Society and Politics in Africa and the Americas*, ed. Arnetha Ball, Sinfree Makoni, Geneva Smitherman, and Arthur K. Spears (London: Routledge, 2005), 155–168.

116 Agata Gluszek and John F. Dovidio, "The Way They Speak: A Social Psychological Perspective on the Stigma of Nonnative Accents in Communication," *Personality and Social Psychology Review* 14, no. 2 (2010): 214–237.

117 Shiri Lev-Ari and Boaz Keysar, "Why Don't We Believe Non-Native Speakers? The Influence of Accent on Credibility," *Journal of Experimental Social Psychology* 46, no. 6 (2010): 1093–1096.

118 Carrie Gillon, interview with the author, January 21, 2022.

119 Rob Drummond, interview with the author, June 25, 2021.

120 Megan Figueroa, interview with the author, January 21, 2022.

121 Gillon, interview with the author.

122 Leonardo Wanderley Lopes et al., "Accent and Television Journalism: Evidence for the Practice of Speech Language Pathologists and Audiologists," *CoDAS* 25, no. 5 (2013): 475–481.

123 Mark Jacob, "Medill Study Finds Preferences for Female Voices and Local Accents," *Medill Local News Initiative*, March 30, 2020, https://localnewsinitiative.northwestern

.edu/posts/2020/03/30/voice-accent-study/#:~:text=Lee%2C%20a%20professor%20
at%20Northwestern's,speaking%20with%20a%20local%20accent.

124 Jacob, "Medill Study Finds Preferences."

125 William Labov, *Dialect Diversity in America: The Politics of Language Change*
(Charlottesville: University of Virginia Press, 2012).

126 Tanya Ott-Fulmore, "Does This Microphone Make Me Sound White? An
Experiment Exploring Race Recognition and Source Credibility in Radio News"
(master's mmasteraster's thesis, University of Alabama, 2020), https://ir-api.ua.edu
/api/core/bitstreams/574cb7ea-883d-4e0f-ba54-04b78cddb3fe/content.

127 Edison Research, *The Infinite Dial 2021*, March 11, 2021, http://www.edisonresearch
.com/wp-content/uploads/2021/03/The-Infinite-Dial-2021.pdf.

128 Izadi, "Why Your Favorite New NPR Show Might Sound a Lot Like a Podcast."

129 Rund Abdelfatah et al., "Who Is NPR (For)?," *Throughline*, June 10, 2021, podcast,
https://www.npr.org/2021/06/07/1004079815/who-is-npr-for

130 Lantigua, interview with the author.

131 Lee Edwards, "Discourse, Credentialism and Occupational Closure in the Communications Industries: The Case of Public Relations in the UK," *European Journal of
Communication* 29, no. 3 (2014): 319–334.

132 Lantigua, interview with the author.

133 Stephanie J. Tobin and Rosanna E. Guadagno, "Why People Listen: Motivations
and Outcomes of Podcast Listening," *PloS One* 17, no. 4 (2022), https://doi.org/10
.1371/journal.pone.0265806.

134 Gans, *Deciding What's News*; Karin Wahl-Jorgensen, "The Construction of the
Public in Letters to the Editor: Deliberative Democracy and the Idiom of Insanity,"
Journalism 3, no. 2 (2002): 183–204.

135 Coddington, Lewis, and Belair-Gagnon, "The Imagined Audience for News"; Gina
Masullo Chen and Paromita Pain, "Journalists and Online Comments," Center for
Media Engagement, August 2016, https://mediaengagement.org/research/journalists
-and-online-comments.

136 Jackson, interview with the author.

137 Teri Finneman and Joy Jenkins, "Sexism on the Set: Gendered Expectations of TV
Broadcasters in a Social Media World," *Journal of Broadcasting & Electronic Media*
62, no. 3 (2018): 479–494.

138 Joe Wertz, interview with the author, June 10, 2021.

139 Terry Gross, "It's Impossible to Fit 'All Things' Ari Shapiro Does into This
Headline," *Fresh Air*, NPR, March 22, 2023, para. 16, https://www.npr.org/2023/03
/22/1165002548/ari-shapiro-npr-pink-martini-best-strangers-world.

140 Scott Detrow (@ScottDetrow), "I am a white dude on the radio, and no one has
ever tweeted at me critiquing my voice," Twitter, July 5, 2019, https://x.com
/scottdetrow/status/1147137833855062016?s=20.

141 Sally Herships, interview with the author, January 11, 2022.

142 Ira Glass, "545: Freedom Fries," *This American Life*, podcast, January 23, 2015,
https://www.thisamericanlife.org/545/if-you-dont-have-anything-nice-to-say-say-it
-in-all-caps/act-two-0.

143 Glass, "545: Freedom Fries."

144 Kris Vera-Phillips, interview with the author, August 15, 2023.

145 Molly Webster, "Don't Fear the Vocal Fry," *Werk It: The Podcast*, WNYC Studios,
June 7, 2015, https://www.wnycstudios.org/podcasts/werkit/episodes/werk-it
-owning-your-voice.

146 Gene Denby, "Talk American," *Code Switch*, podcast, NPR, August 8, 2018,
https://www.npr.org/transcripts/636442508.

147 Shereen Marisol Meraji, Gotham Artists. https://gothamartists.com/shereen-marisol-meraji/

148 Nick Quah, "It's Been a Minute with Sam Sanders," *Servant of Pod*, podcast, LAist, April 19, 2021, https://laist.com/podcasts/servant-of-pod/its-been-a-minute-with-sam-sanders.

149 Catherine Stifter, interview with the author, June 7, 2021.

150 Julie Mazziotta, "Meteorologist Claps Back at Body Shamer Who Tells Her to Cover Her 'Bulge': 'I Like My Body,'" *People*, October 16, 2019, https://people.com/health/meteorologist-claps-back-at-body-shamer-who-tells-her-to-cover-her-bulge-i-like-my-body/.

151 Tahera Rahman, interview with the author, January 16, 2022.

152 Terry Gross, "From Upspeak to Vocal Fry: Are We 'Policing' Young Women's Voices?" *Fresh Air*, NPR, July 23, 2015, para. 19, https://www.npr.org/transcripts/425608745

153 Ann S. Utterback, interview with the author, June 7, 2021.

154 Harrison Hove, interview with the author, August 17, 2023.

155 Goldstein, interview with the author.

156 Javier E. Gómez, interview with the author, September 1, 2021.

157 Mariam Sobh, interview with the author, September 2, 2022.

158 Whitney Miller, interview with the author, February 14, 2022.

159 Coddington, Lewis, and Belair-Gagnon, "The Imagined Audience for News."

160 Gans, *Deciding What's News*; James G. Robinson, "The Audience in the Mind's Eye: How Journalists Imagine Their Readers," *Columbia Journalism Review* 2019, June 26, https://www.cjr.org/tow_center_reports/how-journalists-imagine-their-readers.php.

161 Robinson, "The Audience in the Mind's Eye"; DeWerth-Pallmeyer, *The Audience in the News*; Coddington, Lewis, and Belair-Gagnon, "The Imagined Audience for News."

162 Becker, Caudill, and Fruit, *The Training and Hiring of Journalists*, 100.

163 Paul J. DiMaggio and Walter W. Powell, "The Iron Cage Revisited: Institutional Isomorphism and Collective Rationality in Organizational Fields," *American Sociological Review* 48, no. 2 (1983): 147–160, https://doi.org/10.2307/2095101.

164 Coddington, Lewis, and Belair-Gagnon, "The Imagined Audience for News."

165 Goldstein, interview with the author.

166 Elena Rivera, interview with the author, December 20, 2021.

167 Kathy Tu, interview with the author, March 14, 2022.

168 Headlee, interview with the author.

169 Don Champion, interview with the author, June 3, 2021.

170 Hugo Balta, interview with the author, January 5, 2022.

171 Carolyn Kane, interview with the author, January 18, 2022.

172 Headlee, interview with the author.

173 Betsy Mason, "Curbing Implicit Bias: What Works and Doesn't Work," *Knowable Magazine*, June 4, 2020, https://knowablemagazine.org/article/mind/2020/how-to-curb-implicit-bias.

174 Headlee, interview with the author.

Chapter 5 Consistent and Conventional Appearance

1 Sia Nyorkor, interview with the author, January 22, 2022.

2 Whitney Miller, interview with the author, January 22, 2022.

3 Torey Van Oot, "Why 95.8% of Female Newscasters Have the Same Hair," *InStyle*, August 14. 2018, para. 4, https://www.instyle.com/hair/secret-beauty-rules-of -television-talking-heads.

4 Mary Angela Bock et al., "The Faces of Local TV News in America: Youth, Whiteness, and Gender Disparities in Station Publicity Photos," *Feminist Media Studies* 18, no. 3 (2018): 440–457, https://doi.org/10.1080/14680777.2017.1415950.

5 Matt Carlson, *Journalistic Authority* (New York: Columbia University Press, 2017).

6 Anne Witz, Chris Warhurst, and Dennis Nickson, "The Labour of Aesthetics and the Aesthetics of Organization," *Organization* 10, no. 1 (2003): 33–54.

7 Chris Warhurst and Dennis Nickson, *Aesthetic Labour* (Thousand Oaks, CA: Sage, 2020).

8 Liz Hart, interview with the author, June 17, 2021.

9 Carolyn Kane, interview with the author, January 18, 2022.

10 Alan Stephenson, David Reese, and Mary Beadle, *Broadcast Announcing Worktext: A Media Performance Guide*, 4th ed. (London: Taylor & Francis, 2013).

11 Nyorkor, interview with the author.

12 Dana Adams, interview with the author, January 11, 2022.

13 Dorothy Tucker, interview with the author, January 8, 2022.

14 Vanessa Ruiz, interview with the author, June 3, 2021.

15 Katie Couric, "Rachel Maddow Tells Katie Couric, 'I'm Not Competing on the Pretty-Girl-on-Cable Front,'" *Glamour*, May 1, 2011, para. 11, https://www.glamour .com/story/rachel-maddow-tells-katie-couric-im-not-competing-on-the-pretty-girl -on-cable-front.

16 Libby Lewis, *The Myth of Post-Racialism in Television News* (New York: Routledge, 2015).

17 Miller, interview with the author.

18 Mary Angela Bock et al., "The Faces of Local TV News in America: Youth, Whiteness, and Gender Disparities in Station Publicity Photos," *Feminist Media Studies* 18, no. 3 (2018): 440–457, https://doi.org/10.1080/14680777.2017 .1415950.

19 Bock et al., "The Faces of Local TV News."

20 Tammy L. Anderson et al., "Aesthetic Capital: A Research Review on Beauty Perks and Penalties," *Sociology Compass* 4, no. 8 (2010): 564–575.

21 Ashley Mears, "Aesthetic Labor for the Sociologies of Work, Gender, and Beauty," *Sociology Compass* 8, no. 12 (2014): 1330–1343.

22 Robert M. Entman, "Modern Racism and the Images of Blacks in Local Television News," *Critical Studies in Media Communication* 7, no. 4 (1990): 332–345; Kerner Commission, *Report of the National Advisory Commission on Civil Disorders* (Washington, DC: Government Printing Office, 1967), https://www.ojp.gov/ncjrs /virtual-library/abstracts/national-advisory-commission-civil-disorders-report.

23 Pamela Newkirk, *Within the Veil: Black Journalists, White Media* (New York: New York University Press, 2000), 80-81.

24 Ron Powers, *The Newscasters* (New York: St. Martin's Press, 1977).

25 Valerie Geller, interview with the author, January 14, 2022.

26 Bob Papper and Keren Henderson, "Minority Representation Increases, but Still Lags General Population," RTDNA, November 16, 2022, https://www.rtdna.org /news/minority-representation-increases-but-still-lags-general-population.

27 Amy Jo Coffey, "Challenging Assumptions about Ownership and Diversity: An Examination of US Local On-Air Television Newsroom Personnel," *International Journal on Media Management* 20, no. 4 (2018): 277–305; Amy Jo Coffey,

"Representing Ourselves: Ethnic Representation in America's Television News-rooms," *Howard Journal of Communications* 24, no. 2 (2013): 154–177.

28 Bock et al., "The Faces of Local TV News."

29 Libby Lewis, *The Myth of Post-Racialism in Television News* (New York: Routledge, 2016).

30 Javier E. Gómez, interview with the author, September 1, 2021.

31 Hugo Balta, interview with the author, January 5, 2022.

32 Gómez, interview with the author.

33 Antoinette Lattouf, interview with the author, August 23, 2021.

34 Michael C. Keith, *Broadcast Voice Performance* (Boston: Focal Press, 1989).

35 Keith, *Broadcast Voice Performance*.

36 Powers, *The Newscasters*.

37 Stuart Hyde and Dina A. Ibrahim, *Television and Radio Announcing* (New York: Routledge, 2017).

38 Gordon L. Patzer, *Looks: Why They Matter More than You Ever Imagined* (New York: AMACOM, 2008).

39 Bock et al., "The Faces of Local TV News."

40 Nyorkor, interview with the author.

41 Kimberly Meltzer, *TV News Anchors and Journalistic Tradition: How Journalists Adapt to Technology* (New York: Peter Lang, 2010).

42 Valerie Geller, interview with the author, January 14, 2022.

43 Adam Rhew, "Why News Anchors All Have the Same Look," *Racked*, February 1, 2017, para. 18, https://www.racked.com/2017/2/1/14441128/local-news-anchor-image-consultants.

44 Mears, "Aesthetic Labor."

45 Erika Engstrom, "Looking through a Gendered Lens: Local U.S. Television News Anchors' Perceived Career Barriers," *Journal of Broadcasting & Electronic Media* 44, no. 4 (2000): 614–634, https://doi.org/10.1207/s15506878jobem4404_6.

46 Engstrom, "Looking through a Gendered Lens"; Paromita Pain and Victoria Chen, "This Reporter Is So Ugly, How Can She Appear on TV? Negotiating Gender Online and Offline in Taiwanese Media," *Journalism Practice* 13, no. 2 (2019): 140–158.

47 Samantha Brick, "'Sorry, Some Women Are Too Ugly for TV': So Says that Self-Proclaimed Beauty, and Former TV Executive Samantha Brick," *Daily Mail*, May 1, 2012, https://www.dailymail.co.uk/femail/article-2138177/Samantha-Brick-Sorry-women-ARE-ugly-TV.html.

48 Christine Craft, interview with the author, May 30, 2021.

49 Craft, interview with the author.

50 Meltzer, *TV News Anchors*.

51 Christine Craft, *Too Old, Too Ugly, and Not Deferential to Men* (Rocklin, CA: Prima Pub. and Communications, 1988).

52 Craft, *Too Old, Too Ugly*.

53 Craft, *Too Old, Too Ugly*, 10.

54 Craft, *Too Old, Too Ugly*, 208.

55 Christine Craft, "KMBC Said I Was Too Old and Too Ugly. Newswomen Today Are Still Fighting Discrimination," *Kansas City Star*, March 16, 2019, para. 10, https://www.kansascity.com/opinion/readers-opinion/guest-commentary/article228013579.html.

56 Noor Tagouri, interview with the author, January 19, 2022.

57 Mariam Sobh, interview with the author, September 2, 2022.

58 Tahera Rahman, interview with the author, January 16, 2022.

59 Rahman, interview with the author.

60 Kane, interview with the author.

61 Barbara Allen-Rosser, interview with the author, January 26, 2022.

62 Dara Allen, interview with the author, June 29, 2021.

63 McHugh and Hoffman, "Viewer Attitudes toward Baltimore Televison," 1977, Box 2, Baltimore, 1968-1979, McHugh and Hoffman Records, 1957–1999, Bentley Historical Library, University of Michigan, Ann Arbor (collection referred to hereafter as McHugh and Hoffman Records.

64 Hoffman, "Attitudes toward Buffalo TV," Box 2, Buffalo, 1965-1978, McHugh and Hoffman Records.

65 Craft, *Too Old, Too Ugly*.

66 Craft, *Too Old, Too Ugly*, 41.

67 Craft, Craft, *Too Old, Too Ugly*.

68 Judy Bachrach, "The Complicated History behind the Hair and Makeup of Female News Anchors," *Allure*, November 20, 2017, https://www.allure.com/story/the-looks-behind-the-news.

69 M. Nitz et al., "All the News that's Fit to See? The Sexualization of Television News Journalists as a Promotional Strategy," *Journal of Promotion Management* 13, no. 1–2 (2007): 13–33.

70 Bock et al., "The Faces of Local TV News."

71 Gloria Riviera, interview with the author, January 19, 2022.

72 Lattouf, interview with the author.

73 Viktoria Capek, interview with the author, December 15, 2021.

74 Capek, interview with the author.

75 Capek, interview with the author.

76 Jana Shortal, interview with the author, February 14, 2022.

77 Shortal, interview with the author.

78 Shortal, interview with the author.

79 Bock et al., "The Faces of Local TV News."

80 Bock et al., "The Faces of Local TV News."

81 Christy Zhou Koval and Ashleigh Shelby Rosette, "The Natural Hair Bias in Job Recruitment," *Social Psychological and Personality Science* 12, no. 5 (2021): 741–750.

82 McHugh and Hoffman, "Images of Memphis Television Stations, Newscasts and Newscast Personalities," 1973, Box 13, Memphis, 1976–1979, McHugh and Hoffman Records (quote); Van Oot, "Why 95.8% of Female Newscasters Have the Same Hair."

83 Pamela Newkirk, *Within the Veil: Black Journalists, White Media* (New York: New York University Press, 2000).

84 Newkirk, *Within the Veil*, 84.

85 Brittany Noble, interview with the author, June 17, 2021.

86 Noble, interview with the author.

87 Brittany Noble, "Why I Disappeared from WJTV in Jackson, Mississippi," *Medium*, January 7, 2019, para. 7, https://medium.com/@thenoblejournalist/why-i-disappeared-from-the-news-desk-at-wjtv-in-jackson-mississippi-bd734b1affb3.

88 Treasure Roberts (@TRobertsTV), "Braids are professional," Twitter, August 4, 2020< https://x.com/TRobertsTV/status/1290730651512168448?s=20.

89 Kaci Jones (@KaciONTV), "For the first time in my career i'm wearing braids on air," Twitter, June 15, 2020, https://x.com/KaciONTV/status/1272500327401631744?s=20.

90 Nyorkor, interview with the author.

91 Miller, interview with the author.
92 Whitney Miller, "It's 2020 and Black Reporters Are Still Asking to Wear Their Braids on TV," *WCPO*, August 31, 2020, https://www.wcpo.com/news/opinion /column-its-2020-and-black-reporters-are-still-asking-to-wear-their-braids-on-tv.
93 Miller, interview with the author.
94 Nyorkor, interview with the author.
95 Miller, interview with the author.
96 Geller, interview with the author.

Chapter 6 "Accentless" Speech and Attractive Voices

1 Viktoria Capek, interview with the author, December 15, 2021.
2 Jill Olmsted, interview with the author, June 29, 2021.
3 Tanya Ott, interview with the author, June 17, 2021.
4 Natalie Wolchover, "Why Do All News Anchors Talk the Same?," *NBC News*, October 1, 2011, para. 1, https://www.nbcnews.com/id/wbna44740700.
5 Edward McClelland, *How to Speak Midwestern* (Cleveland, OH: Belt Publishing, 2016); John R. Bittner and Denise A. Bittner, *Radio Journalism* (Englewood Cliffs, NJ: Prentice-Hall, 1977).
6 McClelland, *How to Speak Midwestern*.
7 Carl Hausman, Lewis B. O'Donnell, and Philip Benoit, *Announcing: Broadcast Communicating Today* (Belmont, CA: Wadsworth Publishing, 2000), 37.
8 Cathy Runnels, interview with the author, December 20, 2021.
9 Allan A. Metcalf, *How We Talk: American Regional English Today* (Boston: Houghton Mifflin Harcourt, 2000).
10 Rob Drummond, interview with the author, June 25, 2021.
11 Andrew Tolson, *Media Talk: Spoken Discourse on Radio and TV* (Edinburgh: Edinburgh University Press, 2005).
12 Hausman, O'Donnell, and Benoit, *Announcing*.
13 Sally Prosser, interview with the author, June 7, 2021.
14 Dana Adams, interview with the author, January 11, 2022.
15 Liz Hart, interview with the author, June 17, 2021.
16 Stuart Hyde and Dina A. Ibrahim, *Television and Radio Announcing* (New York: Routledge, 2017); Michael C. Keith, *Broadcast Voice Performance* (Boston: Focal Press, 1989).
17 Jeannette Reyes (@msnewslady), "A mix of Rhode Island . . . plus a little bit of Rosie Perez," TikTok, December 28, 2020, https://www.tiktok.com/@msnewslady/video /6910279401355742470.
18 Anne Karpf, *The Human Voice: How This Extraordinary Instrument Reveals Essential Clues about Who We Are* (New York: Bloomsbury Pub., 2006).
19 Don Champion, interview with the author, June 3, 2021.
20 Hyde and Ibrahim, *Television and Radio Announcing*.
21 William G. Hardy, "Radio and the American Language," *Quarterly Journal of Speech* 24, no. 3 (1938): 464, https://doi.org/10.1080/00335633809380394.
22 Metcalf, *How We Talk*; Bittner and Bittner, *Radio Journalism*, 127.
23 Metcalf, *How We Talk*.
24 Hardy, "Radio and the American Language," 456.
25 Hausman, O'Donnell, and Benoit, *Announcing*.
26 Henry Lee Ewbank and Sherman P. Lawton, *Broadcasting: Radio and Television* (New York: Harper, 1952).

27 Karpf, *The Human Voice*.

28 Shawn VanCour, *Making Radio: Early Radio Production and the Rise of Modern Sound Culture* (Oxford: Oxford University Press, 2018).

29 Lynda Mugglestone, *Talking Proper: The Rise of Accent as Social Symbol*, 2nd ed. (Oxford: Oxford University Press, 2003).

30 Paul Carley, "Arthur Lloyd James and English Pronunciation for Foreign Learners," in *Proceedings of PTLC 2013*, ed. Joann Przedlacka, John Maidment, and Michael Ashby (London: Phonetics Teaching and Learning Conference, 2013), 27–30, https://studylib.net/doc/13896750/arthur-lloyd-james-and-english-pronunciation -for-foreign-.

31 Jürg Rainer Schwyter, *Dictating to the Mob: The History of the BBC Advisory Committee on Spoken English* (New York: Oxford University Press, 2016).

32 Stuart Allan, *News Culture* (Maidenhead, UK: McGraw-Hill Education, 2010).

33 Schwyter, *Dictating to the Mob*.

34 Schwyter, *Dictating to the Mob*.

35 Some consider Good American Speech and American Stage Speech to be varieties of World English.

36 Dudley Knight, "Standard Speech: The Ongoing Debate," in *The Vocal Vision: Views on Voice by 24 Leading Teachers Coaches and Directors*, ed. Marion Hampton and Barbara Acker (New York: Applause, 1997): 177.

37 Hausman, O'Donnell, and Benoit, *Announcing*.

38 Carolyn Kane, interview with the author, January 18, 2022.

39 John Baugh, *Out of the Mouth of Slaves: African American Language and Educational Malpractice* (Austin: University of Texas Press, 1999).

40 McClelland, *How to Speak Midwestern*.

41 Baugh, *Out of the Mouth of Slaves*.

42 Libby Lewis, *The Myth of Post-Racialism in Television News* (New York: Routledge, 2015), 2.

43 Dorothy Tucker, interview with the author, January 8, 2022.

44 Runnels, interview with the author.

45 Huga Balta, interview with the author, January 5, 2022.

46 Kane, interview with the author.

47 Balta, interview with the author.

48 Vanessa Ruiz, interview with the author, June 3, 2021.

49 Adams, interview with the author.

50 Christopher A. Chávez, "'News with an Accent': Hispanic Television and the Re-Negotiation of US Latino Speech," *Communication and Critical/Cultural Studies* 12, no. 3 (2015): 252–270.

51 Balta, interview with the author.

52 Chávez, "News with an Accent."

53 Gretel Kahn, interview with the author, January 14, 2022.

54 Keith, *Broadcast Voice Performance*, 127.

55 Megan Figueroa and Carrie Gillon, "Southern Fried," *Vocal Fries Pod*, podcast, September 12, 2018, https://vocalfriespod.com/2018/09/12/transcript-3-southern-fried/.

56 Joseph Person, "'That is who he is': Marty Smith Found Fame Staying True to His Southern Roots," *The Athletic*, June 19, 2020, https://theathletic.com/1879122/2020 /06/19/that-is-who-he-is-spiked-hair-the-suits-that-accent-its-all-marty-smith/.

57 Antoinette Lattouf, interview with the author, August 23, 2021.

58 Institute of Employment Rights, "Class Still a Significant Factor in Workplace Progression, Research Finds," Institute of Employment Rights, June 22, 2018,

https://www.ier.org.uk/news/class-still-significant-factor-workplace-progression-research-finds/.

59 Lucrece Grehoua, interview with the author, January 25, 2022.

60 Grehoua, interview with the author.

61 Beth Rigby (@BethRigby), "Someone has been kind enough to update my Wikipedia Page," Twitter, September 5, 2019, https://x.com/BethRigby/status/1169543742765842432?s=20.

62 Jo Tweedy, "Sky News Political Editor Beth Rigby Reveals Trolls Hacked Her Wikipedia Page," *Daily Mail*, September 5, 2019, https://www.dailymail.co.uk/femail/article-7431017/Sky-News-political-editor-trolled-speech-impediment.html.

63 Ewbank and Lawton, *Broadcasting*.

64 Hausman, O'Donnell, and Benoit, *Announcing* (quote); Alan Stephenson, David Reese, and Mary Beadle, *Broadcast Announcing Worktext: A Media Performance Guide*, 4th ed. (London: Taylor & Francis, 2013), 14.

65 Jessica Hansen, interview with the author, June 17, 2021.

66 Ott, interview with the author.

67 Nancy Reardon and Tom Flynn, *On Camera: How to Report, Anchor & Interview* (Hoboken, NJ: Taylor & Francis, 2013).

68 Susan Carter, "A Mic of Her Own: Stations, Collectives, and Women's Access to Radio," *Journal of Radio Studies* 11, no. 2 (2004): 169–183, https://doi.org/10.1207/s15506843jrsi1102_3.

69 *Complete Course in the Technique of Broadcasting*, nos. 1–4 (Washington, DC: Floyd Gibbons School of Broadcasting, 1932), part 1, 9–10.

70 Sherman P. Lawton, "The Principles of Effective Radio Speaking," *Quarterly Journal of Speech* 16, no. 3 (1930): 255–277.

71 Hyde and Ibrahim, *Television and Radio Announcing*.

72 Stephenson, Reese, and Beadle, *Broadcast Announcing Worktext*.

73 Jessica Hanse, interview with the author, June 17, 2021.

74 Emily Gasser et al., "Production, Perception, and Communicative Goals of American Newscaster Speech," *Language in Society* 48, no. 2 (2019): 233–259.

75 Gloria Riviera, interview with the author, January 19, 2022.

76 Lattouf, interview with the author.

77 Hyde and Ibrahim, *Television and Radio Announcing*.

78 Charles L. Ponce de Leon, *That's The Way It Is: A History of Television News in America* (Chicago: University of Chicago Press, 2015).

79 Fabio Fasoli, Peter Hegarty, and David M. Frost, "Stigmatization of 'Gay-Sounding' Voices: The Role of Heterosexual, Lesbian, and Gay Individuals' Essentialist Beliefs," *British Journal of Social Psychology* 60, no. 3 (2021): 826–850.

80 *Do I Sound Gay?*, directed by David Thorpe (New York: IFC Films, 2014).

81 Harrison Hove, interview with the author, August 17, 2023.

82 Don Champion, interview with the author, June 3, 2021.

83 Bill Kirkpatrick, "Voices Made for Print: Crip Voices on the Radio," in *Radio's New Wave: Global Sound in the Digital Era*, ed. Jason Loviglio and Michele Hilmes (New York: Routledge, 2013), 106–125.

84 Samantha Warhurst, Patricia McCabe, and CatherineMadill, "What Makes a Good Voice for Radio: Perceptions of Radio Employers and Educators," *Journal of Voice* 27, no. 2 (2013): 217–224.

85 Hausman, O'Donnell, and Benoit, *Announcing*.

86 Keith, *Broadcast Voice Performance*.

87 Kirkpatrick, "Voices Made for Print."

88 Kirkpatrick, "Voices Made for Print."

89 Diane Rehm, *Finding My Voice* (Herndon, VA: Capital Books, 2002).

90 Ben Strauss, "The Radio Reporter Who Lost His Voice but Still Covers Congress," *Politico*, December 15, 2017, https://www.politico.com/magazine/story/2017/12/15 /jamie-dupree-radio-voice-216107/.

91 John Hendrickson, *Life on Delay: Making Peace with a Stutter* (New York: Alfred A. Knopf, 2023), 180.

92 Here and throughout this section, some journalists' names are not provided because they were promised confidentiality.

93 Elia Powers, "The Journalist's Speech: A Phenomenological Study of Stuttering in the Newsroom," *Journalism Studies* 21, no. 9 (2020): 1243–1260, https://doi.org/10 .1080/1461670X.2020.1738953.

94 Powers, "The Journalist's Speech."

95 Katie Ellis and Gerard Goggin, *Disability and the Media*, Key Concerns in Media Studies (New York: Palgrave Macmillan, 2015).

96 Barbara Walters, *Audition* (New York: Vintage Books, 2009).

97 *Gilda Radner's Greatest Moments*, directed by Dennis Rosenblatt, aired in 2002 on ABC, https://archive.org/details/gildaradnersgreatestmoments.

98 *Gilda Radner's Greatest Moments*.

99 Walters, *Audition*; "Charlize Theron/The Black Keys," directed by Don Roy King, *Saturday Night Live*, season 39, episode 20, aired May 10, 2014, on NBC.

100 Walters, *Audition*, 142.

Chapter 7   The Enduring #PubRadioVoice

1 Lulu Garcia-Navarro (@lourdesgnavarro), "Sitting in host chair for first time I channeled white voice from Midwest and lost my own," Twitter, January 29, 2015, https://twitter.com/lourdesgnavarro/status/561112865189691392?ref_src=twsrc %5Etfw.

2 Audie Cornish (@AudieCornish), "People usually don't react to my voice they react to their Google image search," Twitter, January 29, 2015, https://x.com/AudieCornish /status/560945171781918720?s=20.

3 Al Letson (@Al_Letson), "If an org is telling you they believe in diversity, but don't invest in it, what's that belief worth?," Twitter, January 29, 2015, https://x.com/Al _Letson/status/560970727277330432?s=20.

4 "Chenjerai Kumanyika," *Transom Review* 15, no. 2 (2015), para. 2, https://transom .org/wp-content/uploads/2015/01/Chenjerai-Kumanyika-Review.pdf.

5 Chenjerai Kumanyika, "Challenging the Whiteness of Public Radio," *Code Switch*, podcast, NPR, January 29, 2015, para. 2, https://www.npr.org/sections/codeswitch /2015/01/29/382437460/challenging-the-whiteness-of-public-radio.

6 "Chenjerai Kumanyika," para. 19.

7 "Chenjerai Kumanyika."

8 Juan González and Joseph Torres, *News for All the People: The Epic Story of Race and the American Media* (London: Verso, 2011), 201.

9 González and Torres, *News for All the People*; Derek W. Vaillant, "Sounds of Whiteness: Local Radio, Racial Formation, and Public Culture in Chicago, 1921–1935," *American Quarterly* 54, no. 1 (2002): 25–66.

10 González and Torres, *News for All the People*.

11 González and Torres, *News for All the People*.

12 Laura Garbes, "When the 'Blank Slate' Is a White One: White Institutional Isomorphism in the Birth of National Public Radio," *Sociology of Race & Ethnicity* 8, no. 1 (2022): 84.

13 Garbes, "When the 'Blank Slate' Is a White One."

14 Eduardo Bonilla-Silva, Carla Goar, and David G. Embrick, "When Whites Flock Together: The Social Psychology of White Habitus," *Critical Sociology* 32, no. 2–3 (2006): 229–253; Garbes, "When the 'Blank Slate' Is a White One."

15 Garbes, "When the 'Blank Slate' Is a White One."

16 Lisa Napoli, *Susan, Linda, Nina & Cokie: The Extraordinary Story of the Founding Mothers of NPR* (New York: Abrams Press, 2021).

17 Cokie Roberts and Susan Stamberg, *This Is NPR: The First Forty Years* (San Francisco: Chronicle Books, 2010).

18 Napoli, *Susan, Linda, Nina & Cokie*, 71.

19 Napoli, *Susan, Linda, Nina & Cokie*.

20 Kerry Thompson and Erin Slomski-Pritz, "50 and Forward: An Anniversary Celebration of NPR," podcast, NPR. April 30, 2021. https://www.npr.org/2021/04/30/991424624/fifty-and-forward-an-anniversary-celebration-of-npr.

21 Jeff Porter, *Lost Sound: The Forgotten Sound of Radio Storytelling* (Chapel Hill: University of North Carolina Press, 2016).

22 Adam Ragusea, "How Women, People of Color, and Everyone Else Can Sound More Like Themselves on the Radio," *The Pub*, Episode 4, Podcast. February 15, 2015, 2.

23 Christopher Chávez, "When One Way of Speaking Dominates, Who Gets to Tell Their Stories on Public Radio?," *Current*, June 25, 2020. https://current.org/2020/06/when-one-way-of-speaking-dominates-who-gets-to-tell-their-stories-on-public-radio/; Jack W. Mitchell, *Listener Supported: The Culture and History of Public Radio* (Westport, CT.: Praeger, 2005).

24 Jeffrey A. Dvorkin, "Why Doesn't NPR Sound Like the Rest of America?," NPR, May 18, 2005, para. 1, https://www.npr.org/sections/publiceditor/2005/05/18/4656584/why-doesnt-npr-sound-more-like-the-rest-of-america.

25 Brian Montopoli, "All Things Considerate: How NPR Makes Tavis Smiley Sound Like Linda Wertheimer," *Washington Monthly* 35, no. 1/2 (2001): 40–42, https://washingtonmonthly.com/2001/01/01/all-things-considerate/.

26 Christopher Chávez, *The Sound of Exclusion: NPR and the Latinx Public* (Tucson: University of Arizona Press, 2021).

27 Chávez, "When One Way of Speaking Dominates," para. 27.

28 Jessica Hansen, interview with the author, June 17, 2021.

29 Huo Jingnan, interview with the author, March 13, 2023.

30 Michael P. McCauley, *NPR: The Trials and Triumphs of National Public Radio* (New York: Columbia University Press, 2005), 99.

31 Alexis Soloski, "When Podcast Hosts Speak, What Do We Hear?," *New York Times*, February 25, 2021, para. 1, https://www.nytimes.com/interactive/2021/02/25/arts/podcast-voice-sound.html (first quote); Adam Ragusea, "How Women, People of Color, and Everyone Else Can Sound More Like Themselves on the Radio," *The Pub*, podcast, episode 4, February 15, 2015, 2 (second quote).

32 Jason Loviglio, "U.S. Public Radio, Social Change, and the Gendered Voice," in *Electrified Voices: Medial, Socio-Historical and Cultural Aspects of Voice Transfer*, ed. Nils Meise and Dmitri Zakharine (Göttingen: V&R Unipress, 2013), 137–146.

33 Dvorkin, "Why Doesn't NPR Sound Like the Rest of America?"

34 Teddy Wayne, "'NPR Voice' Has Taken over the Airwaves," *New York Times*, October 24, 2015, https://www.nytimes.com/2015/10/25/fashion/npr-voice-has-taken-over-the-airwaves.html.

35 "Chenjerai Kumanyika," para. 3.

36 Chenjerai Kumanyika, interview with the author, June 23, 2021.

37 "Chenjerai Kumanyika," para. 15.

38 Rob Rosenthal, interview with the author, December 15, 2021.

39 Rosenthal, interview with the author.

40 "Chenjerai Kumanyika," para. 15.

41 Alicia Montgomery (@AMontgomery_998), "It's not just race. Class, education, faith experience. . . . Too often we don't sound anything like America," Twitter, January 29, 2015, https://x.com/AMontgomery_998/status/560957940468023297?s=20.

42 Kumanyika, interview with the author.

43 Alison MacAdam, interview with the author, June 21, 2021.

44 Steve Olson, "Often Overlooked, Airchecking Is Essential to Keeping Public Radio's Audience," *Current*, April 14, 2016, https://current.org/2016/04/often-overlooked-airchecking-is-essential-to-keeping-public-radios-audience/.

45 Steve Olson, interview with the author, September 8, 2022.

46 Olson, "Often Overlooked," 2.

47 Olson, interview with the author.

48 Diana Opong, interview with the author, December 21, 2021.

49 Linda Holmes (@LindaHolmes), "Having my delivery so meticulously managed is literally the ONE thing I don't like about doing radio," Twitter, January 29, 2015, https://x.com/lindaholmes/status/560956922372042752?s=20.

50 Catherine Stifter, interview with the author, June 7, 2021.

51 Gabrielle Jones, interview with the author, June 17, 2021.

52 Opong, interview with the author.

53 Celeste Headlee, interview with the author, June 23, 2021.

54 Celeste Headlee, "An Anti-Racist Future: A Vision and Plan for the Transformation of Public Media," *Medium*, January 18, 2021, para. 4, https://celesteheadlee.medium.com/an-anti-racist-future-a-vision-and-plan-for-the-transformation-of-public-media-224149ab37e6.

55 Headlee, interview with the author.

56 Kumanyika, "Challenging the Whiteness of Public Radio," para. 6.

57 Linda Holmes (@lindaholmes), "I think some people in public radio seek to make their voices—and themselves—invisible," Twitter, January 29, 2015, https://x.com/lindaholmes/status/560953979405078528?s=20.

58 Stephanie Foo, interview with the author, June 25, 2021.

59 Dmae Lo Roberts, interview with the author, January 7, 2022.

60 Tamara Keith, "How I Found My #PubRadioVoice," *Adventures in Radioland*, February 6, 2015, para. 8, http://www.tamarakeith.com/2015/02/how-i-found-my-pubradiovoice-spoiler.html.

61 Liana Van Nostrand, "Sounding Like a Reporter—and a Real Person, Too," *NPR Opinion*, August 7. 2019, para. 12, https://www.npr.org/sections/publiceditor/2019/08/07/749060986/sounding-like-a-reporter-and-a-real-person-too.

62 Dvorkin, "Why Doesn't NPR Sound Like the Rest of America?"

63 "Stephanie Foo," *Transom Review* 16, no. 1 (2016): 1–7, https://transom.org/wp-content/uploads/2016/05/StephanieFoo_review.

64 Gisele Regatão, interview with the author, June 4, 2021.

65 Regatão, interview with the author.

66 Jennifer Gerson, "The Voices of NPR: How Four Women of Color See Their Roles as Hosts," *The 19th*, April 26, 2023, https://19thnews.org/2023/04/the-voices-of-npr/.

67 Viki Merrick, interview with the author, January 14, 2022.

68 Abby Goldstein, interview with the author, September 13, 2022.

Chapter 8 Semi-Performative and Vocally Diverse

1 Diana Opong, interview with the author, December 21, 2021.
2 Gene Denby, "Talk American," *Code Switch*, podcast, NPR, August 8, 2018, https://www.npr.org/transcripts/636442508.
3 Huo Jingnan, interview with the author, April 25, 2023.
4 Nicholas Quah, interview with the author, June 17, 2021.
5 Opong, interview with the author, December 21, 2021.
6 Eric Nuzum, *Make Noise: A Creator's Guide to Podcasting and Great Audio Storytelling* (New York: Workman Publishing Company, 2019).
7 Michael Barbaro, "Where's Michael?," *New York Times*, May 28, 2021, https://www.nytimes.com/2021/05/28/podcasts/the-daily-newsletter-michael-barbaro-astead-herndon.html.
8 Edison Research, "The Creators 2022," The Creators, July 8, 2022, accessed February 14, 2023, https://www.edisonresearch.com/the-creators/.
9 Nicholas Quah, "What Went Wrong at Gimlet?," *Vulture*, March 10, 2021, https://www.vulture.com/article/gimlet-reply-all-controversy-spotify-test-kitchen.html.
10 Steve Friess, "Why Are #PodcastsSoWhite?," *Columbia Journalism Review*, March 21, 2017, https://www.cjr.org/the_feature/podcasts-diversity.php.
11 Friess, "Why Are #PodcastsSoWhite?"
12 Ariel Shapiro, "New Podcast Creation Has Fallen Off a Cliff," *The Verge*, January 17, 2023. https://www.theverge.com/2023/1/17/23559638/new-podcasts-down-apple-spotify-amazon-audible-hot-pod-summit.
13 Edison Research, "Weekly Insights 11.10.22 The Steady Climb of Podcasting's Reach in the U.S.," *Edison Weekly Insights*, November 10, 2022, https://www.edisonresearch.com/weekly-insights-11-10-22-the-steady-climb-of-podcastings-reach-in-the-u-s/.
14 Daniela M. Schlütz and Imke Hedder, "Aural Parasocial Relations: Host–Listener Relationships in Podcasts," *Journal of Radio & Audio Media* 29, no. 2 (2022): 457–474.
15 Evo Terra, interview with the author, June 3, 2021.
16 Quah, interview with the author.
17 Viki Merrick, interview with the author, January 14, 2022.
18 Alexis Soloski, "When Podcast Hosts Speak, What Do We Hear?," *New York Times*, February 25, 2021, para. 6, https://www.nytimes.com/interactive/2021/02/25/arts/podcast-voice-sound.htm.
19 Mariam Sobh, interview with the author, September 2, 2022.
20 Eric Nuzum, interview with the author, September 22, 2022.
21 Schlütz and Hedder, "Aural Parasocial Relations."
22 Nuzum, interview with the author.
23 Terra, interview with the author.
24 Mary Chan, interview with the author, May 30, 2021.
25 Terra, interview with the author.
26 Terra, interview with the author.
27 Alison MacAdam, interview with the author, June 21, 2021.
28 Erving Goffman, *The Presentation of Self in Everyday Life* (New York: Doubleday, 1959).
29 Molly Webster, *Werk It: The Podcast*, "Don't Fear the Vocal Fry," June 7, 2015. https://www.wnycstudios.org/podcasts/werkit/episodes/werk-it-owning-your-voice.
30 Kim Fox, interview with the author, June 21, 2021.
31 Gloria Riviera, interview with the author, January 19, 2022.

32 Gustavo Arellano, interview with author, January 11, 2022.

33 Arellano, interview with the author.

34 Shannon Cason, interview with the author, January 13, 2022.

35 Cason, interview with the author.

36 "Chenjerai Kumanyika," *Transom Review*, 15, no. 2 (2015), para. 2, https://transom .org/wp-content/uploads/2015/01/Chenjerai-Kumanyika-Review.pdf.

37 Chenjerai Kumanyika, interview with the author, June 23, 2021.

38 Reggie Ugwu, "Saidu Tejan-Thomas Jr. and the Voices of Resistance," *New York Times*, February 25, 2021, para. 19, https://www.nytimes.com/2021/02/25/arts/saidu -tejan-thomas-jr-resistance.html.

39 Maxie C. Jackson III, interview with the author, January 18, 2022.

40 Sara M. Lomax, interview with the author, January 18, 2022.

41 Kim Fox, David O. Dowling, and Kyle Miller, "A Curriculum for Blackness: Podcasts as Discursive Cultural Guides, 2010–2020," *Journal of Radio & Audio Media* 27, no. 2 (2020): 302.

42 Reggie Ugwu, "Brittany Luse and Eric Eddings of 'For Colored Nerds' Play For Keeps," *New York Times*, November 17, 2021, para. 13, https://www.nytimes.com /2021/11/17/arts/brittany-luse-eric-eddings-for-colored-nerds-podcast.html.

43 Juleyka Lantigua, interview with the author, December 17, 2021.

44 Lantigua, interview with the author.

45 Quah, interview with the author.

46 Beth A. Haller, *Disabled People Transforming Media Culture for a More Inclusive World* (New York: Routledge, 2023).

47 Shin Yu Pai, Whitney Henry-Lester, and Jim Gates, "A Voice Breaks Barriers," *Ten Thousand Things*, podcast, KUOW, June 19, 2023, https://www.kuow.org/stories/a -voice-breaks-barriers.

48 Maya Chupkov, "Trailer: Introducing Proud Stutter," *Proud Stutter*, https://www .proudstutter.com/trailer-information.

49 Nuzum, interview with the author.

50 Tanya Ott, interview with the author, June 17, 2021.

51 Nielsen, "Podcasts Are Resonating with Diverse Audiences," Nielsen, December 2021, https://www.nielsen.com/insights/2021/podcasts-are-resonating-with-diverse -audiences/.

Chapter 9 Legal Protections and Their Limits

1 Employees seeking legal remedies for pressure to cover and employers who want to avoid liability should consult a qualified attorney.

2 Restatement (Third) of Employment 2.01 cmt. b (Am. Law Inst. 2015).

3 Charles J. Muhl, "The Employment-at-Will Doctrine: Three Major Exceptions," *Monthly Labor Review* 124 (2001): 3–4; Brett H. McDonnell and Matthew T. Bodie, "From Mandates to Governance: Restructuring the Employment Relationship," *Maryland Law Review* 81, no. 3 (2022): 896, 944; American Law Institute, "Restatement (Third) of Employment" 5.01, 5.02.

4 Muhl, "The Employment-at-Will Doctrine," 7.

5 Muhl, "The Employment-at-Will Doctrine," 8; American Law Institute, "Restatement (Third) of Employment," 1.01.

6 Julia Tomassetti, "Power in the Employment Relationship: Why Contract Law Should Not Govern At-Will Employment," Economic Policy Institute,

November 19, 2020, https://www.epi.org/unequalpower/publications/the-legal
-understanding-and-treatment-of-an-employment-relationship-versus-a-contract/.

7 Muhl, "Employment-at-Will Doctrine," 10.

8 Equal Employment Opportunities, 42 U.S.C. § 2000e-2(a) (2000).

9 *Bostock v. Clayton Co.*, 140 S. Ct. 1731 (2020).

10 Equal Employment Opportunities, 42 U.S.C. § 2000e-2(e)(1); Heather R. James, "If You Are Attractive and You Know It, Please Apply: Appearance-Based Discrimination and Employers' Discretion," *Valparaiso University Law Review* 42, no. 2 (2008): 646.

11 *UAW v. Johnson Controls, Inc.*, 111 S. Ct. 1196, 1205 (1991); *Western Air Lines v. Criswell*, 472 U.S. 400, 413 (1985); Beatrice Bich-Dao Nguyen, "Accent Discrimination and the Test of Spoken English: A Call for an Objective Assessment of the Comprehensibility of Nonnative Speakers," *California Law Review* 81, no. 5 (1993): 1333.

12 James, "If You Are Attractive," 643.

13 James, "If You Are Attractive," 642.

14 Mari J. Matsuda, "Voices of America: Accent, Antidiscrimination Law, and a Jurisprudence for the Last Reconstruction," *Yale Law Journal* 100, no. 5 (1991): 1376.

15 U.S. Equal Opportunity Employment Commission, "Facts about Race/Color Discrimination," https://www.eeoc.gov/fact-sheet/facts-about-racecolor
-discrimination.

16 James, "If You Are Attractive," 646–647.

17 Title 29, 29 U.S.C. §§ 623(a)(1), 631(a) (2000).

18 Title 29, 29 U.S.C. § 623(f)(1) (2000).

19 Equal Opportunity for Individuals with Disabilities, 42 USC §§ 12112(5)(A) (2009).

20 Christopher J. Kuczynski, "EEOC Informal Discussion Letter: ADA: Job Related and Consistent with Business Necessity / Direct Threat," Equal Employment Opportunity Commission, March 16, 2001, https://www.eeoc.gov/foia/eeoc
-informal-discussion-letter-44.

21 Kenji Yoshino, *Covering: The Hidden Assault on Our Civil Rights* (New York: Random House, 2007), 197, Kindle.

22 Yoshino, *Covering*, 153–154, 188; *Rogers v. American Airlines, Inc.*, 527 F. Supp. 229 (S.D.N.Y. 1981). The court noted that Title VII might protect hair styled in an Afro because banning a natural hairstyle would run afoul of the policies underlying the prohibition of discrimination on the basis of immutable characteristics.

23 Matsuda, "Voices of America," 1332; Nguyen, "Accent Discrimination," 1327, 1328.

24 Matsuda, "Voices of America," 1345; *Kahakua v. Friday*, 876 R2d 896 (9th Cir. 1989).

25 Matsuda, "Voices of America," 1332; Nguyen, "Accent Discrimination," 1335, 1336, 1338.

26 Matsuda, "Voices of America," 1355-1356.

27 Nguyen, "Accent Discrimination," 1346.

28 Matsuda, "Voices of America," 1377; Nguyen, "Accent Discrimination," 1340.

29 Sylvia Calamai and Fabio Ardolino, "Italian with an Accent: The case of 'Chinese Italian' in Tuscan High Schools," *Journal of Language and Social Psychology* 39, no. 1 (2020): 132–147; Howard Giles and Bernadette M. Watson, *The Social Meanings of Language, Dialect and Accent: International Perspectives on Speech Styles* (New York: Peter Lang, 2013).

30 Katarzyna Boduch-Grabka and Shiri Lev-Ari, "Exposing Individuals to Foreign Accent Increases Their Trust in What Nonnative Speakers Say," *Cognitive Science* 45, no. 11 (2021): e 13064, https://doi.org/10.1111/cogs.13064.

31 Jean-Marc Dewaele and James McCloskey, "Attitudes towards Foreign Accents among Adult Multilingual Language Users," *Journal of Multilingual and Multicultural Development*, 36, no. 3 (2015): 221–238.

32 Boduch-Grabka and Lev-Ari, "Exposing Individuals to Foreign Accent."

33 Frank J. Cavico, Stephen C. Muffler, and Bahaudin G. Mujtaba, "Appearance Discrimination in Employment: Legal and Ethical Implications of 'Lookism' and 'Lookphobia,'" *Equality, Diversity and Inclusion* 32, no. 1 (2013): 104.

34 James, "If You Are Attractive," 639, 642; Cavico, Muffler, and Mujtaba, "Appearance Discrimination," 105.

35 James, "If You Are Attractive," 648–649; Cavico, Muffler, and Mujtaba, "Appearance Discrimination," 91.

36 James, "If You Are Attractive," 650.

37 *Price Waterhouse v. Hopkins*, 490 U.S. 228 (1989) (woman's accounting firm thought she was too aggressive and masculine).

38 James, "If You Are Attractive," 645.

39 Cavico, Muffler, and Mujtaba, "Appearance Discrimination," 90.

40 Cavico, Muffler, and Mujtaba, "Appearance Discrimination."

41 Cavico, Muffler, and Mujtaba, "Appearance Discrimination," 104; James, "If You Are Attractive," 633.

42 Cavico, Muffler, and Mujtaba, "Appearance Discrimination," 97; James, "If You Are Attractive," 640.

43 Cavico, Muffler, and Mujtaba, "Appearance Discrimination," 98.

44 42 U.S.C. §§ 12102(2), 12111(8), 12112(a) (2000).

45 29 C.F.R. §1630.2(h)(1) (2005).

46 *School Board of Nassau County v. Arline*, 480 U.S. 273, 284 (1987).

47 James, "If You Are Attractive," 652.

48 Cavico, Muffler, and Mujtaba, "Appearance Discrimination," 95–96.

49 Elliott-Larsen Civil Rights Act, Act 453 of 1976, § 37.2102 (2004), https://www .michigan.gov/-/media/Project/Websites/mdcr/public-act-453-of-1976-elliott-larsen .pdf?rev=c15451b0a9f943d78ae818259a38c8dc.

50 Wash. Rev. Code ch. 49.60 (2018); *Taylor v. Burlington Northern Railroad Holdings, Inc.*, 444 P.3d 606 (Wash. 2019).

51 Human Rights Law, chapter 14, Code of the District of Columbia, § 2–1401.11(a) (2001), https://code.dccouncil.gov/us/dc/council/code/titles/2/chapters/14.

52 Cavico, Muffler, and Mujtaba, "Appearance Discrimination," 99–100.

53 Cavico, Muffler, and Mujtaba, "Appearance Discrimination," 100; Deborah L. Rhode, "The Injustice of Appearance," *Stanford Law Review* 61, no. 5 (2009): 1084.

54 Crown Coalition, "Creating a Respectful and Open World for Natural Hair," accessed February 6, 2024, https://www.thecrownact.com/about.

55 James, "If You Are Attractive," 632–633.

56 James, "If You Are Attractive."

57 Cavico, Muffler, and Mujtaba, "Appearance Discrimination," 112–113, citing Ritu Mahajan, "The Naked Truth: Appearance Discrimination, Employment, and the Law," *Asian-American Law Journal* 14 (2007): 201.

58 James, "If You Are Attractive," 635–36, citing *Craft v. Metromedia, Inc.*, 766 F.2d 1205, 1215 (8th Cir. 1985) (Court allowed reassignment of a television news coanchor to a different position because of her appearance and negative viewer feedback to it).

59 Cavico, Muffler, and Mujtaba, "Appearance Discrimination," 103–104.

60 Cavico, Muffler, and Mujtaba, "Appearance Discrimination," 103; James, "If You Are Attractive," 670, 672.

61 James, "If You Are Attractive," 661.

62 James, "If You Are Attractive," 664; Cavico, Muffler, and Mujtaba, "Appearance Discrimination," 106.

63 Robert J. Barro, "So You Want to Hire the Beautiful. Well, Why Not?," *Business Week*, March 16, 1998, https://scholar.harvard.edu/files/barro/files/bw98_03_16 .pdf.

64 Cavico, Muffler, and Mujtaba, "Appearance Discrimination," 116.

65 Yoshino, *Covering*, 202.

66 Yoshino, *Covering*, 202, 207.

Chapter 10 How Change Happens

1 Harrison Hove, interview with the author, August 17, 2023.

2 Vanessa Ruiz, interview with the author, June 3, 2021.

3 Ruiz, interview with the author.

4 Hove, interview with the author.

5 Kris Vera-Phillips, interview with the author, August 15, 2023.

6 Vera-Phillips, interview with the author.

7 Hove, interview with the author.

8 Ruiz, interview with the author.

9 Hove, interview with the author.

10 Hove, interview with the author.

11 Ruiz, interview with the author.

12 Hove, interview with the author.

13 Vera-Phillips, interview with the author.

14 Tanya Ott, interview with the author, June 17, 2021.

15 Rob Rosenthal, interview with the author, December 15, 2021.

16 Dara Allen, interview with the author, June 29, 2021.

17 Khalon Richard, interview with the author, March 13, 2023.

18 Diana Opong, interview with the author, December 21, 2021.

19 Dana Adams, interview with the author, January 11, 2022.

20 Jessica Hansen, interview with the author, June 17, 2021.

21 Cathy Runnels, interview with the author, December 20, 2021.

22 Chenjerai Kumanyika, interview with the author, June 23, 2021.

23 Robert J. Richardson, "Local TV Newsroom Diversity: Race and Gender of Newscasters and Their Managers," *Journal of Broadcasting & Electronic Media* 66, no. 5 (2022): 823–842.

24 Sara M. Lomax, interview with the author, January 18, 2022.

25 Ariana Martinez, interview with the author, January 13, 2022.

26 Stephanie Foo, interview with the author, June 25, 2021.

27 Mari J. Matsuda, "Voices of America: Accent, Antidiscrimination Law, and a Jurisprudence for the Last Reconstruction," *Yale Law Journal* 100, no. 5 (1991): 1341; Katherine D. Kinzler, *How You Say It: Why You Talk the Way You Do and What It Says about You* (New York: Houghton Mifflin Harcourt, 2020).

28 Matsuda, "Voices of America," 1377.

29 Eric Nuzum, "To Serve Diverse Audiences, You Can't Walk the Walk Until You Know Where You Stand," *Current*, March 10, 2022, https://current.org/2022/03/to -serve-diverse-audiences-you-cant-walk-the-walk-until-you-know-where-you-stand/.

30 Khalon Richard, interview with the author, March 13, 2023.

31 Elena Rivera, interview with the author, December 20, 2021.

32 Viki Merrick, interview with the author, January 14, 2022.
33 Jill Olmsted, interview with the author, June 29, 2021.
34 Valerie Geller, interview with the author, January 14, 2022.
35 Kumanyika, interview with the author.
36 Agata Gluszek and John F. Dovidio, "The Way They Speak: A Social Psychological Perspective on the Stigma of Nonnative Accents in Communication," *Personality and Social Psychology Review* 14, no. 2 (2010): 229.
37 Tahera Rahman, interview with the author, January 16, 2022.
38 Hove, interview with the author.

Bibliography

Abdelfatah, Rund, Ramtin Arablouei, Jamie York, Julie Caine, Laine Kaplan-Levenson, Lawrence Wu, Darius Rafieyan, and Victor Yvellez. "Who Is NPR (For)?" *Throughline*, June 10, 2021. Podcast. https://www.npr.org/2021/06/07/1004079815/who-is -npr-for.

Alamo-Pastrana, Carlos, and William Hoynes. "Racialization of News: Constructing and Challenging Professional Journalism as 'White Media.'" *Humanity & Society* 44, no. 1 (2020): 67–91. https://doi.org/10.1177/0160597618820071.

Allan, Stuart. *News Culture*. UK: McGraw-Hill Education, 2010.

Allen, Craig. "Consultants: Role in Newsroom." In *The International Encyclopedia of Journalism Studies*, edited by T. P. Vos, F. Hanusch, D. Dimitrakopoulou, M. Geertsema-Sligh, and A. Sehl, 1–8. Wiley Online Library, 2019. https://doi.org/10 .1002/9781118841570.iejs0223.

———. "Discovering 'Joe Six Pack' Content in Television News: The Hidden History of Audience Research, News Consultants, and the Warner Class Model." *Journal of Broadcasting & Electronic Media* 49, no. 4 (2005): 363–382.

———. "Gender Breakthrough Fit for a Focus Group: The First Women Newscasters and Why They Arrived in Local TV News." *Journalism History* 28, no. 4 (2003): 154–162.

———. *News Is People: The Rise of Local TV News and the Fall of News from New York*. Ames: Iowa State University Press, 2001.

Anderson, Tammy L., Catherine Grunert, Arielle Katz, and Samantha Lovascio. "Aesthetic Capital: A Research Review on Beauty Perks and Penalties." *Sociology Compass* 4, no. 8 (2010): 564–575.

Ang, Ien. *Desperately Seeking the Audience*. New York: Routledge, 1991.

Atkinson, Joe. "Performance Journalism: A Three-Template Model of Television News." *International Journal of Press/Politics* 16, no. 1 (2011): 102–129.

Bachrach, Judy. "The Complicated History behind the Hair and Makeup of Female News Anchors." *Allure*, November 20, 2017. https://www.allure.com/story/the -looks-behind-the-news.

Balon, Robert E., Joseph C. Philport, and Charles F. Beadle. "How Sex and Race Affect Perceptions of Newscasters." *Journalism Quarterly* 55, no. 1 (1978): 160–164. https:// doi.org/10.1177/107769907805500125.

Bandura, Albert. *Social Learning Theory*. Englewood Cliffs, NJ: Prentice Hall, 1977. https://doi.org/10.1177/105960117700200317.

Barbaro, Michael. "Where's Michael?" *New York Times*, May, 28, 2021. https://www.nytimes.com/2021/05/28/podcasts/the-daily-newsletter-michael-barbaro-astead-herndon.html.

Barnhurst, Kevin G., and John Nerone. *The Form of News: A History*. New York: Guilford Press, 2002.

Barro, Robert J. "So You Want to Hire the Beautiful. Well, Why Not?" *Business Week* 3, no. 16, March 16, 1998. https://scholar.harvard.edu/files/barro/files/bw98_03_16.pdf.

Barthel, Michael, Elizabeth Grieco, and Elisa Shearer. "Older Americans, Black Adults and Americans with Less Education More Interested in Local News." Pew Research Center, August 14, 2019. https://www.pewresearch.org/journalism/2019/08/14/older-americans-black-adults-and-americans-with-less-education-more-interested-in-local-news/.

Baugh, John. "Linguistic Profiling." In *Black Linguistics: Language, Society and Politics in Africa and the Americas*, edited by Arnetha F. Ball, Sinfree Makoni, Geneva Smitherman and Arthur K. Spears, 155–168. New York: Routledge, 2005.

———. *Out of the Mouth of Slaves: African American Language and Educational Malpractice*. Austin: University of Texas Press, 1999.

Becker, Lee B., Jeffrey W. Fruit, Susan L. Caudill, Sharon L. Dunwoody, and Leonard P. Tipton. *The Training and Hiring of Journalists*. Norwood, NJ: Ablex Pub. Corp., 1987.

Belair-Gagnon, Valerie, Avery E. Holton, and Oscar Westlund. "Space for the Liminal." *Media and Communication* 7, no. 4 (2019): 1–7.

Bhargava, Deepti, and Petra Theunissen. "The Future of PR Is 'Fantastic,' 'Friendly' and 'Funny': Occupational Stereotypes and Symbolic Capital in Entry-Level Job Advertisements." *Public Relations Review* 45, no. 4 (2019): article 101822. https://doi.org/10.1016/j.pubrev.2019.101822.

Bittner, John R., and Denise A. Bittner. *Radio Journalism*. Englewood Cliffs, NJ: Prentice-Hall, 1977.

Bock, Mary Angela. "Smile More: A Subcultural Analysis of the Anchor/Consultant Relationship in Local Television News Operations." PhD diss., Drake University, 1986.

Bock, Mary Angela, Lourdes Miriam Cueva Chacón, Hyeri Jung, Heloisa Aruth Sturm, and Ever J. Figueroa. "The Faces of Local TV News in America: Youth, Whiteness, and Gender Disparities in Station Publicity Photos." *Feminist Media Studies* 18, no. 3 (2018): 440–457. https://doi.org/10.1080/14680777.2017.1415950.

Boduch-Grabka, Katarzyna, and Shiri Lev-Ari. "Exposing Individuals to Foreign Accent Increases Their Trust in What Nonnative Speakers Say." *Cognitive Science* 45, no. 11 (2021): e 13064. https://doi.org/10.1111/cogs.13064.

Bonilla-Silva, Eduardo, Carla Goar, and David G. Embrick. "When Whites Flock Together: The Social Psychology of White Habitus." *Critical Sociology* 32, no. 2–3 (2006): 229–253.

Boudana, Sandrine. "Impartiality Is Not Fair: Toward an Alternative Approach to the Evaluation of Content Bias in News Stories." *Journalism* 17, no. 5 (2016): 600–618.

Bourdieu, Pierre. *Distinction: A Social Critique of the Judgement of Taste*. Cambridge, MA: Harvard University Press, 2018.

———. *The Logic of Practice*. Stanford, CA: Stanford University Press, 1990.

Boyd A., Paul Stewart, and Ray Alexander. *Broadcast Journalism: Techniques of Radio and Television News*. 6th ed. New York: Routledge, 2008.

Brann, Maria, and Kimberly Leezer Himes. "Perceived Credibility of Male versus Female Television Newscasters." *Communication Research Reports* 27, no. 3 (2010): 243–252.

Breed, Warren. "Social Control in the Newsroom: A Functional Analysis." *Social Forces* 33, no. 4 (May 1955): 326–335. https://doi.org/10.2307/2573002.

Brick, Samantha. "'Sorry, Some Women Are Too Ugly for TV': So Says that Self-Proclaimed Beauty, and Former TV Executive Samantha Brick." *Daily Mail*, May 1, 2012. https://www.dailymail.co.uk/femail/article-2138177/Samantha-Brick-Sorry -women-ARE-ugly-TV.html.

Broersma, Marcel. "Journalism as Performative Discourse: The Importance of Form and Style in Journalism." In *Journalism and Meaning-Making: Reading the Newspaper*, edited by Verica Rupar, 15–35. New York: Hampton Press, 2010.

Burgoon, Judee K. "Attributes of the Newscaster's Voice as Predictors of His Credibility." *Journalism Quarterly* 55, no. 2 (1978): 276–300.

Calamai, Silvia, and Fabio Ardolino. "Italian with an Accent: The Case of 'Chinese Italian' in Tuscan High Schools." *Journal of Language and Social Psychology* 39, no. 1 (2020): 132–147.

Cameron, Deborah. "Language: Designer Voices." *Critical Quarterly* 43, no. 4 (2004): 81–84.

Carbado, Devon W., and Mitu Gulati. *Acting White? Rethinking Race in Post-Racial America*. New York: Oxford University Press, 2013.

———. "Working Identity." *Cornell Law Review* 85, no. 5 (2000): 1259–1308.

Carley, Paul. "Arthur Lloyd James and English Pronunciation for Foreign Learners." In *Proceedings of PTLC 2013*, edited by Joann Przedlacka, John Maidment, and Michael Ashby, 27–30. London: Phonetics Teaching and Learning Conference, 2013. https://studylib.net/doc/13896750/arthur-lloyd-james-and-english-pronunciation-for -foreign-.

Carlson, Matt. *Journalistic Authority*. New York: Columbia University Press, 2017.

Carter, Susan. "A Mic of Her Own: Stations, Collectives, and Women's Access to Radio." *Journal of Radio Studies* 11, no. 2 (2004): 169–183. https://doi.org/10.1207 /s15506843jrs1102_3.

Cathcart, William L. "Viewer Needs and Desires in Television Newscasters." *Journal of Broadcasting & Electronic Media* 14, no. 1 (1969): 55–62.

Cavico, Frank J., Stephen C. Muffler, and Bahaudin G. Mujtaba. "Appearance Discrimination in Employment: Legal and Ethical Implications of 'Lookism' and 'Lookphobia.'" *Equality, Diversity and Inclusion: An International Journal* 32, no. 1 (2013): 83–119.

Chantler, Paul, and Peter Stewart. *Basic Radio Journalism*. New York: Routledge, 2013.

Charnley, Mitchell Vaughn. *News by Radio*. New York: Macmillan Co., 1948.

Chávez, Christopher. "'News with an Accent': Hispanic Television and the Re-Negotiation of US Latino Speech." *Communication and Critical/Cultural Studies* 12, no. 3 (2015): 252–270.

———. *The Sound of Exclusion: NPR and the Latinx Public*. Tucson: University of Arizona Press, 2021.

———. "When One Way of Speaking Dominates, Who Gets to Tell Their Stories on Public Radio?" *Current*, June 25, 2020. https://current.org/2020/06/when-one-way -of-speaking-dominates-who-gets-to-tell-their-stories-on-public-radio/.

Chen, Gina Masullo, and Paromita Pain. "Journalists and Online Comments." Center for Media Engagement, August 2016. https://mediaengagement.org/research /journalists-and-online-comments/.

"Chenjerai Kumanyika." *Transom Review* 15, no. 2 (2015). https://transom.org/wp-content/uploads/2015/01/Chenjerai-Kumanyika-Review.pdf.

Coddington, Mark, Seth C. Lewis, and Valerie Belair-Gagnon. "The Imagined Audience for News: Where Does a Journalist's Perception of the Audience Come From?" *Journalism Studies* 22, no. 8 (2021): 1028–1046.

Coffey, Amy Jo. "Challenging Assumptions about Ownership and Diversity: An Examination of US Local on-Air Television Newsroom Personnel." *International Journal on Media Management* 20, no. 4 (2018): 277–305.

———. "Representing Ourselves: Ethnic Representation in America's Television Newsrooms." *Howard Journal of Communications* 24, no. 2 (2013): 154–177.

Coleman, Renita, and H. Denis Wu. "More than Words Alone: Incorporating Broadcasters' Nonverbal Communication into the Stages of Crisis Coverage Theory—Evidence from September 11th." *Journal of Broadcasting & Electronic Media* 50, no. 1 (2006): 1–17.

Complete Course in the Technique of Broadcasting. No. 1–4. Washington DC: Floyd Gibbons School of Broadcasting, 1932.

Corrigan, Patrick W., and Deepa Rao. "On the Self-Stigma of Mental Illness: Stages, Disclosure, and Strategies for Change." *The Canadian Journal of Psychiatry* 57, no. 8 (2012): 464–469.

Couric, Katie. "Rachel Maddow Tells Katie Couric, 'I'm Not Competing on the Pretty-Girl-on-Cable Front'" *Glamour*, May 1, 2011. https://www.glamour.com/story/rachel-maddow-tells-katie-couric-im-not-competing-on-the-pretty-girl-on-cable-front.

Craft, Christine. "KMBC Said I Was Too Old and Too Ugly. Newswomen Today Are Still Fighting Discrimination." *Kansas City Star*, March 16, 2019. https://www.kansascity.com/opinion/readers-opinion/guest-commentary/article228013579.html.

———. *Too Old, Too Ugly, and Not Deferential to Men.* Rocklin, CA: Prima Pub. and Communications, 1988.

Cramerotti, Alfredo. *Aesthetic Journalism: How to Inform without Informing.* Bristol, UK: Intellect Books, 2009.

Crown Coalition. "Creating a Respectful and Open World for Natural Hair." Accessed October 6, 2023. https://www.thecrownact.com/about.

Deavours, Danielle. "Written All over Their Faces: Neutrality and Nonverbal Expression in Sandy Hook Coverage." *Electronic News* 14, no. 3 (2020): 123–142.

Denby, Gene. "Talk American." *Code Switch*. NPR. Podcast. August 8, 2018. https://www.npr.org/transcripts/636442508.

Deuze, Mark. *Media Work.* New York: Wiley, 2007.

Dewaele, Jean-Marc, and James McCloskey. "Attitudes towards Foreign Accents among Adult Multilingual Language Users." *Journal of Multilingual and Multicultural Development* 36, no. 3 (2015): 221–238.

DeWerth-Pallmeyer, Dwight. *The Audience in the News.* New York: Routledge, 2013.

DiMaggio, Paul J., and Walter W. Powell. "The Iron Cage Revisited: Institutional Isomorphism and Collective Rationality in Organizational Fields." *American Sociological Review* 48, no. 2 (1983): 147–160. https://doi.org/10.2307/2095101.

Donsbach, Wolfgang. "Journalism as the New Knowledge Profession and Consequences for Journalism Education." *Journalism* 15, no. 6 (2014): 661–677.

Dunn, Amina. "Younger, College-Educated Black Americans Are Most Likely to Feel Need to 'Code-Switch.'" Pew Research Center, September 24, 2019. https://www.pewresearch.org/fact-tank/2019/09/24/younger-college-educated-black-americans-are-most-likely-to-feel-need-to-code-switch/.

Dvorkin, Jeffrey A. "Why Doesn't NPR Sound Like the Rest of America?" NPR, May 18, 2015. https://www.npr.org/sections/publiceditor/2005/05/18/4656584/why -doesnt-npr-sound-more-like-the-rest-of-america.

Edison Research. "The Creators 2022." The Creators, July 8, 2022. Accessed February 14, 2023. https://www.edisonresearch.com/the-creators/.

——. *The Infinite Dial 2021.* March 11, 2021. http://www.edisonresearch.com/wp -content/uploads/2021/03/The-Infinite-Dial-2021.pdf.

——. "Weekly Insights 11.10.22 The Steady Climb of Podcasting's Reach in the U.S." *Edison Weekly Insights,* November 10, 2022. https://www.edisonresearch.com /weekly-insights-11-10-22-the-steady-climb-of-podcastings-reach-in-the-u-s/.

Edwards, Lee. "Discourse, Credentialism and Occupational Closure in the Communications Industries: The Case of Public Relations in the UK." *European Journal of Communication* 29, no. 3 (2014): 319–334.

Ellis, Katie, and Gerard Goggin. *Disability and the Media.* New York: Palgrave Macmillan, 2015.

Elmen-Gruys, Kjerstin. "Properly Attired, Hired, or Fired: Aesthetic Labor and Social Inequality." PhD diss., University of California, Los Angeles, 2014.

Engstrom, Erika. "Looking through a Gendered Lens: Local U.S. Television News Anchors' Perceived Career Barriers." *Journal of Broadcasting & Electronic Media* 44, no. 4 (2000): 614–634. https://doi.org/10.1207/s15506878jobem4404_6.

Entman, Robert M. "Modern Racism and the Images of Blacks in Local Television News." *Critical Studies in Media Communication* 7, no. 4 (1990): 332–345.

Ewbank, Henry Lee, and Sherman P. Lawton. *Broadcasting: Radio and Television.* New York: Harper, 1952.

Fairclough, Norman. *Discourse and Social Change.* Cambridge, MA: Polity Press, 1992.

Falk, Tyler. "Drop in Younger Listeners Makes Dent in NPR News Audience." *Current,* October 16, 2015. https://current.org/2015/10/drop-in-younger-listeners-makes-dent -in-npr-news-audience/.

Fasoli, Fabio, Peter Hegarty, and David M. Frost. "Stigmatization of 'Gay-Sounding' Voices: The Role of Heterosexual, Lesbian, and Gay Individuals' Essentialist Beliefs." *British Journal of Social Psychology* 60, no. 3 (2021): 826–850.

Figueroa, Megan, and Carrie Gillon. "I Ain't Messing with You." *The Vocal Fries Pod.* Podcast. June 28, 2021. https://vocalfriespod.com/2021/06/28/i-aint-messing-with -you/.

——. "Southern Fried." *The Vocal Fries Pod.* Podcast. September 12, 2018. https:// vocalfriespod.com/2018/09/12/transcript-3-southern-fried/.

Finneman, Teri, and Joy Jenkins. "Sexism on the Set: Gendered Expectations of TV Broadcasters in a Social Media World." *Journal of Broadcasting & Electronic Media* 62, no. 3 (2018): 479–494.

Fox, Kim, David O. Dowling, and Kyle Miller. "A Curriculum for Blackness: Podcasts as Discursive Cultural Guides, 2010–2020." *Journal of Radio & Audio Media* 27, no. 2 (2020): 298–318.

Friess, Steve. "Why Are #PodcastsSoWhite?" *Columbia Journalism Review,* March 21, 2017. https://www.cjr.org/the_feature/podcasts-diversity.php.

Gans, Herbert J. *Deciding What's News: A Study of CBS Evening News, NBC Nightly News, Newsweek, and Time.* New York: Pantheon Books, 1979.

Garbes, Laura. "'I Just Don't Hear It': How Whiteness Dilutes Voices of Color at Public Radio Stations." The American Prospect, August 18, 2020. https://prospect.org /culture/i-just-dont-hear-it-voices-of-color-npr-public-radio/.

———. "When the "Blank Slate" Is a White One: White Institutional Isomorphism in the Birth of National Public Radio." *Sociology of Race & Ethnicity* 8, no. 1 (2022): 79–94.

Gasser, Emily, Byron Ahn, Donna Jo Napoli, and Z. L. Zhou. "Production, Perception, and Communicative Goals of American Newscaster Speech." *Language in Society* 48, no. 2 (2019): 233–259.

Gerson, Jennifer. "The Voices of NPR: How Four Women of Color See Their Roles as Hosts." *The 19th*, April 26, 2023. https://19thnews.org/2023/04/the-voices-of-npr/.

Giles, Howard, and Bernadette M. Watson. *The Social Meanings of Language, Dialect and Accent: International Perspectives on Speech Styles*. New York: Peter Lang, 2013.

Glass, Ira. "545: Freedom Fries." *This American Life*. Podcast. January 23, 2015. https://www.thisamericanlife.org/545/if-you-dont-have-anything-nice-to-say-say-it-in-all-caps/act-two-0.

Glasser, Theodore, L. "The Aesthetics of News." *ETC: A Review of General Semantics* 37 (1980): 238–247.

———. "Professionalism and the Derision of Diversity: The Case of the Education of Journalists." *Journal of Communication* 42, no. 2 (1992): 131–140.

Gluszek, Agata, and John F. Dovidio. "The Way They Speak: A Social Psychological Perspective on the Stigma of Nonnative Accents in Communication." *Personality and Social Psychology Review* 14, no. 2 (2010): 214–237.

Goffman, Erving. *Forms of Talk*. University of Pennsylvania Press, 1981.

———. *The Presentation of Self in Everyday Life*. New York: Doubleday, 1959.

———. *Stigma: Notes on the Management of Spoiled Identity*. New York: Simon & Schuster, 1963.

Gong, Zijian Harrison, and James Eppler. "Exploring the Impact of Delivery Mistakes, Gender, and Empathic Concern on Source and Message Credibility." *Journalism Practice* 16, no. 8 (2022): 1653–1672.

González, Juan, and Joseph Torres. *News for All the People: The Epic Story of Race and the American Media*. London: Verso, 2011.

Gould, Samuel B., and Sidney Dimond. *Training the Local Announcer*. New York: Longmans, Green and Co., 1950.

Grabe, Maria Elizabeth, and Lelia Samson. "Sexual Cues Emanating from the Anchorette Chair: Implications for Perceived Professionalism, Fitness for Beat, and Memory for News." *Communication Research* 38, no. 4 (2011): 471–496.

Gravengaard, Gitte, and Lene Rimestad. "Socializing Journalist Trainees in the Newsroom: On How to Capture the Intangible Parts of the Process." *Nordicom Review* 35, no. s1 (2014): 81–96. https://doi.org/10.2478/nor-2014-0105.

Gross, Terry. "'It Was Just Thrilling': 2 NPR Founders Remember the First Days, 50 Years Ago." Excerpt from *Fresh Air*. NPR, April 28, 2021. https://www.npr.org/2021/04/28/991268881/it-was-just-thrilling-2-npr-founders-remember-the-first-days-50-years-ago.

———. "It's Impossible to Fit 'All Things' Ari Shapiro Does into This Headline." *Fresh Air*, NPR, March 22, 2023, para. 16. https://www.npr.org/2023/03/22/1165002548/ari-shapiro-npr-pink-martini-best-strangers-world.

Grove, Lloyd. "The Bland Leading the Bland." *Washington Post*, November 6, 1983. https://www.washingtonpost.com/archive/lifestyle/magazine/1983/11/06/the-bland-leading-the-bland/50e8264e-ade1-4a62-b074-4df404bfc53b/.

Haller, Beth A. *Disabled People Transforming Media Culture for a More Inclusive World*. New York: Routledge, 2023.

Hamilton, James T. *All The News that's Fit to Sell: How the Market Transforms Information into News*. Princeton, NJ: Princeton University Press, 2004.

Hanitzsch, Thomas, and Tim P. Vos. "Journalistic Roles and the Struggle over Institutional Identity: The Discursive Constitution of Journalism." *Communication Theory* 27, no. 2 (2017): 115–135. https://doi.org/10.1111/comt.12112.

Hardin, Marie, and Ann Preston. "Inclusion of Disability Issues in News Reporting Textbooks." *Journalism & Mass Communication Educator* 56, no. 2 (2001): 43–54.

Hardy, William G. "Radio and the American Language." *Quarterly Journal of Speech* 24, no. 3 (1938): 453–464. https://doi.org/10.1080/00335633809380394.

Hartley, John. *Understanding News*. New York: Routledge, 2013.

Hausman, Carl, Lewis B. O'Donnell, and Philip Benoit. *Announcing: Broadcast Communicating Today*. Belmont, CA: Wadsworth Publishing, 2000.

Headlee, Celeste. "An Anti-Racist Future: A Vision and Plan for the Transformation of Public Media." *Medium*, January 18, 2021. https://celesteheadlee.medium.com/an-anti-racist-future-a-vision-and-plan-for-the-transformation-of-public-media-224149ab37e6.

Hellmueller, Lea, Tim P. Vos, and Mark A. Poepsel. "Shifting Journalistic Capital? Transparency and Objectivity in the Twenty-First Century." *Journalism Studies* 14, no. 3 (2013): 287–304.

Hendrickson, John. *Life on Delay: Making Peace with a Stutter*. New York: Alfred A. Knopf, 2023.

Holt, Kristoffer. "Authentic Journalism? A Critical Discussion about Existential Authenticity in Journalism Ethics." *Journal of Mass Media Ethics* 27, no. 1 (2012): 2–14. https://doi.org/10.1080/08900523.2012.636244.

Horwitz, Paul. "Uncovering Identity." *Michigan Law Review* 105, no. 6 (2007): 1283–1300.

Houlberg, Rick. "The Audience Experience with Television News: A Qualitative Study." Paper presented at the 64th Annual Meeting of the Association for Education in Journalism, East Lansing, MI, August 9–11, 1981. https://eric.ed.gov/?id=ED204756.

Hutchinson, Kevin L. "The Effects of Newscaster Gender and Vocal Quality on Perceptions of Homophily and Interpersonal Attraction." *Journal of Broadcasting & Electronic Media* 26, no. 1 (1982): 457–467.

Hyde, Stuart, and Dina A. Ibrahim. *Television and Radio Announcing*. New York: Routledge, 2017.

Institute of Employment Rights. "Class Still a Significant Factor in Workplace Progression, Research Finds." Institute of Employment Rights, June 22, 2018. https://www.ier.org.uk/news/class-still-significant-factor-workplace-progression-research-finds/.

"Ira Glass." *Here's the Thing*. Podcast episode hosted by Alec Baldwin. WNYC Studios. November 23, 2014, https://www.wnycstudios.org/podcasts/heresthething/episodes/ira-glass-interview.

Izadi, Elahe. "Why Your Favorite New NPR Show Might Sound a Lot Like a Podcast." *Washington Post*, May 3, 2021. https://www.washingtonpost.com/lifestyle/media/npr-50thanniversary-podcast-audience/2021/05/03/afod49a0-a8fa-11eb-8d25-7b30e74923ea_story.html.

Jablin, Fredric M. "Organizational Entry, Assimilation, and Disengagement/Exit." In *The New Handbook of Organizational Communication: Advances in Theory, Research, and Methods*, edited by F. M. Jablin and J.. Putnam, 732–818. Thousand Oaks, CA: Sage, 2001.

Jacob, Mark. "Medill Study Finds Preferences for Female Voices and Local Accents." *Medill Local News Initiative*, March 30, 2020. https://localnewsinitiative.northwestern .edu/posts/2020/03/30/voice-accent-study/#:~:text=Lee%2C%20a%20professor%20 at%20Northwestern's,speaking%20with%20a%20local%20accent.

Jacobs, Andrew. "Novice Newscasters Get Voice Therapy." *New York Times*, June 16, 1997. https://www.nytimes.com/1997/06/16/business/novice-newscasters-get-voice -therapy.html.

Jacobs, Jerry. *Changing Channels: Issues and Realities in Television News*. Mountain View, CA: Mayfield Pub. Co., 1990.

James, Heather R. "If You Are Attractive and You Know It, Please Apply: Appearance-Based Discrimination and Employers' Discretion." *Valparaiso University Law Review* 42, no. 2 (2008): 629–674.

Karpf, Anne. *The Human Voice: How This Extraordinary Instrument Reveals Essential Clues about Who We Are*. New York: Bloomsbury Pub., 2006.

Keith, Michael C. *Broadcast Voice Performance*. Boston: Focal Press, 1989.

Keith, Tamara. "How I Found My #PubRadioVoice." *Adventures in Radioland*, February 6, 2015. http://www.tamarakeith.com/2015/02/how-i-found-my -pubradiovoice-spoiler.html.

Kern, Jonathan. *Sound Reporting: The NPR Guide to Audio Journalism and Production*. University of Chicago Press, 2012.

Kerner Commission. *Report of the National Advisory Commission on Civil Disorders*. Washington, DC: Government Printing Office, 1967. https://www.ojp.gov/ncjrs /virtual-library/abstracts/national-advisory-commission-civil-disorders-report.

Kinzler, Katherine D. *How You Say It: Why You Talk the Way You Do and What It Says about You*. New York: Houghton Mifflin Harcourt, 2020.

Kirkpatrick, Bill. "Voices Made for Print: Crip Voices on the Radio." In *Radio's New Wave: Global Sound in the Digital Era*, edited by Jason Loviglio and Michele Hilmes, 106–125. New York: Routledge, 2013.

Knight, Dudley. "Standard Speech: The Ongoing Debate." In *The Vocal Vision: Views on Voice by 24 Leading Teachers Coaches and Directors,* edited by Marion Hampton and Barbara Acker, 155–184. New York: Applause, 1997.

Koval, Christy Zhou, and Ashleigh Shelby Rosette. "The Natural Hair Bias in Job Recruitment." *Social Psychological and Personality Science* 12, no. 5 (2021): 741–750.

Kuczynski, Christopher J. "EEOC Informal Discussion Letter: ADA: Job Related and Consistent with Business Necessity / Direct Threat." U.S. Equal Employment Opportunity Commission, March 16, 2001. https://www.eeoc.gov/foia/eeoc -informal-discussion-letter-44.

Kumanyika, Chenjerai. "Challenging the Whiteness of Public Radio." *Code Switch*. Podcast. NPR, January 29, 2015. https://www.npr.org/sections/codeswitch/2015/01 /29/382437460/challengingthe-whiteness-of-public-radio.

Labov, William. *Dialect Diversity in America: The Politics of Language Change*. Charlottesville: University of Virginia Press, 2012.

Lawton, Sherman P. "The Principles of Effective Radio Speaking." *Quarterly Journal of Speech* 16, no. 3 (1930): 255–277.

———. *Radio Speech*. Boston: Expression Company, 1932.

Lev-Ari, Shiri, and Boaz Keysar. "Why Don't We Believe Non-Native Speakers? The Influence of Accent on Credibility." *Journal of Experimental Social Psychology* 46, no. 6 (2010): 1093–1096.

Lewis, Libby. *The Myth of Post-Racialism in Television News*. New York: Routledge, 2015.

Litt, Eden. "Knock, Knock. Who's There? The Imagined Audience." *Journal of Broadcasting & Electronic Media* 56, no. 3 (2012): 330–345.

Lopes, Leonardo Wanderley, Ivonaldo Leidson Barbosa Lima, Eveline Gonçalves Silva, Larissa Nadjara Alves de Almeida, and Anna Alice Figueiredo de Almeida. "Accent and Television Journalism: Evidence for the Practice of Speech Language Pathologists and Audiologists." *CoDAS* 25, no. 5 (2013): 475–481.

Loviglio, Jason. "U.S. Public Radio, Social Change, and the Gendered Voice." In *Electrified Voices: Medial, Socio-Historical and Cultural Aspects of Voice Transfer,* edited by Nils Meise and Dmitri Zakharine, 137–146. Göttingen: V&R Unipress, 2013.

Lowery, Wesley. "A Reckoning over Objectivity, Led by Black Journalists." *New York Times,* June 23, 2020. https://www.nytimes.com/2020/06/23/opinion/objectivity -black-journalists-coronavirus.html.

Mahajan, Ritu. "The Naked Truth: Appearance Discrimination, Employment, and the Law." *Asian American Law Journal* 14 (2007): 165–213.

Mason, Betsy. "Curbing Implicit Bias: What Works and Doesn't Work." *Knowable Magazine,* June 4, 2020. https://knowablemagazine.org/article/mind/2020/how-to -curb-implicit-bias.

Matsa, Katerina Eva. "Fewer Americans Rely on TV News; What Type They Watch Varies by Who They Are." Pew Research Center, January 5, 2018. https://www .pewresearch.org/short-reads/2018/01/05/fewer-americans-rely-on-tv-news-what -type-they-watch-varies-by-who-they-are/.

Matsuda, Mari J. "Voices of America: Accent, Antidiscrimination Law, and a Jurisprudence for the Last Reconstruction." *Yale Law Journal* 100, no. 5 (1991): 1329–1407.

Mazziotta, Julie. "Meteorologist Claps Back at Body Shamer Who Tells Her to Cover Her 'Bulge': 'I Like My Body.'" *People,* October 16, 2019. https://people.com/health /meteorologist-claps-back-at-body-shamer-who-tells-her-to-cover-her-bulge-i-like-my -body/.

McCauley, Michael P. *NPR: The Trials and Triumphs of National Public Radio.* New York: Columbia University Press, 2005.

McClelland, Edward. *How to Speak Midwestern.* Cleveland, OH: Belt Publishing, 2016.

McDonnell, Brett H., and Matthew T. Bodie. "From Mandates to Governance: Restructuring the Employment Relationship." *Maryland Law Review* 81, no. 3 (2022): 887–950.

McNab, Kaitlyn. "Black Newscasters Are Redefining What It Means To 'Look Professional' On-Air." *Allure,* April 4, 2021. https://www.allure.com/story/black -news-anchors-braids-natural-hair.

Mears, Ashley. "Aesthetic Labor for the Sociologies of Work, Gender, and Beauty." *Sociology Compass* 8, no. 12 (2014): 1330–1343.

Meltzer, Kimberly. *TV News Anchors and Journalistic Tradition: How Journalists Adapt to Technology.* New York: Peter Lang, 2010.

Metcalf, Allan A. *How We Talk: American Regional English Today.* Boston: Houghton Mifflin, 2000.

Miller, Whitney. "It's 2020 and Black Reporters Are Still Asking to Wear Their Braids on TV." *WCPO,* August 31, 2020. https://www.wcpo.com/news/opinion/column-its -2020-and-black-reporters-are-still-asking-to-wear-their-braids-on-tv.

Mitchell, Jack W. *Listener Supported: The Culture and History of Public Radio.* Westport, CT.: Praeger, 2005.

Mitra, Barbara, Mike Webb, and Claire Wolfe. "Audience Responses to the Physical Appearance of Television Newsreaders." *Participations Journal of Audience & Reception Studies* 11, no. 2 (2014): 45–57.

Montgomery, Martin. "Defining 'Authentic Talk.'" *Discourse Studies* 3, no. 4 (2001): 397–405. https://doi.org/10.1177/1461445601003004004.

Montopoli, Brian. "All Things Considerate: How NPR Makes Tavis Smiley Sound Like Linda Wertheimer." *Washington Monthly* 35, no. 1/2 (2001): 40–42.

Morris, Michael. "Standard White: Dismantling White Normativity." *California Law Review* 104, no. 4 (2016): 949–978.

Mosley, Tonya. "The Neutrality vs. Objectivity Game Ends." Nieman Foundation, January 5, 2020. https://www.niemanlab.org/2020/01/the-neutrality-vs-objectivity -game-ends/.

Mugglestone, Lynda. *Talking Proper: The Rise of Accent as Social Symbol.* 2nd ed. Oxford: Oxford University Press, 2007.

Muhl, Charles J. "The Employment-at-Will Doctrine: Three Major Exceptions." *Monthly Labor Review* 124 (2001): 3.

Myskow, Wyatt, and Piper Hansen. "Incoming Cronkite Dean Has Alleged History of Racist, Homophobic Comments toward Students." *The State Press*, June 5, 2020. https://www.statepress.com/article/2020/06/spcommunity-incoming-cronkite -dean-has-alleged-history-of-racist-homophobic-comments-toward-students.

Nadler, Anthony. *Making the News Popular: Mobilizing U.S. News Audiences.* Champaign: University of Illinois Press, 2016.

Napoli, Lisa. *Susan, Linda, Nina & Cokie: The Extraordinary Story of the Founding Mothers of NPR.* New York: Abrams Press, 2021.

Negrin, Llewellyn. *Appearance and Identity: Fashioning the Body in Postmodernity.* New York: Palgrave Macmillan, 2008.

Nelson, Jacob. L. *Imagined Audiences: How Journalists Perceive and Pursue the Public.* New York: Oxford University Press, 2021.

Newkirk, Pamela. *Diversity, Inc.: The Failed Promise of a Billion-Dollar Business.* New York: Bold Type Books, 2019.

———. *Within the Veil: Black Journalists, White Media.* New York University Press, 2000.

Nguyen, Beatrice Bich-Dao. "Accent Discrimination and the Test of Spoken English: A Call for an Objective Assessment of the Comprehensibility of Nonnative Speakers." *California Law Review* 81, no. 5 (1993): 1325–1361.

Nickson, Dennis, Chris Warhurst, Anne Marie Cullen, and Allan Watt. "Bringing in the Excluded? Aesthetic Labour, Skills and Training in the 'New' Economy." *Journal of Education and Work* 16, no. 2 (2003): 185–203.

Nielsen. "Podcasts Are Resonating with Diverse Audiences." Nielsen. December 2021. https://www.nielsen.com/insights/2021/podcasts-are-resonating-with-diverse -audiences/.

Nightingale, Virginia. "Introduction." In *The Handbook of Media Audiences*, edited by Virginia Nightengale, 1–16. Malden, MA: Wiley-Blackwell, 2011.

Nissen, Shawn, Quint B. Randle, Jared L. Johnson, and Jenny Lynes. "Prosodic Elements for Content Delivery in Broadcast Journalism: A Quantitative Study of Vocal Pitch." *Electronic News* 14, no. 2 (2020): 63–77.

Nitz, Michael, Tom Reichert, Adonica Schultz Aune, and André Vander Velde. "All the News that's Fit to See? The Sexualization of Television News Journalists as a Promotional Strategy." *Journal of Promotion Management* 13, no. 1–2 (2007): 13–33.

Noble, Brittany. "Why I Disappeared from WJTV in Jackson, Mississippi." *Medium*, January 7, 2019. https://medium.com/@thenoblejournalist/why-i-disappeared-from -the-news-desk-at-wjtv-in-jackson-mississippi-bd734b1affb3.

Nuzum, Eric. *Make Noise: A Creator's Guide to Podcasting and Great Audio Storytelling.* New York: Workman Publishing, 2019.

———. "To Serve Diverse Audiences, You Can't Walk the Walk Until You Know Where You Stand." *Current*, March 10, 2022. https://current.org/2022/03/to-serve-diverse-audiences-you-cant-walk-the-walk-until-you-know-where-you-stand/.

Ojala, Markus. "Is the Age of Impartial Journalism Over? The Neutrality Principle and Audience (Dis)trust in Mainstream News." *Journalism Studies* 22, no. 15 (2021): 2042–2060.

Olson, Steve. "Often Overlooked, Airchecking Is Essential to Keeping Public Radio's Audience." *Current*, April 14, 2016. https://current.org/2016/04/often-overlooked-airchecking-is-essential-to-keeping-public-radios-audience/.

Ott-Fulmore, Tanya. "Does This Microphone Make Me Sound White? An Experiment Exploring Race Recognition and Source Credibility in Radio News." MA thesis, University of Alabama, 2020. https://ir-api.ua.edu/api/core/bitstreams/574cb7ea-883d-4e0f-ba54-04b78cddb3fe/content.

Pai, Shin Yu, Whitney Henry-Lester, and Jim Gates. "A Voice Breaks Barriers." *Ten Thousand Things*. Podcast. KUOW. June 19, 2023. https://www.kuow.org/stories/a-voice-breaks-barriers.

Pain, Paromita, and Victoria Chen. "This Reporter Is So Ugly, How Can She Appear on TV? Negotiating Gender Online and Offline in Taiwanese Media." *Journalism Practice* 13, no. 2 (2019): 140–158.

Papper, Bob, and Keren Henderson. "Minority Representation Increases, but Still Lags General Population." RTDNA, November 16, 2022. https://www.rtdna.org/news/minority-representation-increases-but-still-lags-general-population.

Patton, Michael Quinn. *Qualitative Research & Evaluation Methods*. 3rd ed. Sage, 2002.

Patzer, Gordon. *Looks: Why They Matter More Than You Ever Imagined*. New York: AMACOM, 2008.

———. "Source Credibility as a Function of Communicator Physical Attractiveness." *Journal of Business Research* 11, no. 2 (1983): 229–241.

Person, Joseph. "'That is who he is': Marty Smith Found Fame Staying True to His Southern Roots." *The Athletic*, June 19, 2020. https://theathletic.com/1879122/2020/06/19/that-is-who-he-is-spiked-hair-the-suits-that-accent-its-all-marty-smith/.

Pitkin, Hanna. *The Concept of Representation*. Berkeley: University of California Press, 1967.

Ponce de Leon, Charles L. *That's The Way It Is: A History of Television News in America*. University of Chicago Press, 2015.

Porter, Jeff. *Lost Sound: The Forgotten Sound of Radio Storytelling*. University of North Carolina Press, 2016.

Powell, Tracie. "Are Podcasts the New Path to Diversifying Public Radio?" *Columbia Journalism Review* (2015). https://www.cjr.org/analysis/are_podcasts_the_new_path_to_diversifying_public_radio.php.

Powers, Elia. "The Journalist's Speech: A Phenomenological Study of Stuttering in the Newsroom." *Journalism Studies* 21, no. 9 (2020): 1243–1260. https://doi.org/10.1080/1461670X.2020.1738953.

———. "Seeking 'Skilled, Poised, Fluent' Verbal Communicators: Aesthetic Labor and Signaling in Journalism Job Advertisements." *Newspaper Research Journal* 42, no. 1 (2021): 12–28. https://doi.org/10.1177/0739532921989884.

Powers, Elia, and Beth Haller. "Journalism and Mass Communication Textbook Representations of Verbal Media Skills: Implications for Students with Speech Disabilities." *Journal of Media Literacy Education* 9, no. 2 (2017): 58–75. https://doi.org/10.23860/JMLE-2019-09-02-05.

Powers, Ron. *The Newscasters*. New York: St. Martin's Press, 1977.

Prato, Lou. "TV News Refrain: Talk to My Agent." *American Journalism Review* 18, no. 1 (1996): 56–57.

PwC and Interactive Advertising Bureau. "Internet Advertising Revenue Report: Full-Year 2022 Results." April 2022. https://www.iab.com/wp-content/uploads/2022/04/IAB_Internet_Advertising_Revenue_Report_Full_Year_2021.pdf.

Quah, Nicholas. "It's Been a Minute with Sam Sanders." *Servant of Pod.* Podcast. LAist. April 19, 2021. https://laist.com/podcasts/servant-of-pod/its-been-a-minute-with-sam-sanders.

———. "What Went Wrong at Gimlet?" *Vulture*, March 10, 2021. https://www.vulture.com/article/gimlet-reply-all-controversy-spotify-test-kitchen.html.

Raemy, Patric. "A Theory of Professional Identity in Journalism: Connecting Discursive Institutionalism, Socialization, and Psychological Resilience Theory." *Communication Theory* 31, no. 4 (2021): 841–861.

Ragusea, Adam. "How Women, People of Color, and Everyone Else Can Sound More Like Themselves on the Radio." *The Pub*, episode 4. Podcast. February 15, 2015.

Reardon, Nancy, and Tom Flynn. *On Camera: How to Report, Anchor & Interview.* Taylor & Francis, 2013.

Rehm, Diane. *Finding My Voice.* Herndon, VA: Capital Books, 2002.

Rhew, Adam. "Why News Anchors All Have the Same Look." *Racked*, February 1, 2017. https://www.racked.com/2017/2/1/14441128/local-news-anchor-image-consultants.

Rhode, Deborah L. "The Injustice of Appearance." *Stanford Law Review* 61, no. 5 (2009): 1033–1101.

Richardson, Robert J. "Local TV Newsroom Diversity: Race and Gender of Newscasters and Their Managers." *Journal of Broadcasting & Electronic Media* 66, no. 5 (2022): 823–842.

Roberts, Cokie, and Susan Stamberg. *This Is NPR: The First Forty Years.* San Francisco: Chronicle Books, 2010.

Robinson, James G. "The Audience in the Mind's Eye: How Journalists Imagine Their Readers." *Columbia Journalism Review*, June 26, 2019. https://doi.org/10.7916/d8-drvj-wjo6.

Robinson, Russell K. "Uncovering Covering." *Northwestern University Law Review.* 101 (2007): 1809–1850.

Rueckert, Veronica. *Outspoken: Why Women's Voices Get Silenced and How to Set Them Free.* New York: HarperCollins, 2019.

Sanders, Keith P., and Michael Pritchett. "Some Influences of Appearance on Television Newscaster Appeal." *Journal of Broadcasting & Electronic Media* 15, no. 3 (1971): 293–302.

Schlütz, Daniela, and Imke Hedder. "Aural Parasocial Relations: Host–Listener Relationships in Podcasts." *Journal of Radio & Audio Media* 29, no. 2 (2022): 457–474.

Schumacher-Matos, Edward. "Black, Latino, Asian and White: Diversity at NPR." NPR, April 10, 2012. https://www.npr.org/sections/publiceditor/2012/04/10/150367888/black-latino-asian-and-white-diversity-at-npr.

Schwyter, Jürg Rainer. *Dictating to the Mob: The History of the BBC Advisory Committee on Spoken English.* New York: Oxford University Press, 2016.

Shapiro, Ariel. "New Podcast Creation Has Fallen Off a Cliff." *The Verge*, January 17, 2023. https://www.theverge.com/2023/1/17/23559638/new-podcasts-down-apple-spotify-amazon-audible-hot-pod-summit.

Shimpach, Shawn. "Viewing." In *The Handbook of Media Audiences*, edited by Virginia Nightingale, 62–85. Malden, MA: Wiley-Blackwell, 2011.

Smith, Jonathan A., Paul Flowers, and Michael Larkin. *Interpretative Phenomenological Analysis: Theory, Research, and Method.* Thousand Oaks, CA: Sage, 2009.

Smith, Jonathan A., and Mike Osborn. "Interpretative Phenomenological Analysis as a Useful Methodology for Research on the Lived Experience of Pain." *British Journal of Pain* 9, no. 1 (2015): 41–42.

Soloski, Alexis. "When Podcast Hosts Speak, What Do We Hear?" *New York Times*, February 25, 2021. https://www.nytimes.com/interactive/2021/02/25/arts/podcast-voice-sound.html.

Spence, Michael. "Job Market Signaling." In *Uncertainty in Economics: Readings and Exercises*, edited by Peter A. Diamond and Michael Rothschild, 281–306. New York: Academic Press, 1978.

Stavitsky, Alan G. "'Guys in Suits with Charts': Audience Research in US Public Radio." *Journal of Broadcasting & Electronic Media* 39, no. 2 (1995): 177–189.

Steinmetz, Johanna. "'Mr. Magic'—The TV Newscast Doctor." *New York Times*, October 12, 1975. https://www.nytimes.com/1975/10/12/archives/mr-magicthe-tv-newscast-doctor-mr-magicthe-newscast-doctor.html.

"Stephanie Foo." *Transom Review* 16, no. 1 (2016). https://transom.org/wp-content/uploads/2016/05/StephanieFoo_review.pdf.

Stephane, Joanne, Heather McBride Leef, Sameen Affaf, Kenji Yoshino, and David Glasgow. "Uncovering Culture: A Call to Action for Leaders. *Deloitte and the Meltzer Center for Diversity, Inclusion, and Belonging.* Last modified November 14, 2023, https://www2.deloitte.com/content/dam/Deloitte/us/Documents/about-deloitte/dei/us-uncovering-culture-a-call-to-action-for-leaders.pdf?dl=1.

Stephenson, Alan, David Reese, and Mary Beadle. *Broadcast Announcing Worktext: A Media Performance Guide.* 4th ed. London: Taylor & Francis, 2013.

Stone, Vernon. "Attitudes toward Television Newswomen." *Journal of Broadcasting* 18, no. 1 (1973): 49–62.

Strauss, Ben. "The Radio Reporter Who Lost His Voice but Still Covers Congress." *Politico*, December 15, 2017. https://www.politico.com/magazine/story/2017/12/15/jamie-dupree-radio-voice-216107/.

Thompson, Kerry, and Erin Slomski-Pritz. "50 and Forward: An Anniversary Celebration of NPR." Podcast. NPR. April 30, 2021. https://www.npr.org/2021/04/30/991424624/fifty-and-forward-an-anniversary-celebration-of-npr.

Tobin, Stephanie J., and Rosanna E. Guadagno. "Why People Listen: Motivations and Outcomes of Podcast Listening." *PloS One* 17, no. 4 (2022): https://doi.org/10.1371/journal.pone.0265806.

Tolson, Andrew. *Media Talk: Spoken Discourse on Radio and TV.* Edinburgh: Edinburgh University Press, 2005.

Tomassetti, Julia. "Power in the Employment Relationship: Why Contract Law Should Not Govern At-Will Employment." Economic Policy Institute, November 19, 2020. https://www.epi.org/unequalpower/publications/the-legal-understanding-and-treatment-of-an-employment-relationship-versus-a-contract/.

Tweedy, Jo. "Sky News Political Editor Beth Rigby Reveals Trolls Hacked Her Wikipedia Page." *Daily Mail*, September 5, 2019. https://www.dailymail.co.uk/femail/article-7431017/Sky-News-political-editor-trolled-speech-impediment.html.

Ugwu, Reggie. "Brittany Luse and Eric Eddings of 'For Colored Nerds' Play For Keeps," *New York Times*, November 17, 2021, para. 13. https://www.nytimes.com/2021/11/17/arts/brittany-luse-eric-eddings-for-colored-nerds-podcast.html.

———. "Saidu Tejan-Thomas Jr. and the Voices of Resistance." *New York Times*, February 25, 2021. https://www.nytimes.com/2021/02/25/arts/saidu-tejan-thomas-jr -resistance.html.

U.S. Equal Opportunity Employment Commission. "Facts about Race/Color Discrimination," https://www.eeoc.gov/fact-sheet/facts-about-racecolor-discrimination.

Usher, Nikki. *News for the Rich, White, and Blue: How Place and Power Distort American Journalism*. New York: Columbia University Press, 2021.

Utterback, Ann S. *Broadcast Voice Handbook: How to Polish Your On-Air Delivery*. Santa Monica, CA: Bonus Books, Inc., 2005.

Vaillant, Derek W. "Sounds of Whiteness: Local Radio, Racial Formation, and Public Culture in Chicago, 1921–1935." *American Quarterly* 54, no. 1 (2002): 25–66. http://www.jstor.org/stable/30042215.

Van Nostrand, Liana. "Sounding Like a Reporter—and a Real Person, Too." NPR, August 7. 2019. https://www.npr.org/sections/publiceditor/2019/08/07/749060986 /sounding-like-a-reporter-and-a-real-person-too.

Van Oot, Torey. "Why 95.8% of Female Newscasters Have the Same Hair." *InStyle*, August 14, 2018. https://www.instyle.com/hair/secret-beauty-rules-of-television -talking-heads.

VanCour, Shawn. *Making Radio: Early Radio Production and the Rise of Modern Sound Culture*. Oxford: Oxford University Press, 2018.

Vonk, Laura. "Peer Feedback in Aesthetic Labour: Forms, Logics and Responses." *Cultural Sociology* 15, no. 2 (2021): 213–232. https://doi.org/10.1177/1749975520962368.

Wahl-Jorgensen, Karin. "The Construction of the Public in Letters to the Editor: Deliberative Democracy and the Idiom of Insanity." *Journalism* 3, no. 2 (2002): 183–204.

Wallace, Lewis. "Objectivity Is Dead, and I'm OK with It." *Medium*, January 27, 2017. https://medium.com/@lewispants/objectivity-is-dead-and-im-okay-with-it -7fd2b4b5c58f.

Walters, Barbara. *Audition*. New York: Vintage Books, 2009.

Warhurst, Chris, and Dennis Nickson. *Aesthetic Labour*. Thousand Oaks, CA: Sage, 2020.

———. *Looking Good, Sounding Right*. London: Industrial Society, 2001.

Warhurst, Chris, Dennis Nickson, Anne Witz, and Anne Marie Cullen. "Aesthetic Labour in Interactive Service Work: Some Case Study Evidence from the 'New' Glasgow." *Service Industries Journal* 20, no. 3 (2000): 1–18.

Warhurst, Samantha, Patricia McCabe, and Catherine Madill. "What Makes a Good Voice for Radio: Perceptions of Radio Employers and Educators." *Journal of Voice* 27, no. 2 (2013): 217–224.

Warhurst, Samantha, Patricia McCabe, Edwin Yiu, Robert Heard, and Catherine Madill. "Acoustic Characteristics of Male Commercial and Public Radio Broadcast Voices." *Journal of Voice* 27, no. 5 (2013): e1–7. https://doi.org/10.1016/j.jvoice.2013.04.012.

Wayne, Teddy. "'NPR Voice' Has Taken over the Airwaves." *New York Times*, October 24, 2015. https://www.nytimes.com/2015/10/25/fashion/npr-voice-has-taken -over-the-airwaves.html.

Webster, Molly. "Don't Fear the Vocal Fry." *Werk It: The Podcast*. WNYC Studios. June 7, 2015. https://www.wnycstudios.org/podcasts/werkit/episodes/werk-it -owning-your-voice.

Weibel, David, Bartholomäus Wissmath, and Rudolf Groner. "How Gender and Age Affect Newscasters' Credibility—an Investigation in Switzerland." *Journal of Broadcasting & Electronic Media* 52, no. 3 (2008): 466–484.

Wiedeman, Reeves. "Ambiguously Genuine." *New Yorker*, November 10, 2013. https://www.newyorker.com/magazine/2013/11/18/ambiguously-genuine.

Wiik, Jenny. "Internal Boundaries: The Stratification of the Journalistic Collective." In *Boundaries of Journalism*, edited by Matt Carlson, Seth C. Lewis, 118–133. New York: Routledge, 2015.

Williams, Christine L., and Catherine Connell. "'Looking Good and Sounding Right': Aesthetic Labor and Social Inequality in the Retail Industry." *Work & Occupations* 37, no. 3 (2010): 349–377. https://doi.org/10.1177/0730888410373744.

Witz, Anne, Chris Warhurst, and Dennis Nickson. "The Labour of Aesthetics and the Aesthetics of Organization." *Organization* 10, no. 1 (2003): 33–54.

Wolchover, Natalie. "Why Do All News Anchors Talk the Same?" *NBC News*, October 1, 2011. https://www.nbcnews.com/id/wbna44740700.

Wolfe, Claire, and Barbara Mitra. "Newsreaders as Eye Candy: The Hidden Agenda of Public Service Broadcasting." *Journalism Education* 1, no. 1 (2012): 92–99.

Yoshino, Kenji. *Covering: The Hidden Assault on Our Civil Rights*. New York: Random House, 2007. Kindle.

Yoshino, Kenji, and Christie Smith. "Uncovering Talent: A New Model of Inclusion." Deloitte University. Last modified December 6, 2013. http://www.law.nyu.edu/sites/default/files/upload_documents/Uncovering_talent_A_new_model_of_inclusion.pdf.

Zelizer, Barbie. *Covering the Body: The Kennedy Assassination, the Media, and the Shaping of Collective Memory*. Chicago: University of Chicago Press, 1992.

———. "Journalists as Interpretive Communities." *Critical Studies in Media Communication* 10, no. 3 (1993): 219–237.

Index

About the Author

ELIA POWERS is an associate professor of journalism at Towson University. He has a PhD in journalism studies from the University of Maryland, a master's degree in American culture studies from Washington University in St. Louis, and a bachelor's degree in journalism from Northwestern University. Formerly a reporter for publications such as the *Los Angeles Times*, *Inside Higher Ed*, and the *St. Louis Beacon*, he is now a contributing editor at the *Baltimore Watchdog* and an independent podcast producer/host. A proud Seattle native, he lives in Washington, DC, with his wife and two sons.

About the Author.